The Skillful Soul of the Psychotherapist

The Skillful Soul of the Psychotherapist

Edited by
George S. Stavros and Steven J. Sandage

ROWMAN & LITTLEFIELD
Lanham • Boulder • New York • London

Published by Rowman & Littlefield
A wholly owned subsidiary of The Rowman & Littlefield Publishing Group, Inc.
4501 Forbes Boulevard, Suite 200, Lanham, Maryland 20706
www.rowman.com

16 Carlisle Street, London W1D 3BT, United Kingdom

British Library Cataloguing in Publication Information Available

Library of Congress Cataloging-in-Publication Data

The skillful soul of the psychotherapist / [edited by] George S. Stavros and Steven J Sandage. pages cm
p. cm.
Includes index.
ISBN 978-1-4422-3448-2 (cloth : alk. paper) 1. Psychotherapist and patient. 2. Psychotherapy. 3. Psychotherapy--Religious aspects. I. Stavros, George, and Sandage, Steven J., editors.
RC480.8.S55 2014
616.89'14--dc23
2014023907

∞™ The paper used in this publication meets the minimum requirements of American National Standard for Information Sciences Permanence of Paper for Printed Library Materials, ANSI/NISO Z39.48-1992.

Printed in the United States of America

This book is dedicated to Merle Jordan
Teacher, Mentor, and Friend

Contents

Foreword

Hospitality and Discovery

The Danielsen Institute was established in 1952 within Boston University's School of Theology with the task of training ordained clergy in psychotherapeutic skills and technique, in order to enhance their pastoral effectiveness in the face of the complex emotional, relational, and spiritual suffering of their parishioners. Over the past sixty years, the Institute has moved beyond that original mission to one that is focused on the practice, training, and research of relationally-oriented depth psychotherapy informed by and integrated with religious, spiritual, existential, and theological perspectives. And, the Danielsen Institute's unique engagement with religion and spirituality in clinical practice is based upon maintaining a hospitable orientation toward the role of religion and spirituality in the provision, teaching, and research of psychotherapeutic care. Dr. Merle Jordan, Professor Emeritus of Pastoral Psychology at Boston University's School of Theology, and former Executive Director of The Danielsen Institute at Boston University, embodies this hospitality, as a clinician, teacher, supervisor, scholar, mentor, and friend.

The Skillful Soul of the Psychotherapist, as a product of the Danielsen Institute's Merle Jordan Conference, is a volume that contains the efforts of master clinicians who have accepted the offer and challenge to make more explicit the connections between their religious and spiritual perspectives, lives, and histories in relation to their clinical work and theories. The intention of this project is to create a hospitable space within which this process of discovery can occur. Nouwen (1986) writes,

> Hospitality, therefore, means primarily the creation of a free space where the stranger can enter and become a friend instead of an enemy. Hospitality is not

> to change people, but to offer them space where change can take place. It is not to bring men and women over to our side, but to offer freedom not disturbed by dividing lines. The paradox of hospitality is that it wants to create emptiness, not a fearful emptiness, but a friendly emptiness where strangers can enter and discover themselves as created free (pp. 71-72).

In other words, the authors have been invited to both discover and articulate some of the formative and transformative spiritual roots of their psychotherapeutic practice. This volume is an attempt to steer clear of hard lines of demarcation, "dividing lines," between psychotherapy and spirituality. It is an attempt, through the courageous and creative self-disclosure of master psychotherapists, to discover a resonant core of experience that encompasses both spiritual and clinical sensibilities.

Our hypothesis in approaching the spirituality-psychotherapy relationship in this way is that these master clinicians will demonstrate compelling insights for clinical practice and training through making their implicit spiritual identities and experiences more explicit. What these authors have helped us to realize is that, very often, our most authentic and vulnerable responses to the spirituality-psychotherapy question contain information that is deeply personal, tied to some of the most important and poignant parts of our developmental, relational, and spiritual experiences and history. And simultaneously, these responses can be connected to many of our most profound capacities for clinical effectiveness and excellence.

Nancy McWillams, David Wallin, Salman Akhtar, Phillis Sheppard, Marie Hoffman, Daniel Shaw, Celia Brickman, Tom Cottle, and Chris Schlauch each offer a precious piece of themselves to this task. And the fruits of their labor prove to be sustaining and nourishing for psychotherapists across a spectrum of experience and theoretical orientation. This is a group of master clinicians who have been willing to explore in rich and often personal ways things like the connection between a Protestant upbringing and a vocation as a psychoanalytic psychotherapist and teacher; the connection between a mystical meditative experience, Judaism, and attachment in psychotherapy; and, the connection between vision, survival, and faith in psychoanalytic attitude.

Why is this important from a teaching and training standpoint? A great deal of the conversation between psychotherapy and spirituality has been focused on the skills and knowledge necessary to treat religiously committed clients. Others have focused on the utilization of spiritual practices and techniques within psychotherapy to provide symptom relief. Yet emerging research on spiritual and religious competencies for clinicians also highlights the need for practitioners to be "aware of how their own spiritual and/or religious background and beliefs may influence their clinical practice" (Vieten, Scammell, Pilato, Ammondson, Pargament, & Lakoff, 2013, p. 135). What we have found over decades of training at the Danielsen Institute is that our psychology, social work, and psychiatry fellows are not only hungry for the necessary theory and skills to be spiritually adept psychotherapists. They are equally hungry, and legitimately so, to know whom it is they are learning from and why these people are teaching them in the ways that they are. Our fellows want to know from us why we believe that this strange form of human interaction, relationally-oriented depth psychotherapy, is something worthwhile, both to learn and to offer to others as a form of healing.

The authors in this volume demonstrate that there are powerful ways of answering this question of "Who is teaching me?" And, their use of clinical material combined with often very personal accounts of their religious and spiritual histories demonstrates and models a generous and effective vehicle for teaching and training in psychotherapy. The authors steer clear of a need to define religion and spirituality in bounded and categorical ways, moving rather to a more expansive place where clinical work and things of depth human experience resist categorization and marginalization. While the authors represent diverse disciplines, perspectives, and social locations, there is an *implicit relationality* to the process of their self-reflection regarding the sacred, combined with disclosure and therapeutic integration. We suggest this process of skillful spiritual relationality, within a professional community of dialogue, can move us toward greater clinical wisdom and effectiveness.

We want to express our sincere appreciation to Merle and Barbara Jordan and their family, to the staff and Board of Governors of the Danielsen Institute, to Lauren Kehoe, for her relentless and invaluable work with the manuscript, to our editor Amy King, and to our wives, Despina and Danielle, for the unfailing support we received in carrying this volume through to completion.

George Stavros and Steven Sandage

REFERENCES

Nouwen, H.J.M. (1986). *Reaching out: The three movements of the spiritual life*. New York: Doubleday.

Vieten, C., Scammell, S., Pilato, R., Ammondson, I., Pargament, K.I., 7 Lukoff, D. (2013). Spiritual and religious competencies for psychologists. *Psychology of Religion and Spirituality*, 5, 129–144.

Chapter One

The Skillful Soul of the Psychotherapist

George Stavros and Steven Sandage

RELIGION AND SPIRITUALITY IN PSYCHOTHERAPY

For much of the last century, the relationship between religion and psychotherapy as distinct disciplines has often been characterized by territoriality and tense mutual mistrust. Simultaneously, a more subtle, positive, practical, and enduring relationship between religion and psychotherapy has quietly managed to exist, taking many forms in many different cultures that value the healing power of human relationship, counsel, and shared wisdom. Scholars have described this more synergistic relationship between psychotherapy and religion in the context of multiple ancient religious traditions, including Islam (Haque, 2004), Buddhism (Epstein, 2013), Judaism (Rich, 2008), Hinduism (Akhilananda, 2012), and Christianity (Miller & Delaney, 2005), among others.

In the modern Western context, psychotherapy has developed as a therapeutic practice which seeks to facilitate emotional, cognitive, behavioral, relational, and systemic change and healing for those who seek the aid of a psychotherapist. The place of religion and spirituality in this healing enterprise continues to be considered and debated. On the one hand, there is increasing evidence that the field of psychotherapy is moving to a place of accountability, acceptance, and openness to religious and spiritual matters. For example, it is considered a matter of ethical clinical practice that mental health clinicians treat the religious and spiritual practices and beliefs of their clients with respect, cultural sensitivity, and openness (American Psychological Association, 2010; National Association of Social Workers, 2008). Additionally, it is a matter of ethical practice that mental health professionals be aware of potential personal biases they may have regarding religion and spirituality, so as to minimize any negative impact their bias may have in treating their clients (Bartoli, 2007; Vieten et al., 2013; Wiggins, 2009). Surveys in the United States show approximately 79 percent to 88 percent of the population considers religion "very important" or "fairly important in their lives," and the numbers would likely increase if the focus were on "spirituality" (Gallup, 2012). There is also empirical evidence that a majority of psychotherapy clients hold important religious and spiritual beliefs and prefer to have these considered as part of their psychotherapeutic treatment (Rose et al., 2008). Post and Wade (2009) note findings on a similar openness to spirituality and religion on the part of therapists and state,

> Research indicates that therapists are open to religious/spiritual issues, that clients want to discuss these matters in therapy, and that the use of religious/spiritual interventions for some clients can be an effective adjunct to traditional therapy interventions (p. 131).

On the other hand, psychotherapy continues to carry forward a significant anti-religious legacy, even to the present day. From the narrowly defined empirical imperatives of logical positivism (Friedman, 1999) to Freud's (1927; 1933) characterization of religion as "an illusion" and "comparable to a childhood neurosis," the challenges to a spirituality-psychotherapy alliance are woven into psychotherapy's development throughout the last century. And while there are many more pockets of hospitality and openness to the role of religion and spirituality than at any time in the past one hundred years, there also remain formidable strains of antagonism, suspicion, or avoidance (Bartoli, 2007). Gonsiorek, Richards, Pargament, & McMinn (2009) state,

> Dealing with religious and spiritual issues in psychotherapy is inherently messy. Why? In part, because religion and science are not totally separable. Although we can draw contrasts between contemporary psychology and religious traditions, these contrasts can be overdone . . . Working with religious and spiritual issues in psychotherapy is also messy because the spiritual dimension is inextricably inter-woven into the character of psychotherapy—in clients, in psychotherapists, and in the process of psychotherapy itself (pp. 391–392).

While therapists may sometimes feel ambivalence about engaging discussions of the sacred, it is interesting to consider the perspective of clients. One study found psychotherapy clients reported initiating discussions of spirituality more frequently than did their therapists (Ganje-Fling, Veach, Kuang, & Houg, 2000). In some cases this may reflect an intention to allow clients to take the lead on sensitive topics. However, it seems likely this can also sometimes represent various forms of therapist ambivalence about spirituality and religion or confusion on how to effectively engage those dynamics in psychotherapy. Yet clinical outcomes can be at stake given evidence that highly religious or spiritually committed clients (a) tend to show superior outcomes when treatment involves explicit integration of religion or spirituality (Worthington, Hook, Davis, & McDaniel, 2011) and (b) can report negative experiences in psychotherapy if they perceive the therapist to oppose their religious views or to avoid discussing spiritual and religious issues (Cragun & Friedlander, 2012).

RELIGION AND SPIRITUALITY IN THE PSYCHOTHERAPIST

While much of the available research highlights the importance of issues of the sacred to highly religious or spiritually committed clients, we have found clinically that it is impossible to predict the variety of implicit associations clients may make to religion and spirituality regardless of their explicitly stated beliefs. Consider this clinical example:

> Megan, a female psychotherapist, in her early 40s, was in the process of ending treatment with a young adult, male client who was preparing to leave the region for a job and whom she had been seeing since the client was an adolescent. The treatment had lasted almost six years, and during that time, the therapist and client had negotiated multiple therapeutic ruptures, much acting out and emotional suffering by the client, including dangerous substance abuse and sexual activity, frequent periods of hopelessness, suicidality, and intense family conflicts. The alliance between the therapist and client, forged in much relational rupture and repair, was strong, and both the client and therapist felt great sadness about their work ending and great satisfaction about the work they had done together. During the course of their treatment, issues of religion and spirituality were never explicitly discussed, though both therapist and client would acknowledge a "deep" sense of connection to one another. The therapist, prior to entering training as a psychologist, had obtained a Master's degree in theology and kept her diploma hanging on her office wall. In the final few minutes of their last session, the following exchange occurred:
>
> **Client**: So, I noticed that diploma from theology school on your wall.
> **Therapist**: (Surprised) You just noticed that today?
> **Client**: No. I noticed it the first day I met you.
> **Therapist**: (Befuddled) What? What did you think about it? You never said anything about it until now.
> **Client**: At first, it made me think you would be a pushover. Or that you were going to try to convert me, or something.
> **Therapist**: (Smiling) Probably a good thing I didn't go there (Client smiles, then drops his eyes). What is it?
> **Client**: (Slowly, tearfully) Well . . . it's just. It's just that when things would get really bad. When I would be suicidal or getting high all the time. Sometimes I would look at the diploma when I walked in, and I would think, "Okay, I can trust Megan. She'll stick with me." Thanks for sticking with me.

Therapist: (Moist eyes) Thanks for sticking with me . . . with us.
Client and therapist get up from their chairs to say goodbye, embrace briefly, and end the session.

Be Prepared for Surprises

In the above clinical vignette, one might wonder how such an important detail within the clinical process went unspoken for so long. Given the overall therapeutic outcome, it would be inaccurate to think of that as unusual, or even necessarily problematic. Perhaps this particular client appreciated the space to hold his own internal spiritual attachment associations with the therapist. At the same time, one could see the potentially rich clinical territory that might have been opened up, particularly in the termination process, were religious and spiritual considerations more easily and explicitly discussed. Attending to religion and spirituality in psychotherapy requires a holding of tensions, between the spoken and unspoken, between structure and spontaneity, between explicit and implicit ways of knowing, believing, relating, and understanding. Griffith and Griffith (2003) describe working with these tensions when a moment of profound spiritual significance emerged between an Indian mother and daughter in family therapy:

> What did the therapy have to do with the entry into this spirituality? For us, this is the crucial question. It seemed to "just happen," a moment of mystery that cannot be fully understood, and certainly could not have been orchestrated. Nevertheless, we want to understand as much about it as possible (p. 4).

The vignette also opens up other important questions about the formation and training of psychotherapists. For instance, in what ways did the therapist draw upon her own religious and spiritual resources over the course of a difficult and trying treatment process, and how aware was she of doing so? Or, what was it about working with this particular client that contributed to the therapist keeping her beliefs more implicit (with the exception of the diploma)? Would there be value in this therapist more closely examining and articulating her religious and spiritual beliefs as they are relevant for her clinical role and practice, both for herself and as a model for training other therapists to do the same? And how might the therapist have responded to a more problematic spiritual or religious transference, such as one in which a client eventually revealed negative associations or assumptions about the therapist's spiritual or religious orientation?

An important operating assumption in this volume is that it is not only ethically necessary, but clinically vital, for psychotherapists to explore and be aware of their own religious and spiritual sensibilities, histories, practices, and beliefs and to consider carefully how religion and spirituality inform, affect, guide, and influence their clinical work. To this point, Pargament (2011) argues,

> Knowingly or unknowingly, the spirituality of the therapist permeates his or her understanding of people, problems, and change. Spiritually integrated psychotherapy makes explicit the importance of the therapist's own orientation to spirituality (p. 187).

This idea can be articulated using language from various clinical traditions, for example "managing countertransference" or, more broadly and constructively, "self-of-therapist" awareness and growth. Quantitative research on the integration of spirituality into clinical training has identified spiritual self-of-therapist awareness as associated with relational dynamics in supervision and in the therapist's own support system (Miller, Korinek, & Ivey, 2006). Qualitative research on counselor's confidence in addressing spiritual and religious issues with clients has pointed to the importance of opportunities to process and relationally construct an understanding of their own spiritual journey (Tillman, Dinsmore, Hof, & Chasek, 2013). These findings reinforce Pargament's invitation for therapists to gain awareness and make meaning out of their own orientation to spirituality.

Psychotherapists also bear tremendous responsibility for being accountable for the power dynamics in the therapeutic relationship involving religion and spirituality. This is especially true in relation to major risks associated with religion, spirituality, and psychotherapy, namely biased pathologizing or idealizing of a client's spirituality and power-based advancing of the therapist's religious and spiritual beliefs in a proselytizing way. At the same time, psychotherapists also bear responsibility for utilizing all that is at their disposal, through clinical training, life experience, and personhood, for the therapeutic benefit of their psychotherapy clients. This must include appropriate aspects of their own spiritual and religious resources. Thus, psychotherapists require awareness and training that enables them to discern effective timing, context, and purpose for interventions and interactions that include implicit or explicit connections to religion and spirituality (Keeling, Dolbin-MacNab, Ford, & Perkins, 2010; Griffith & Griffith, 2003). In an article that exemplifies spiritual self-of-therapist awareness, Aron (2004) offers the following reflection:

> I assume that other analysts have been shaped and influenced by their own experience with God, and I am suggesting that an examination and comparison of these influences would be productive. It should be added that just as my religious background has affected my psychoanalytic vision, so too, my psychoanalytic experience has influenced my spiritual values and ideals (p. 449).

This bi-directional, relational understanding of spiritual and psychological influence on clinical practice fits the "integrative paradigm" we see as extremely promising for the mental health fields (Pargament, Mahoney, Exline, Jones, & Shafranske, 2013, p. 3). The goal is not to assimilate spirituality or psychology into one another in some reductionistic fashion, but rather to find ways to explore points of connection and potentially integrate differentiated perspectives, languages, and practices.

Practice and Training Work in Tandem

In considering religion and spirituality as potentially rich resources within psychotherapy and to psychotherapists, it is important to consider how these resources might be delivered and utilized in clinical training. A recent study of over five hundred clinical and counseling psychology trainees showed nearly all believed clients should be asked about spirituality and religion (Saunders, Petrik, & Miller, 2014). However, nearly one-fourth of trainees reported having received no training whatsoever in this area and just over 30 percent reported training that was part of a course or seminar. Despite the growing recognition of the clinical significance of spirituality and religion among trainees and established professionals, there is a widespread lack of systematic training aimed at developing even entry levels of spiritual and religious clinical competence (Hathway, 2013; Shafranske, 2013).

Training efforts aimed at knowledge and skills domains of spiritual and religious competence are vital, but our self-of-therapist focus in this volume is centered on the attitude dimension which is optimally cultivated through healthy and supportive relational experiences. Sorenson's (2004) programmatic research on the process of integrating spirituality and psychology among doctoral trainees across numerous religiously-affiliated clinical psychology programs showed a common implicit process similar to the clinical vignette above. Across four different programs, many trainees reported a recurring theme of seeking to integrate by forming implicit, sometimes unspoken, relationships or attachments with faculty and drawing upon the sense of authentic spirituality revealed by any faculty members. Of course, the quality of those relational training experiences of faculty accessibility and modeling were varied with corresponding implications for trainee reports in success with spiritual integration.

These findings invite a question: what would it look like for trainees and seasoned clinicians intentionally to share a relational holding environment that fostered authentic processing of challenging spiritual and religious dimensions of psychotherapy? The following offers a brief example:

> The members of a small group psychotherapy seminar consisting of five members, three of whom were training psychotherapists (a female, culturally Jew-

ish social work fellow; a female, South Asian psychology intern; a male, non-practicing Protestant Christian psychology post-doc) and two of whom are clinically licensed group supervisors (a female, Roman Catholic clinical psychologist; a male, Reformed Jewish social worker) were engaged in a discussion. One of the training fellows, the psychology post-doc, was discussing his personal response to the intensity of emotional suffering that one of his patients was experiencing in the context of their treatment. As he shared the frequent emotional dysregulation, self-hatred, acute suicidality, and self-destructive behavior of his client, the therapist became tearful and paused briefly from his presentation to the others. The psychology post-doc also shared that there seemed to be some small signs of progress and alliance building in the treatment. Given that the group had been working together for eight months, they were familiar with the case and the relentless suffering presented by this client, and they were also familiar with one another, having built a solid group process and sense of mutual trust.

Psychology Intern: It's almost like it's your job to tolerate his agony.
Psychology Post-doc: Yeah. It feels like that a lot. But it also feels like I'm supposed to give him something. We're always working on distress tolerance and emotion regulation skills, and they seem to help in small ways. But there are times when he just seems gone, and all I can do is try to make contact with him. It can be brutal.
Social Work Supervisor: You're doing a good job with him, Michael. He's more connected, to you and the rest of his team than ever before. He's managed to keep his job and apartment. And his work with you has had a lot to do with that. But it sounds like it's taking a toll on you. It's hard to imagine it wouldn't.
Social Work Fellow: (Turning to the two supervisors) Is it fair to ask what we're supposed to do with this "toll of agony"?
Psychology Supervisor: Yeah, it's fair to ask, but it might not be fair to think that a lot of clinical experience spares us from it, or makes us any more able to withstand it.
Psychology Intern: (In "mock" exasperation) Lovely.
Social Work Supervisor: Maybe we'd have better luck turning to the group's wisdom on this. Do any of us have images or ideas that we hold or know that connect with the idea of living with this "toll of agony"?
Psychology Intern: Well, this may sound overly simplistic. I have always loved the image of the lotus flower growing out of the muck. It's not that I've seen that many lotus flowers open up in my office, but that image just makes sense to me for what we're trying to do. Michael's dealing with a lot of muck, but I like to think there might be powerful things that are happening between him and his client that hold the stuff that generates that blossom.
Psychology Post-doc: I like that.
Social Work Fellow: Well, I'm not religious, at all. But when I'm out on my bike on the coast, riding with my brother, and there's no one else around, there are times where it feels like all the burden and agony just burns off temporarily. And it's not like it's just an absence of agony. It feels like something good

> flows into that space. Like I'm good. Or the world is good. Something like that.
>
> **Psychology Supervisor**: I remember when I had a patient suicide. The only time in my career. It was agony and there were a few really rough weeks afterwards. It's not like the hurt has ever left me, but I remember experiencing something that helped me turn a corner. I was talking with a colleague about it, and he noticed I wasn't using the patient's name. He pushed me a little bit, and it connected me to the way my church does memorial services and keeps praying for the deceased. I'm not sure what it was about that, but it helped settle me down.
>
> **Psychology Post-doc**: That's scary and comforting all at the same time.
>
> **Psychology Intern**: Welcome to psychotherapy training.
>
> **Social Work Supervisor**: How about for you, Michael? Does anything connect?

Without sacrificing a commitment to the exposure of training psychotherapists to evidence-based research and literature, the above vignette illustrates a powerful experiential and relational component which increases awareness and utilization of religious and spiritual considerations in psychotherapy. Given the important differences amongst training and practicing clinicians' religious and spiritual backgrounds, comfort levels, and experiences, it becomes crucial that institutions and supervisors provide a hospitable and non-judgmental container within which to explore these issues (Worthington et al., 2009). In fact, we suggest it may be ideal for trainees and established clinicians, over time, to experience multiple relational containers for processing clinically relevant spiritual and religious dynamics (e.g., peer supervision, individual supervision, coursework, personal therapy, professional seminars, etc.). With questions about whether available training resources in religion, spirituality, and psychotherapy are consistently finding their way into the hands of psychotherapists (Bartoli, 2007), creative and accessible vehicles for this kind of training take on great importance. Miller and Athan (2007) offer a description of this type of process when it is working effectively:

> Students are welcomed into bringing private, raw, neglected, and often discredited stories of lived experience to the foreground. Students and instructors together explore and integrate their impact, receive healing, and in turn envision how to tap this transcendent ground for others. Direct experience and imagination are given primacy along with logical positivist analysis and serve to create dynamic discussions with a life of their own (p. 17).

RELATIONAL SPIRITUALITY, ATTACHMENT, AND DIFFERENTIATION

Relational Psychoanalytic Psychotherapy

It is likely spiritual and religious integration in psychotherapy will look different depending on theoretical orientation. The theoretical and clinical lens emphasized in this volume is longer-term, depth-oriented, relational psychoanalytic psychotherapy. This is for two reasons. The first is that many persons who seek out psychotherapy have experienced traumatically disrupted attachment relationships. A relational psychoanalytic approach lends itself well to working with the intense and disorienting affects, relational dynamics, and rupture and repair cycles which are so characteristic of the therapeutic process with these clients. There is now a large body of empirical evidence showing relational dynamics are a major influence on psychotherapy outcomes (Norcross, 2011). The second reason is that relational psychoanalytic psychotherapy provides a robust conversation partner for religion and spirituality, in that they each provide maps, symbols, and language for the longing, pain, and hope which lie deepest within the human heart. Aron (2004) writes,

> The effort to talk openly and directly about religious differences and the implications for psychoanalysis is enormously complicated and filled with a variety of dangers. Religious conflict, repression, and deep fears about religion pervade the history of psychoanalysis. As psychoanalysts, we should recognize that some of our cherished ideals are central to religious traditions and that in analyzing forms of aliveness and deadness, and thus in helping our patients to choose life, we are performing a sacred task (p. 449).

Mitchell and Aron (1999) trace the beginnings of the relational psychoanalytic model to several converging streams of clinical theory. These include American interpersonal psychoanalysis of the 1930s and 1940s, British object relations theory, Bowlby's work on attachment, Kohut's self psychology in the late 1970s, and American psychoanalytic feminism in the late 1970s and early 1980s. At the heart of what they refer to as the "relational turn" in psychoanalysis is the idea that the heart of human motivation lies in something fundamentally relationship-oriented, as opposed to being drive or instinct-oriented. Mitchell (1988) states:

> Libido is not pleasure seeking, but object seeking. The superordinate need of the child is not for pleasure or need gratification, but for an intense relationship with another person. If the caretakers provide opportunities for pleasurable experiences, pleasure is sought, not as an end in itself, but as a vehicle for interaction with others. If only painful experiences are provided, the child does not give up and look for pleasurable experiences elsewhere, but seeks the pain

> as a vehicle for interaction with the significant other. It is the contact, not the pleasure, which is primary (p. 27).

Thus, a crucial way of understanding the psychotherapeutic task with relationally traumatized clients is in appreciating how a history of loss, neglect, abuse, coercion, seduction, exploitation, or abandonment continues to play itself out, or become reenacted, through cycles of relational rupture and repair in present-day relationships, including with the psychotherapist. According to Bromberg (2006), the patient's "capacity to trust human relationship must first be slowly restored—in some cases built for the first time" (p. 109). A key way in which relational psychoanalytic clinicians approach this task of rebuilding their patients' capacity to trust is through an inevitable and relentless process of repairing ruptures to the therapeutic alliance (Colli & Lingiardi, 2009; Muran et al., 2009; Safran, Muran, & Proskurov, 2009; Stern, et al 1998). Shaw (2010) elegantly offers a description of some of the reparative processes which can be brought to bear in this cycle of rupture and repair:

> The reparative processes—acknowledging fallibility, being accountable for doing harm, apologizing, forgiving, expressing and receiving gratitude—are shame diminishing, "subjectifying" processes. They stand in contradistinction to the objectifying, narcissistic processes of coercive projection and belittling diminishment, the purposes of which are to induce shame and establish domination. Narcissistic, objectifying processes are often employed covertly, in ways that are unconscious or disavowed. Reparative, "subjectifying" processes, on the other hand, are usually more effective, I would assert, when overtly employed. The reparative processes can instill hope, and perhaps even faith, in the possibility that disruptions do not have to be catastrophic or terminal, but can be meaningfully repaired, and that one's badness, and the badness in others, can exist along with, and not override and destroy goodness (p. 56).

Relational Spirituality

A relational view of psychotherapy readily integrates with a relational understanding of spirituality. The growing literature on spirituality in the social sciences utilizes a myriad of definitions, and the authors in this volume also offer diverse perspectives. We have been helped by the work of Hill and Pargament (2003, p. 65) who have offered a psychological definition of spirituality as related to "a search for the sacred." The sacred can include "a divine being, divine object, Ultimate Reality, or Ultimate Truth" that is "set apart" as holy and beyond the ordinary (p. 65), and "search" implies an active quest for the sacred. By defining spirituality in relation to whatever a person considers sacred, this phenomenological orientation allows for wide-ranging diversity in understandings of the sacred. Clinically, it orients attention to ideals or whatever is deeply important to a client, which Kohut linked to relational influences on the self. Clients who may not consider themselves "spiritual" or "religious" often hold certain ideals or values, however implicit, which can potentially serve as powerful sources of affect and motivation. Frequently, these sacred ideals show links to relational experiences and patterns, and some clients have ruptured or conflicted relationships with the sacred or consider themselves "in recovery" from religion and spirituality.

Shults and Sandage (2006) adapted the definition of spirituality offered by Hill and Pargament to fit a relational theoretical orientation by defining *relational spirituality* as "ways of relating to the sacred" (p. 161). In theistic spiritual traditions, the sacred includes personal Divine Beings, spirits, and ancestors with whom humans can relate. Yet spiritual traditions which are not explicitly theistic also offer rituals and practices for relating with the sacred and, thus, can be viewed through a relational framework. In this sense, people can relate to God and the sacred in a variety of ways, including trust, avoidance, devotion, disappointment, questioning, hostility, surrender, narcissistic identification, and many other relational categories. Relational themes of spirituality are woven throughout the chapters to follow in this volume.

Attachment

Attachment theory is not only one of the most empirically supported theories of human development but has also become a leading framework in the psychology of religion and spirituality (Granqvist & Kirkpatrick, 2013). The relational dynamics of spirituality can fit coherently within attachment theory based on human needs for (a) safe havens of security and emotional support and (b) a secure base for confident exploration of the world. The limbic-based attachment system is most readily activated in situations of anxiety or vulnerability, so attachment functions are intended to help regulate anxiety and promote adaptive functioning and processing of meaning. From an attachment perspective, forms of relational spirituality which can foster psychological healing and growth will involve spiritual and existential resources to provide safe haven experiences for affect regulation and secure base grounding to promote confident exploration.

One of the empirical strengths of attachment theory is the identification of individual differences in relational behavior based on developmental experiences. Research using attachment categories in the psychology of religion and spirituality has identified both correspondence and compensation effects through comparing interpersonal and spiritual attachment patterns. Correspondence effects refer to a similarity in interpersonal and spiritual attachment styles for an individual, such as an avoidantly-attached adult who avoids closeness or emotional vulnerability with both human relational partners and with the sacred. An example of a compensation effect would be an individual who reports a very close and warm attachment with the sacred which seems to be an attempt to compensate for a total lack of such attachments in the human realm. If it is an anxiety-driven compensation effect, the person's relational spirituality may not lead to more secure interpersonal attachments and this can be a source of dissonance or distress. This attention to relational subjectivity and its mediation through the limbic brain makes attachment and other relational perspectives particularly useful for attending to spirituality and religion in clinical practice.

Differentiation of Self

Differentiation of self represents a healthy configuration of self-other relations characterized by the ability to balance (a) emotional and cognitive functioning and (b) intimacy and autonomy in relationships. Individuals with a high degree of differentiation of self are less emotionally reactive to others and have greater flexibility and self-awareness than those with low self-differentiation. Differentiation of self, therefore, represents a mature relational capacity to handle the anxiety of both closeness (intimacy) and difference (otherness) (Shults & Sandage, 2006). Differentiation and related concepts such as individuation have been critiqued for seeming to represent highly individualistic cultural values; however, it is now more widely understood in the family systems field that differentiation of self includes the ability to connect *both* with others and to self-regulate (Jankowski & Sandage, 2012). In a parallel fashion, numerous spiritual writers have described this important dialectic of being able to function well in community and also value the spiritual practice of solitude. In short, differentiation of self represents a capacity for spiritual and psychological wholeness through balancing the emotional regulation that leads to well-being and the distress tolerance of suffering that can lead to maturity.

Numerous empirical studies have demonstrated significant association between differentiation of self and various indices of spiritual development and virtue (see Jankowski, Sandage, & Hill, 2013; Jankowski & Sandage, in press; Sandage & Jankowski, 2013), including spiritual well-being, spiritual maturity, meditative prayer, forgiveness, hope, humility, intercultural competence, and social justice commitment. We find it helpful to include both attachment and differentiation of self in our understanding of the clinical dynamics of relational spirituality. Technically, secure attachment and differentiation of self are overlapping constructs in that each references healthy developmental capacities for (a) balancing connection and autonomy and (b) emotional regulation. However, in popular clinical use, it seems the concept of attachment more often references notions of healthy connection and relational regulation, while differentiation of self often connotes the ability to self-regulate emotions and to be sufficiently secure in one's own self-identity to appreciate interpersonal differences. In our view, relational psychoanalytic psychotherapy can effectively engage the relational dynamics of spirituality with a goal of fostering corrective experiences of secure attachment and constructive development of differentiation.

In the chapters that follow in this volume, authors will offer a range of relational psychoanalytic perspectives and employ differing clinical theories and terms; however, connections to the themes of relational spirituality, attachment, and differentiation will emerge in various ways. Psychotherapy should offer clients a relationship of safe connection and support, and differentiated therapists are able to accept client differences and cultivate the emotional freedom to explore new terrain, whether that terrain is understood to be sacred or profane. These are the core relational and spiritual dynamics of the *skillful soul of the psychotherapist.*

REFERENCES

Akhilananda, S. (2012). *Hindu psychology: Its meaning for the west.* New York: Routledge.

Akhtar, S. (2010). *Matters of life and death: Psychoanalytic reflections.* London: Karnac Books.

Akhtar, S., & Parens, H. (2001). *Does God help: Developmental and clinical aspects of religious belief.* Lanham, MD: Jason Aronson.

American Psychological Association. (2010). Ethical principles of psychologists and code of conduct. Retrieved 11/27/13, from http://www.apa.org/ethics/code/index.aspx.

Aron, L. (2004). God's influence on my psychoanalytic vision and values. *Psychoanalytic Psychology, 21*(3), 442–451.

Aron, L., & Mitchell, S.A. (Eds.). (1999). Relational psychoanalysis, Volume 14: The emergence of a tradition. New York: Routledge/Taylor & Francis Group.

Bartoli, E. (2007). Religious and spiritual issues in psychotherapy practice: Training the trainer. *Psychotherapy: Theory, Research, Practice, Training, 44*(1), 54–65.

Bromberg, P. (2006). *Awakening the Dreamer: Clinical Journeys.* Mahway, NJ: The Analytic Press.

Colli, A., & Lingiardi, V. (2009). The Collaborative Interactions Scale: A new transcript-based method for the assessment of therapeutic alliance ruptures and resolutions in psychotherapy. *Psychotherapy Research, 19*(6), 718–734.

Cragun, C. L. & Friedlander, M. L. (2012). Experiences of Christian clients in secular psychotherapy: A mixed-methods investigation. *Journal of Counseling Psychology, 59*(3), 379–391.

Epstein, M. (2013). *Thoughts without a thinker: Psychotherapy from a Buddhist perspective.* New York: Basic Books.

Friedman, M. (1999). *Reconsidering logical positivism.* New York: Cambridge University Press.

Gallup. (2012). Religion (Poll). Retrieved 11/19/2012, from http://www.gallup.com/poll/1690/religion/aspx.

Ganje-Fling, M., Veach, P. M., Kuang, H., & Houg, B. (2000). Effect of childhood sexual abuse on client spiritual well-being. *Counseling and Values, 44*(2), 84–91.

Gonsiorek, J. C., Richards, P. S., Pargament, K. I., & McMinn, M. R. (2009). Ethical challenges and opportunities at the edge: Incorporating spirituality and religion into psychotherapy. *Professional Psychology: Research and Practice, 40*(4), 385–395.

Granqvist, P., & Kirkpatrick, L. A. (2013). Religion, spirituality and attachment. In K. I. Pargament, J. J. Exline & J. W. Jones (Eds). *APA handbook of psychology, religion, and spirituality (Vol. 1): Context, theory, and research.* (pp. 139–155). Washington, DC: American Psychological Association.

Griffith, J. L., & Griffith, M. E. (2003). *Encountering the sacred in psychotherapy: How to talk with people about their spiritual lives*. New York: Guilford Press.

Haque, A. (2004). Psychology from Islamic perspective: Contributions of early Muslim scholars and challenges to contemporary Muslim psychologists. *Journal of Religion and Health, 43*(4), 357–377.

Hathaway, W. (2013). Pathways toward graduate training in the clinical psychology of religion and spirituality: A spiritual competencies model. In K. I. Pargament, A. Mahoney, and E. P. Shafranske (Eds.) *APA handbook of psychology, religion, and spirituality (Vol. 2): An applied psychology of religion and spirituality.* (pp. 635–649). Washington, DC, US: American Psychological Association.

Hill, P. C., & Pargament, K. I. (2003). Advances in the conceptualization and measurement of religion and spirituality: Implications for physical and mental health research. *American Psychologist, 58,* 64–74.

Hoffman, M. (2004). From enemy combatant to strange bedfellow: The role of religious narratives in the work of W. R. D. Fairbairn and D. W. Winnicott. *Psychoanalytic Dialogues, 14*(6), 769–804.

Hoffman, M. T. (2010). *Toward mutual recognition: Relational psychoanalysis and the Christian narrative*. New York: Taylor & Francis.

Jankowski, P. J., & Sandage, S. J. (in press). Attachment to God and dispositional humility: Indirect effect and conditional effects model. *Journal of Psychology and Theology.*

Jankowski, P. J., & Sandage, S. J. (2012). Spiritual dwelling and well-being: The mediating role of differentiation of self in a sample of distressed adults. *Mental Health, Religion, & Culture, 15,* 417–434.

Jankowski, P. J., Sandage, S. J., & Hill, P. C. (2013). Differentiation-based models of forgivingness, mental health, and social justice commitment: Mediator effects of differentiation of self and humility. *Journal of Positive Psychology.* DOI: 17439760.2013.820337

Keeling, M. L., Dolbin-MacNab, M. L., Ford, J., & Perkins, S. N. (2010). Partners in the spiritual dance: Learning clients' steps while minding all our toes. *Journal of Marital and Family Therapy, 36*(2), 229–243.

Miller, L., & Athan, A. (2007). Spiritual awareness pedagogy: The classroom as spiritual reality. *International Journal of Children's Spirituality, 12*(1), 17–35.

Miller, M. M., Korinek, A. W. & Ivey, D. C. (2006). Integrating spirituality into training: The Spiritual Issues in Supervision Scale. *The American Journal of Family Therapy, 34,* 355–372.

Miller, W. R., & Delaney, H. D. (2005). *Judeo-christian perspectives on psychology: Human nature, motivation, and change.* Washington, D.C.: American Psychological Association.

Muran, J. C., Safran, J. D., Gorman, B. S., Eubanks-Carter, C., Winston, A., & Samstag, L. W. (2009). The relationship of early alliance ruptures and their resolution to process and outcome in three time-limited psychotherapies for personality disorders. *Psychotherapy: Theory, Research, Practice, Training, 46*(2), 233–248.

National Association of Social Workers. (2008). Code of Ethics of the National Association of Social Workers. Retrieved 10/1/2013 from http://www.naswdc.org/pubs/code/code.asp.

Norcross. J. C. (Ed.) (2011). *Psychotherapy relationships that work: Evidence-based responsiveness* (2nd ed). New York: Oxford University Press.

Nouwen, H. J. M. (1986). *Reaching out: The three movements of the spiritual life*. New York: Random House.

Pargament, K. I. (2011). *Spiritually integrated psychotherapy: Understanding and addressing the sacred.* New York: Guilford Press.

Post, B. C., & Wade, N. G. (2009). Religion and spirituality in psychotherapy: A practice-friendly review of research. *Journal of Clinical Psychology, 65*(2), 131–146.

Rich, M. S. (2008). *Jews in psychology and the psychology of Judaism*. Piscataway, NJ: Tigris/Gorgias Press.

Rose, E. M., Westefeld, J. S., & Ansley, T. N. (2008). Spiritual issues in counseling: Clients' beliefs and preferences. *Psychology of Religion and Spirituality, 1,* 18–33.

Safran, J. D. (2002). Brief relational psychoanalytic treatment. *Psychoanalytic Dialogues: The International Journal of Relational Perspectives 12(2),* 171–196.

Safran, J. D., Muran, J. C., & Proskurov, B. (2009). Alliance, negotiation, and rupture resolution. In R. A. Levy & J. S. Ablon (Eds.), *Handbook of evidence-based psychodynamic psychotherapy* (pp. 201–225). Totowa, NJ: Humana Press.

Sandage, S.J., & Jankowski, P.J. (2013). Spirituality, social justice, and intercultural competence: Mediator effects for differentiation of self. *International Journal for Intercultural Relations, 37,* 366–374.

Saunders, S. M., Petrik, M. L. & Miller, M. L. (2014). Psychology doctoral students persepctives on addressing spirituality and religion with clients: Associations with personal preferences and training. *Psychology of Religion and Spirituality, 6,* 1–8.

Schlosser, L. Z., & Safran, D. A. (2009). Implementing treatments that incorporate clients' spirituality. In J. D. Aten & M. M. Leach (Eds.), *Spirituality and the therapeutic process: A comprehensive resource from intake to termination.* (pp. 193–216). Washington, DC: American Psychological Association.

Shafranske, E. P., & Cummings, J. P. (2013). Religious and spiritual beliefs, affiliations, and practices of psychologists. In K. I. Pargament, A. Mahoney, & E. P. Shafranske (Eds.), *APA handbook of psychology, religion, and spirituality: Vol. 2. An applied psychology of religion and spirituality* (pp. 23–41). Washington, DC: American Psychological Association.

Shaw, D. (2010). Enter ghosts: The loss of intersubjectivity in clinical work with adult children of pathological narcissists. *Psychoanalytic Dialogues, 20*(1), 46–59.

Shults, F. L., & Sandage, S. J. (2006). *Transforming spirituality: Integrating theology and psychology.* Grand Rapids, MI: Baker Academic.

Sorenson, R. L. (2004). *Minding spirituality.* Hillsdale, NJ: The Analytic Press.

Stern, D. N., Bruschweiler-Stern, N., Harrison, A. M., Lyons-Ruth, K., Morgan, A. C., Nahum, J. P., & Tronick, E. Z. (1998). The process of therapeutic change involving implicit knowledge: Some implications of developmental observations for adult psychotherapy. *Infant Mental Health Journal, 19*(3), 300–308.

Tillman, D. R., Dinsmore, J. A., Hof, D. D, & Chasek, C. L. (2013). Becoming confident in addressing client spiritual or religious orientation in counseling: A grounded theory understanding. *Journal of Spirituality in Mental Health, 15,* 239–255.

Vieten, C., Scammell, S., Pilato, R., Ammondson, I., Pargament, K. I. & Lukoff D. (2013). Spiritual and religious competencies for psychologists. *Psychology of Religion and Spirituality, 5*(3), 129–144.

Wallin, D. (2007). *Attachment in psychotherapy.* New York: Guilford Press.

Wiggins, M. I. (2009). Therapist self-awareness of spirituality. In J. D. Aten & M. M. Leach (Eds.), *Spirituality and the therapeutic process: A comprehensive resource from intake to termination.* (pp. 53–74). Washington, DC: American Psychological Association.

Worthington, E. L. Jr., Hook J. N., Davis D. E. & McDaniel M. A. (2011). Religion and spirituality. *Journal of Clinical Psychology, 67(2),* 204–214.

Worthington, E. L. Jr., Sandage, S. J., Davis, D. E., Hook, J. N., Miller, A. J., Hall, M. E. L., & Hall, T. W. (2009). Training therapists to address spiritual concerns in clinical practice and research. In J. D. Aten & M. M. Leach (Eds.), *Spirituality and therapeutic process: A comprehensive resource from intake to termination.* (pp. 267–291). Washington, DC: American Psychological Association.

Chapter Two

Reflections on the Effects of a Protestant Girlhood

Nancy McWilliams

BACKGROUND

In formulating links between my religious sensibility and my vocation as a therapist, I find myself starting, in standard psychoanalytic fashion, with my personal history. The earliest home I remember was in a New England suburb where I lived from age two until age eleven. My family belonged to the First Congregational Church in Longmeadow, MA, and although we attended regularly, I do not recall my parents putting much emphasis on my religious education. My mother, who loved to sing, was in the choir there, and as soon as I was old enough, I joined the junior choir. The words of the hymns we sang can return to me intact decades later. I thought the church was beautiful (I still do; it is a typically spare, elegant, white, steepled New England house of worship). I recall liking the picture on the wall of the Sunday school classroom: a kind-looking Jesus surrounded by children.

I enjoyed Bible stories from a young age, especially "Joseph and the Coat of Many Colors" and "David and Goliath." I suspect that my psychologically astute mother read me those stories in an effort to mitigate my suffering from my older sister's occasional envious attacks on me for having displaced her. This may have been the template for my later consulting scripture in times of trouble. I remember my maternal grandmother teaching me the Lord's Prayer when I was about three. It was a source of much amusement in my family that my grandparents bickered constantly, *except* when reading the Bible aloud to each other every morning and evening. They usually read psalms, and I became familiar with some of their favorites.

Interestingly, my maternal grandmother was a convert to Christian Science. The story was that as a toddler, my mother contracted scarlet fever and was at death's door. All the doctors had given up on her. In desperation, my grandmother hired a Christian Science practitioner, who led a long, bedside prayer vigil. My mother survived, and my grandmother credited Christian Science with her recovery. She was an oddly practical Scientist, however, who explained that if material existence is an illusion, it doesn't matter whether one takes medicine or not (and how could it hurt?). Her father had been a doctor, and I think she could not fully devalue his profession. So during my childhood, Grandma would talk in phrases from Mary Baker Eddy's (2006, orig. 1875) *Science and Health with Key to the Scriptures*, urge us to appreciate that physical treatments for illness were unnecessary, and then make sure we followed the doctor's orders. As a child I did not find this peculiar; as an adult I find it an interesting example of a common tendency for people to find in a religious tradition only what is convenient to take in.

My father, a deep-dyed moralist, told me when I was an adult that he had once considered going into the ministry but had decided against it because he worried about the kind of life his wife would be expected to live as the spouse of a pastor. When I was a teenager, he once surprised me by remarking that theologically, he was more of a Jew than a Christian (my older sister remembers him saying this more than once, as well), meaning that he regarded Jesus as a great teacher but not a divine being or a resurrected one. So he had evidently thought a lot about religious matters. But I remember few childhood references to God, and prayers only at bedtime ("Now I lay me down to sleep . . .") and on occasions such as Thanksgiving when we would say grace.

I must have asked many questions about death and evil and other things that trouble children, but only one theologically related conversation stands out from my earliest years. At about age five, having witnessed my mother's pregnancy with my younger sister and knowing that babies grow inside women, I wanted to understand the role of men in conception. I asked my mother why only women with husbands had babies (in 1950s white suburbia, single mothers were invisible). She replied that God would not want a child to grow up without a father. I remember clearly that this was an unsatisfying answer; I was asking about ontology, and she had responded with teleology. But I also got the message that God cared about children.

When I was seven, my mother was diagnosed with ovarian cancer and was forthright about her grave prognosis. Knowing she would die, I went to the Bible for solace. I remember opening it randomly, hoping my eye would fall on a message from God, but nothing I read seemed to be speaking to me. Still, it was comforting to have that book in my hands. My mother's death two years later was a terrible loss, especially because my father fell apart horribly afterward. My sanity in that difficult time was saved by a loving African-American woman he hired to take care of me and my younger sister. Anna was with us only a few months, but she assured me with conviction that I was going to be okay, and I believed her. She also talked about a sister who worked with the mentally retarded, and for the first time I began imagining a career helping others with psychological problems. This was not simply altruism: Anna's sister reportedly earned $25 a day, which seemed to me a magnificent salary; I knew that my father paid Anna, who was worth a fortune to me, $40 a week plus room and board for herself and her toddler son.

One lesson of my bereavement was the searing realization that life is capricious, that we can all die at any time, and that given the ongoing possibility of sudden loss or change, we must live as well and fully as possible in the here-and-now. A deep sense of gratitude for the things I still had (health, intelligence, people who loved me, the memory of a good mother), became a constant companion. I idealized my dead mother, who was known for her sympathetic kindness. Around this time, the Good Samaritan story became important to me, and I self-consciously tried to live my life by the Golden Rule. I also identified with my father's moralism, probably in an effort to make sure I was acceptable to the one parent I had left, and became very concerned about trying to live up to a Christian ethical code.

From age nine on I went every summer to a Girl Scout camp in western Massachusetts, where we campers had late-night discussions comparing our religious beliefs. My Irish Catholic tent-mates assured me that I was going to Hell, because unlike ignorant pagans, who could spend eternity in Limbo, I had been exposed (by them) to the One True Faith and had rejected it. The Jewish campers considered us Christians a little loopy in our assumption that the Messiah had already come. I envied my Catholic friends, who could confess and be temporarily purified—we Protestants had to live with unremitting sinfulness. (Jesus may have taken on our sins and relieved us of them in his suffering on the cross, but I understood my church's message to be that our original sinfulness also somehow remained and was not erasable by good deeds or ritual. This theological position confirmed my internal sense that I had somehow damaged my mother and could never undo that.) I also envied my Jewish friends, for being the Chosen People.

The camp staff, influenced by the lesbian couple who administered the camp and who valued respectful explorations of difference, encouraged such discussions. Camp Bonnie Brae was a safe space to ponder the big questions about life that young people need to ask. The diversity there—of ethnicity, religion, race, sexual orientation, and socioeconomic status—was a welcome antidote to my white-bread suburban existence the rest of the year.

A year after my mother's death, my father married a kindhearted woman who adopted me and my younger sister and stepped gracefully into the maternal role. Because of a change in my father's job, we moved when I was eleven to New Canaan, CT, a painful relocation for me at a hard age to leave old friends and find my way in a new and much larger school where the students seemed not particularly interested in the new girl. We joined the Congregational Church there, and I sang in the youth choir and sometimes played the piano to accompany the hymns. At least I felt at home in another classic white, steepled church, with a familiar liturgy.

When I was thirteen, another change in my father's job took us to a predominantly Pennsylvania Dutch community, a suburb of Reading, where there were no Congregational churches. Most of my classmates went to Atonement Lutheran, but my parents preferred the First Presbyterian Church—not white, no steeple, a disappointment. But there I attended a weekly youth discussion group, in which members of the small Presbyterian minority in my high school talked earnestly about ethical questions. I enjoyed those meetings and my new friends in this community, which was smaller, stabler, and more welcoming than the New Canaan cliques had been. But I was also homesick for New England. I began collecting postcards of white churches with steeples. My stepmother, noting this interest, gave me a book (for my birthday or Christmas, I think) about the architecture and history of such churches, and also gave me a painting of such a church. I still have them. Perhaps I was homesick not only for a particular setting but also for a kind of confidence in my faith, which I began to question in the ways that adolescents question all the certainties they inherit.

Because my parents felt that joining a religious denomination was a decision that should not be made in childhood (reflecting itself a Protestant orientation toward religious issues), I was not baptized into the faith until my thirties, when my husband and I joined the Presbyterian church in which we would bring up our children. I was struggling with many epistemological, eschatological, and moral questions in high school, however, and I looked to my religion for answers. I read the New Testament carefully and tried to follow Jesus's teachings. Probably because of my enduring love for our housekeeper Anna, and because the Calvinist injunction to do good works had gotten in pretty deep, I was powerfully drawn to the Civil Rights movement, especially to its passionate Christian message of non-violent protest. I made a close (and continuing) friendship with an African-American girl I met in the local high school chapter of the National Council for Christians and Jews, and I occasionally went with her and her family to the Presbyterian church that Reading's African-American community attended. I loved the energy there, especially the joyful singing.

In 1962, I applied to, and was accepted by, Oberlin College. My older sister had urged me to go to a good co-ed school (she had attended a women's college in the era when such institutions expected their students to learn to be intelligent extensions of powerful males, and she regretted her choice), and there was fine music there, which was a big plus from my perspective. But mostly I was attracted to Oberlin's history of concern for social justice. It was the first American college to admit women on an equal basis with men and blacks on an equal basis with whites. It had been founded in the context of a passionate, evangelical abolitionism and had been a major stop on the Underground Railroad. (James McBride captures this sensibility and its relationship to Oberlin, also his alma mater, in his recent [2013] fictional treatment of John Brown's raid on Harper's Ferry.) Mid-sixties Oberlin students were active in current civil rights issues, and Martin Luther King, Jr. occasionally came to campus.

When I applied to Oberlin, the college brochure still described it as an explicitly Christian institution, and this depiction appealed to me. (That epithet disappeared within a couple of years, as the Jewish students expressed their irritation at being marginalized; the turning point as I remember it was when a consciously well-intentioned Dean of Women referred to Jewish students in print as "guests" and was surprised that they felt this as less than wholehearted inclusion.) The college brochure wasn't really wrong: The climate of Social Gospel evangelism in which Oberlin was founded still pervades the place in subtle ways. It produces legions of serious scholars and passionate do-gooders, and I am struck by how many of my classmates have found their way to careers in psychotherapy.

I met my husband at Oberlin. He was a young professor of political science, a "radical from Berkeley." The first time I heard him speak was at a chapel talk. I had attended it out of curiosity: it did not fit my stereotypes that a Berkeley leftist would be giving a sermon. Carey McWilliams was a spellbinder, and I decided to take some courses with him, which led to my majoring in his field and choosing him as my faculty advisor. I fell in love with him when he reached out to me in the context of my beloved stepmother's terminal cancer diagnosis when I was eighteen, a traumatic repetition for my family. Carey also encouraged me to read Freud, handing me a copy of *Civilization and Its Discontents* (Freud, 1930) and suggesting that I do my junior thesis on Freud's political theory "because you're pretty psychological." I soon fell in love with psychoanalysis and began imagining a career as a clinical psychologist.

We married at the beginning of my senior year—this was before the era when faculty-student romances were regarded as inherently exploitive. Despite the age difference, we had a lot in common, including a Calvinist sensibility. Carey was a deeply religious and brilliant man, a serious and learned Christian, but also a kind of walking ecumenical movement: He had studied with Jesuits and with a leading rabbi as well as within the Protestant tradition in which he was raised. He read Hebrew, taught courses on religion and politics, and knew a great deal about theology. I envied both his erudition and the depth of his faith. Now several years after his death, I still miss my conversations with him on these topics.

In Carey's personal library were many psychoanalytic books, including some that dealt with religious topics. I was particularly taken with several books by Theodor Reik, who was talented at writing for nonprofessional readers as well as for other analysts. What stood out most sharply to me in his work were his comments about female psychology—he was the first writer on sex differences I had ever read who did not convey an assumption of female inferiority—but I was also fascinated by his psychoanalytic writing about religious matters (e.g., Reik, 1945, 1946). When I decided to consider analysis for myself, taking advantage of its availability once we had moved to Brooklyn just after my graduation from Oberlin, I sought Reik out; he was then an old man, living in Manhattan and still practicing a little. He sent me for an intake interview at the clinic of the National Psychological Association for Psychoanalysis, which he had founded in reaction against the medical domination of psychoanalysis in the United States, and where I eventually trained as an analyst.

When I went through psychoanalysis in my twenties—a profoundly therapeutic experience with a warm, Jewish social-worker analyst who ran a settlement house on the Lower East Side of Manhattan—I became aware that I struggle with unconscious oedipal guilt (did my badness somehow kill my mother?) and guilt in general. Perhaps because of that tendency, the Protestant notion of radical moral equality, that we are all equal in our sinfulness, has always seemed self-evident—and comforting—to me. I remember struggling as a teenager with the problem of the sin of pride. How could one conquer that sin? As soon as I felt I was succeeding in being less prideful, I noted that I was taking pride in my humility. I now think about such questions in the psychoanalytic language of infantile omnipotence and narcissistic entitlement. But it was the Christian terms that framed my first efforts to understand the complexity of being.

In my analysis, I noticed the difference in temperament between me and my analyst: Like many self-critical Protestants, I was always looking for the "right" path of service and trying to resist "self-indulgence." (When I read *The Protestant Ethic and the Spirit of Capitalism* in college [see Weber, Baehr, & Wells, 2002], I was astonished that Max Weber could put words to a sensibility that had been water to the fish for me.) The Jewish sense of paradox, irony, trade-off, the "on the one hand, on the other" rabbinic outlook, was a welcome corrective to my tendency toward being self-righteous and opinionated. Training as an analyst in New York in the 1970s, I felt treated as a curious minority, and I joked that I practically had to learn Yiddish to graduate from my institute.

The cultural differences between me and my Jewish colleagues, and the overall Jewish sensibility informing psychoanalysis itself, were sources of fascination to my young-adult self. As a system of thought, however, I found psychoanalysis quite resonant with my understanding of Presbyterian theology. Freud's concept of psychic determinism, for example, did not feel too different from Calvin's idea of predestination, a much misunderstood concept that I had thought a lot about. I was not surprised to learn that Freud had had warm, intellectually stimulating friendships with Protestant theists such as Oskar Pfister and James Jackson Putnam.

Later, as a therapist serving patients of diverse religious sensibilities, I discovered Robert Lovinger's (1984) *Working with Religious Issues in Therapy*. The depiction there of the sensibilities characterizing the major religions in the United States deepened my understanding of my clients. For example, Lovinger explored how guilt might be experienced differently by individuals of different faith backgrounds, depending on the context in which their religion had developed. He observes, for example, that Protestants tend, with Martin Luther as perhaps the icon of this sensibility, to feel guilty when they are not brave enough to stand alone on matters of conscience and resist the pull of a community they see as corrupt; in contrast, Jews tend to feel guilty about separation and other threats to the maintenance of a community that has been historically beleaguered. Lovinger attributed the devaluation of faith that was common among therapists not only to their identification with Freud's effort to frame religion as an "illusion," but also to the fact that most people's religious education ends at about age twelve. That felt right to me. It is easy to conceive of religion as "childish" if one has stopped learning from religious teachers at an age when one is still thinking like a child.

PERSONAL IMPLICATIONS

As I consider my religious background and its effect on my work, I suspect its strongest influence has been on my overall moral sensibility. I loved Jesus's tendency to hang out with prostitutes and low-lifes. The Judeo-Christian emphasis on the dignity of every person rings true to me. The Golden Rule, or simple kindness, still seems to me a pretty good guide for living, though a friend of mine who studies Judaic texts has told me that there is an earlier rule, "Do *not* do unto others what you would *not* have them do to you." I like that even better.

The ethic of respect, the I-Thou, subject-to-subject connection that I hope characterizes my clinical work, derives directly from the Judeo-Christian tradition (Buber, 1953). The concept of grace, that God loves us despite our not deserving this love, has always moved me. I distrust worldly authority and cherish the radical egalitarianism of Christianity and the back-to-basics drive of the Protestant movement. I enjoy the writing of sensitive religious thinkers such as Karen Armstrong (e.g., 1994, 2007) and Marilyn Robinson (e.g., 1998, 2004, 2008). I am also interested in trying to understand the psychology of Jesus as a human being (e.g., Aslan, 2013; Crosson, 1992), in making sense of the psychological power of the Christian narrative (e.g., Parnini, 2013), and in making connections between Christian themes and psychoanalytic ones (e.g., Hoffman, 2010).

I am not observant. I do not pray or meditate regularly, but I am ongoingly aware of the presence of God—or whatever we call that which is unimaginably greater than ourselves. I experience my spirituality mostly in two areas, awe and gratitude. Awe takes me over whenever I witness the magnificence and beauty of things that defy mortal comprehension. When a patient makes a surprising discovery, or has survived a traumatic background with more resilience than I would have thought possible, or in mysteriously synchronistic moments when my client and I have a similar dream or find ourselves with the same mental image, or when I witness sudden growth after a stretch of mutual frustration and deadness, I feel awe. In the natural world I can be overwhelmed by the numinous; snorkeling at the Great Barrier Reef a few years ago, I felt dumb with wonder at the beauty of the vast, silent, magnificent underwater universe.

I am often possessed by gratitude. I find myself saying spontaneous prayers of thanks for my life, for my family, for friends, for bodily pleasures, for moments of joy, for natural beauty, for meaningful work, for all the people who have nurtured me. I am keenly aware that although I have worked hard to succeed as a therapist and teacher, I have had innumerable advantages of which I was no more deserving than anyone else. I have written about gratitude and remorse as the "glue" that supports and repairs relationships, and I understand narcissistic psychopathology in terms of the absence of the capacities for genuine appreciation and apology (McWilliams & Lependorf, 1990). It seems that I am circling back to the topic of the sin of pride and the value of recognizing the futility of human efforts to be perfect or omnipotent. The notion that we are all, in Sullivan's words, "more simply human than otherwise," and, as Lacan noted, we are all "broken" has a deep appeal to me.

CLINICAL RAMIFICATIONS

I have worked therapeutically with many people of faith and several practicing clergy. They seem to have radar for professionals who disdain religious belief, and they may find their way to me because they have picked up in my writing my respect for the spiritual. Most of my more religious patients have been observant Protestants, Catholics, and Jews in the mainstream of their respective traditions. I have also worked with committed Quakers, Eastern Orthodox clients, fundamentalist Protestants, Hindus, and Buddhists. I have had Muslim students—Turkish, Palestinian, Pakistani, and Lebanese—who taught me a lot, but I cannot recall ever working intensively with an observant Muslim client.

Much of psychotherapy, at least as I see it, is simply bearing witness. Unbearable suffering and the inability to imagine anything better require a relationship in which grief can be tolerated and hope can emerge. When I was bereaved as a child, I was comforted not by those who tried to distract me or gave me glib reassurances but by those who could bear my pain and tell me the truth. The language of my religious tradition captures this universal human need for honest engagement with suffering, as in Isaiah's "man of sorrows . . . acquainted with grief." I have appreciated writers who construe therapy as a mourning process (e.g., Stark, 1994), and I am allergic to facile efforts to fix what ails us most deeply. I have welcomed the now extensive empirical research showing that it is the relationship, not the technique, that heals (e.g., Wampold, 2010).

Psychotherapy feels to me like a sacred trust. Like Jerome Frank (Frank & Frank, 1993), I see therapists in secular and diverse societies as having a priestly function (one that is under threat these days, but that is a different paper). The 45- or 50-minute session and the other conventional boundaries of treatment provide a container in which both patient and therapist can tolerate the pain that we must process in bits and pieces in order to heal from our psychic injuries and begin growing again. I resonate to theories that emphasize our shared humanity, our inability to know fully someone else's mind, our inevitable wounding of each other, and the cycle of rupture and repair that characterizes therapeutic progress (e.g., Benjamin, 2010).

I think that for me, psychoanalysis has become a kind of religion. Not in the sense of being doctrinal or dogmatic, but in the sense of offering a worldview and an ethic of honesty. Sometimes I muse that I have become an evangelist for psychoanalytic ways of understanding human psychology and emotional suffering. I identified with my father's moralism and my mother's compassion, and (notwithstanding the notorious arrogance of many in the analytic community, especially in the heyday of American ego psychology) I cherish the attitude of humility that I think is inherent in theories that emphasize how much of our behavior is unconsciously motivated. This feels like a familiar spiritual surrender (cf. Ghent, 1990), a continuation of my Judeo-Christian preoccupation with smallness in the face of the infinite. My late colleague Herbert Strean was once interviewed by a reporter who challenged, "Isn't psychoanalysis really just another religion?" "Oh no!" Dr. Strean protested. "Psychoanalysis differs from all *other* religions in that . . . ." I could completely identify with that slip.

Many of my patients struggle with issues of faith. Here are a few vignettes from my practice in which religious issues played a big part. One of my most rewarding clients was a woman who worked as a pastoral counselor for a fundamentalist evangelical denomination that emphasized the sinfulness of homosexuality. She had read one of my books and felt I might respect her religious convictions (though as the transference elaborated, she was in constant expectation of my contempt, the attitude with which her mother had typically responded to her individuality). This woman knew she was gay, but she believed God did not sanction homoerotic love, and she was committed to a heterosexual marriage—a difficult one with an abusive husband. She could not imagine improving her life, given her theology, but she told me she wanted someone to know who she really was, and she wanted to feel alive again.

This was a long treatment in which I watched her slowly feel seen and accepted as she was. Although I never took a position about what she should do, she eventually gave up her hatred of her sexual orientation. Ultimately, she addressed her situation with courage, left her husband safely, dealt honestly and effectively with her children, and only then met a Christian lesbian partner whom she eventually married. During this therapy of many years duration, the first thing she reported as changing internally was her relationship to God. She realized that she had experienced him as a judgmental, punitive male, and she noted that she was beginning to experience God as also merciful and motherly.

She began participating in discussions with other members of her church who were struggling with sexual orientation issues and trying to "stay straight." The longer they talked together, the more they all acknowledged the failure of this solution. Eventually, and probably several weeks or months after the change had taken place internally, she told me her theology had evolved, that she believed that God loves people as they are. She began the wrenching process of leaving her marriage, her disapproving church community, and her restricted life. She retains her deep faith and her spiritual practices but worships now with her same-sex spouse in a new, accepting environment.

Another of my patients is a man who grapples with significant paranoia. He was reared by secular Jewish (and I think also anti-Semitic) parents who literally terrorized him, when they wanted to control him, with the threat, "Hitler is coming back, and next time he'll be coming for *you*." Not surprisingly, he associates his Jewish heritage with humiliation and sadism. Attending a Buddhist temple has helped him to relax and get some respite from the otherwise constant hypervigilence and agitation to which he is prone. Like my lesbian patient, he also suffered from diffuse and relentless parental contempt and finds himself, despite all evidence to the contrary, worried that I will assail his spiritual interests and devalue his Buddhist meditation.

With every improvement in his life, this man expects envious attack, and I do not believe that he could have tolerated his own successes without the spiritual disciplines he has adopted. When he read a draft of this paper (because I needed his permission to publish what I have just described), he noticed with amazement that even after years of work with me, he was surprised to learn that I *really* do not, like his parents, have contempt for faith, that my stance supporting his spiritual quest is not simply an assumed professional façade of acceptance, and that in fact I have derived great strength from the religious tradition in which I was brought up.

A charismatic minister once came to me with the agenda of becoming a better person. It would not be too hard for most of us to have been better than he had been: In his younger days he had led a drug-dealing ring of thieves. He had the charm and manipulativeness of the psychopath, but in his fifties, with all his old friends either dead or in jail, he had become curious about an alternative, more ethically conventional way of life. Having along the way developed a severe substance use disorder, he had finally gone to Alcoholics Anonymous, where he had found God. He then trained as a minister in an evangelical Protestant sect, and he had become the pastor of a small church. The immediate precipitant to his seeking therapy was an occasion when one of the elders in his church had disagreed with him, and he had decked the guy—a response that his parishioners deemed not very ministerial and regarded as grounds for some professionally guided introspection.

What intrigued me about this man was that his childhood had been so abusive, negligent, and inconsistent that even the hypothetical concept of treating people well was new to him. The only reasonably competent adult in his history was an uncle who was good with his fists (hence his reaction to the unfortunate elder). He resembled an anthropologist attempting to figure out the mores of an alien tribe of ethical people. He was trying to be faithful to his wife—an unfamiliar practice—and to be a good parent to their young children. His religion and AA had given him a new language for how to live one's life, and he could see that those precepts offered more potential satisfaction than he had known before. I worked with him for about eighteen months, at which point he was called to a bigger church in another state.

In our last session, I did my usual "exit interview," asking him what he felt he had gotten from our work, and what had disappointed him. He responded that he was unambivalently pleased with and proud of his progress. When I pressed for specifics, he declared, "I sat across from a woman I was attracted to for a year and a half and didn't put the make on you!" At first, I was deflated by this version of his experience (what about all my sensitive interpretations?), but then I realized that for him, it was a significant, life-changing achievement to have related to another person without exploitating or manipulating her.

I find that individuals differ greatly as to how central or experience-near the spiritual is to them. Many patients find it harder to talk about their religious attitudes than to talk about lust or greed or vanity or homicidal wishes. For believers, their spirituality is a matter of the tenderest intimacy.

When I work with clients whose religion is important to them yet relatively unfamiliar to me, I often ask them to give me something to read so that I can understand the spiritual part of their mental life better. (Sometimes they offer such items spontaneously, out of their intuition that I will not understand them well enough without a window on their religious sensibility.) I do this out of my own wish to learn but also to convey that this dimension of their psychology is important for us to recognize together. Once they feel relatively safe with me, they often recount to me their spiritual practices, their conversations with God, and their efforts to deepen their relationship with the divine.

Sometimes religious issues are at the epicenter of a person's suffering. It is not uncommon for people to seek therapy after taking their problems to their faith community and running into insuperable internal resistances to the help they are offered there. For example, an African-American Protestant woman came to me because she was angry with God for allowing her to suffer a series of terrible losses; she was not comforted by her community's reassurance that He would not give her more than she could bear. A Hindu man came because he had worked hard within his ashram on his attitude toward his wife, and despite his efforts to accept her as she was, he was still impatient and irritated with her.

A teacher who had been groomed by his Southern white parents to be a great evangelist—a vocation he had embraced until he reached puberty and realized that avoiding sin is not so easy once sexual desire enters the picture—came to treatment because despite his gratifying career, he felt he had failed his family. Gay and lesbian believers often come to negotiate a painful coming-out process, which may mean for them the loss not only of their parents' support but also of their whole religious community.

CONCLUDING COMMENTS

I have tried to account for my own spiritual inclinations and to connect them with my therapeutic stance and my experiences with patients of varying religious sensibilities and beliefs. I think the legacy of my Protestant background includes an ethic of respect, a sense of the presence of both good and evil (especially evil) in everyone, a tilt toward gratitude, the habit of compassion in the face of suffering, a tolerance of painful emotional states such as grief, and a sense of awe about phenomena that are far beyond human control or influence. I think that these attitudes are often not fully conscious and that they infiltrate my work with patients in mostly silent but probably powerfully consequential ways.

REFERENCES

Armstrong, K. (1994). *A history of God: The 4000-year quest of Judaism, Christianity, and Islam*. New York: Ballantine Books.

Armstrong, K. (2007). *The quiet transformation: The beginning of our religious traditions*. New York: Anchor.

Aslan, R. (2013). *Zealot: The life and times of Jesus of Nazareth*. New York: Random House.

Benjamin, J. (2010). Where's the gap and what's the difference? The relational view of intersubjectivity, multiple selves, and enactments. *Contemporary Psychoanalysis, 46*, 112–119.

Buber, M. (1953) *I and thou*. London: T & T Clark.

Crosson, J. D. (1992). *The historical Jesus: The life of a Mediterranean peasant*. Ontario, Canada: Harpercollins.

Eddy, M. B. (2006). *Science and health with key to the scriptures*. Boston, MA: Christian Science Board of Directors. Originally published in 1875.

Frank, M. D., & Frank, J. B. (1993). *Persuasion and healing: A comparative study of psychotherapy*. Baltimore, MD: Johns Hopkins.

Freud, S. (1930). Civilization and its discontents. In J. Strachey (Ed.), *Standard Edition of the Complete Psychological Works of Sigmund Freud, vol. 21* (pp. 64–145).

Ghent, E. (1990). Masochism, submission, surrender—Masochism as a perversion of surrender. *Contemporary Psychoanalysis, 26*, 108–136.

Hoffman, M. T. (2010). *Toward mutual recognition: Relational psychoanalysis and the Christian narrative*. New York: Routledge.

Lovinger, R. (1984). *Working with religious issues in therapy*. New York: Aronson.

McBride, J. (2013). *The good lord bird*. New York: Riverhead.

McWilliams, N., & Lependorf, S. (1990). Narcissistic pathology of everyday life: The denial of remorse and gratitude. *Contemporary Psychoanalysis, 26*, 430–451.

Parini, J. (2013). *Jesus: The human face of God*. New York: Houghton Mifflin Harcourt.

Reik, T. (1945). *The compulsion to confess*. New York: Wiley.

Reik, T. (1946). *Ritual*. New York: Farrar, Straus & Giroux.

Robinson, M. (1998). *The death of Adam: Essays on modern thought*. New York: Houghton Mifflin.

Robinson, M. (2004). *Gilead*. New York: Farrar, Straus, & Giroux.

Robinson, M. (2008). *Home*. Ontario, Canada: Harpercollins.

Stark, M. (1994). *Working with resistance*. Northvale, NJ: Aronson.

Wampold, B. E. (2010). *The basis of psychotherapy: An introduction to theory and practice*. Washington, DC: American Psychological Association.

Weber, M., Baehr, P. R., & Wells, G. C. (2002). *The Protestant ethic and the spirit of capitalism and other writings*. New York: Penguin.

Chapter Three

The Welcome Return of the Suppressed

Religion and Psychoanalysis in Dialogue

Marie T. Hoffman

In my discussion of Dr. McWilliams' chapter, I will first consider the role of religion in psychoanalysis. I will briefly describe its *suppression* in psychoanalytic history, and highlight those prominent psychoanalysts who precede Dr. McWilliams in the integration of faith into their work. Dr. McWilliams has profoundly impacted contemporary psychoanalysis with her magnificently comprehensive contributions to the practice of psychoanalysis (1994, 1999, 2004, 2006, 2011). With much gratitude, I will interact with Dr. McWilliams' chapter, and will offer a much-deserved recognition of the *expression* of her faith in her clinical practice.

THE SUPPRESSION OF RELIGION IN PSYCHOANALYTIC HISTORY

Freud and His Followers

There is no lack of knowledge concerning Freud's disdain of religion, but there is a lack of consideration of his ample reasons for its dismissal. While painfully aware of centuries of anti-Semitism, Freud himself experienced ongoing prejudice promulgated by the Hapsburg Church-state marriage. Anti-Semitism not only limited his professional ambitions, but foisted humiliations upon him, his father, and his children. Like many Jews of his era, Enlightenment secularism became a far more attractive alternative.

Although Freud noted that his beliefs regarding religion were personal—he nonetheless established a godless trajectory for psychoanalysis that his disciples followed. One exception was Freud's lifelong friend, Swiss pastor Oskar Pfister. Most psychoanalysts know of their close friendship and Pfister's response to Freud's *Future of an Illusion.* Less known are numerous other analysts who were attracted to psychoanalysis because of the embedded Judaic and Christian values that Pfister alludes to in the following remark:

> It is not the religious creed that is the true criterion for a Christian; in John 13:35 another is given. "By this love you have for one another, everyone will know that you are my disciples." ... I dare to assert again that Freud, in the light of these words, with his view of life, and his life's work has preeminence over many a certified church-Christian who considers him a heathen...(Roazen, 1993, p. 578).

Psychoanalysts Influenced by Christianity

In Freud's shadow, most analysts of religious persuasion kept it a private matter. Notwithstanding, more than a few early psychoanalysts were influenced by the Christian narrative which informed their thinking. In *Toward Mutual Recognition: Relational Psychoanalysis and the Christian Narrative* (2011), I have explored the Christian influences in the lives of these early psychoanalysts, and have demonstrated how the Christian narratives contributed to the tectonic paradigm shift in psychoanalysis from Freud's search for quiescence for primordial drive impulses to recognition of the developing nascent, innate motivation to seek relationship.

Greenberg and Mitchell (1983) succinctly articulated this paradigm shift:

> The most significant tension in the history of psychoanalytic ideas has been the dialectic between the original Freudian mode, which takes as its starting point the instinctual drive, and an alternative comprehensive model initiated in the work of Fairbairn and Sullivan, which evolves structure from the individual's relations with other people (Greenberg and Mitchell, 1983, p. 20).

Mitchell consistently asserted throughout his relational corpus that drive theory and the alternative model are incompatible and cannot be integrated because they derive from two different views of human nature. Mitchell endorsed, "Fairbairn [who] was suggesting that object seeking ... is not the vehicle for satisfaction of a specific need, but the expression of our very nature, the form through which we become specifically *human beings* [emphasis in original]" (1988, p. 117). Mitchell understood that "the very nature of [a human person is] wired to be actualized only through exchanges with other minds" (1988, p. 121). The Judaic and Christian narratives from which British object relations theory derives did not escape Margaret Black [Mitchell's spouse and writing partner] who encouraged her husband to explore the religious elements of his relational thinking (personal communication 2011). For a further exploration of Mitchell and the Christian narrative, see L. Hoffman (2014, forthcoming).

In Scotland, W. R. D. Fairbairn lived a private, life-long Christian faith, as documented in his diaries, and the tenets of this faith permeate his theory of endopsychic structure (1952). My husband and I enjoyed the privilege of perusing Fairbairn's diaries and personal papers for several days at the Fairbairn archives at the Library of Scotland in Edinburgh, and have written a compilation of our findings in a forthcoming book chapter (Hoffman, M. & Hoffman, L., 2014). Fairbairn's lifespan church attendance and friendships confirm the significance of Christian faith in his life.

According to Sutherland (1989), weekly Sunday morning and evening church attendance with his parents, Thomas and Cecilia Fairbairn, was not bothersome to their only child, Ronald. His upbringing in the Free Church of Scotland undoubtedly included his memorization of catechisms and voluminous passages of Scripture. Fairbairn's entire primary and secondary education was in the Merchiston Castle Preparatory School and Upper School (Birtles & Scharff, 1994, p.462). Merchiston Castle was founded in 1833 by Charles Chalmers, also a founder of the Free Church of Scotland in 1844. As a preparatory school *par excellence,* Merchiston's curriculum was formulated by respect for science and Christian faith.

Fairbairn studied philosophy at Edinburgh University under the tutelage of Professor Andrew (Seth) Pringle-Pattison. Professor Pattison's robust Christian faith is recorded in his 1912–1913 Gifford Lectures entitled "The Idea of God in Light of Recent Philosophy" (1920). Apparently Fairbairn was deeply influenced by Pringle-Pattison as evidenced by his enrollment in divinity studies in preparation for Christian ministry. After serving in World War I in the Egyptian theater, Fairbairn returned to Scotland and commenced his psychoanalytic training. He completed his training analysis with E. H. Connell, who was analyzed by Ernest Jones, and whom Sutherland described as "a very full-blooded Christian" (1989, p. 7).

In more than twenty significant professional papers spanning the years 1927–1962, Fairbairn integrated his Christian faith with his psychoanalytic thinking. He systematically developed a theory that understood the human infant as seeking the parent, not merely in the Darwinian sense for survival, but in the Judaic and Christian sensibility that humans are created for relationship. "In language that mirrors Calvinist [Christian] theology, Fairbairn attended to the (1) 'fracture' of the internal world, (2) 'enslavement' to bad objects, and (3) 'alienation'—the schizoid condition that underlies all psychopathology.... Recapitulating the Calvinist narrative, Fairbairn's agency for redemption is personal relationship offered by a caring 'other'" (Hoffman & Hoffman, 2014, p. 81).

Throughout his childhood and youth, D. W. Winnicott had been nourished by the English Wesleyanism of his father, J. Frederick Winnicott. The elder Winnicott was an active member and teacher at the King Street Wesleyan Church, and was a founding member and served on the synod of the Wesleyan Church on Mutley Plain (Rodman, 2003, p. 383). Not only D. W.'s parents, J. Frederick and Elizabeth Winnicott, but also his ancestors dating back to the 1700s, were known as "leading lights in the church" and "profoundly religious" (Goldman, 1993, pp. 116–117). Young Donald Winnicott at age fourteen was enrolled at the Leys School, a Methodist boarding school founded for the express purpose of integrating faith and academic scholarship (Rodman, 2003, p. 23).

D. W. Winnicott faithfully attended the Methodist (Wesleyan) Church until age twenty-seven when he converted to the Anglican Church, the church of his mother and his first wife. He discovered psychoanalysis through reading a book written by the Swiss Reformed minister and Christian friend of Freud, Oskar Pfister. In middle adulthood, Winnicott's church attendance declined, but he continued to value "what can be characterized as a lingering religiosity" (Goldman, 1993, p. 115). According to Rodman (2003), "From at least the mid-1940's to the mid-1960's, Jesus Christ was clearly a figure with whom he identified" (p. 291). Winnicott's identification with Jesus intensified after the mid-1960's when he became fascinated by the books *King Jesus* and *Nazarene Gospel Restored,* and he corresponded with their author, Robert Graves (Phillips, 1988, p. 29). Concurrent with this fascination with the person of Jesus, Winnicott wrote his final and most influential paper, "The Use of an Object and Relating through Identifications" (1968), which describes the developmental process of the destruction and survival of the object. D. W. Winnicott bravely posited a place for religion in potential space during a time when the British Psychoanalytic Association was still in the grips of vehement opposition to religion.

Hugh Crichton-Miller founded Tavistock Clinic in London in 1920 and not only sought to live out his Christian calling by helping traumatized World War I veterans, but wrote a book for clergy about psychoanalysis. "Tavistock was a free clinic that offered services to all people suffering bereavement after the war, regardless of their ability to pay. The innovative and unorthodox therapeutic approaches of Tavistock were derived from what became known as the 'school of British eclectics.'" (L. Hoffman, unpublished, p. 4). Many of the eclectics at Tavistock were distinct in "their commitment to the Christian religion .... Crichton-Miller and H. A. Hadfield, who worked at Tavistock ... exemplified [this] commitment.... The Tavistock Clinic itself was sometimes referred to as the 'parsons' clinic' because many staff members were deeply religious" (Newcombe & Lerner, 1981, pp. 5–6). John Rickman (1938), a Quaker who was at the nucleus of the "eclectics" at Tavistock, wrote "Need for a Belief in God." Other notable Christian psychoanalysts at Tavistock included Ian Suttie and Sylvia Payne. While at Tavistock, Wilfred Bion, whose family's crest read "Without God there is no purpose," was drawn to John Rickman and entered a training analysis with him. Tragically, Rickman died at the end of the second year of the analysis.

Michael Balint converted to a distinctively Christian Hungarian Unitarian Church. According to Andre Haynal (personal communication, 2009), this was a shift of religious persuasion more than one to avoid anti-Semitism.

Harold Guntrip was a Congregational minister who popularized Fairbairn's ideas. During his analysis with Fairbairn, "he sought to bring together the new orientation [of psychoanalysis] with his religious experience in a new book, *Mental Pain and the Cure of Souls* (1956)" (Hazell, 1994, p. 9). Sutherland considered Fairbairn, Winnicott, Guntrip, and Balint to be the four primary innovators of British object relations theory.

In Scotland, Ian and Jane Suttie (1935) wrote *Origins of Love and Hate*, a book based on their Christian ideals. Jane Suttie (1952) also translated Sandor Ferenczi's *Further Contributions*, Vol. 2. A boldness to challenge Freud's ideas and a commitment to Christian faith "were abundantly evident in the work of Ian Suttie, who did the most of any of the eclectics to forge theoretical alternatives to Freudianism" (Newcombe & Lerner, 1981, p. 5). John Bowlby was much influenced by Suttie's views during the years both were at Tavistock, and Bowlby wrote the foreword to the 1988 reprint of Suttie's *The Origin of Love and Hate.* Bowlby explained why Suttie's work did not achieve prominence in the psychoanalytic community: "It was unfortunate that, in his strong disagreement with Freud's early metapsychology (now largely forgotten), Suttie became polemical ... this tended to alienate potential friends (though not without influencing them first)" (Suttie, 1988, p. xvii). In an interview with Jeffrey Lerner in 1976, Bowlby discussed a second reason for the marginalization of Suttie's work: "Suttie devoted much effort to the discussion of religion, arguing for a return to a Christianity of the canonical gospels, which he believed had emphasized matriarchal as well as patriarchal concerns, and thus constituted a form of psychotherapy" (Newcombe & Lerner, 1981, p. 11).

In the United States psychoanalysts with ties to Christian faith include James Jackson Putnam, first president of the American Psychoanalytic Association. Clara Thompson was raised Baptist and once aspired to become a medical missionary. Harry Stack Sullivan likely enacted a revolt against his Catholic upbringing by focusing on demystification, and challenging the Freudian papacy. Heinz Kohut wrote about religion and converted to a Christian expression of Unitarianism. He even requested that Martin Luther's "A Mighty Fortress Is Our God" be played at his funeral. Erik Erikson's mother read Christian philosopher Soren Kierkegaard to him while *in utero* and during his childhood, urging him to "revere the existential core of Christianity" (Carveth, 2008, p. 109). Karen Horney was raised Lutheran and her early diaries reveal a deep faith. In adulthood, though no longer observant, she was a devoted friend of theologian Paul Tillich, Tillich delivering the eulogy at her funeral.

Collectively, these psychoanalysts profoundly influenced the development of psychoanalysis. However, these religious influences were hidden or suppressed by a psychoanalytic community whose bias against religion was yet potent.

THE EXPRESSION OF RELIGION IN PSYCHOANALYTIC PRACTICE

In order to contextualize my remarks, I will begin by describing my own religious tradition. I will then explore the expression of religion in Dr. McWilliams' chapter by referencing three couplets that appear in her final paragraph. Utilizing the first couplet, I will reflect on Dr. McWilliams' perspectives on *human nature* and their expression in her work. Using Dr. McWilliams' second couplet, I will address *human experience* from the vantage point of analyst and patient, and consider a psychotherapy practiced with the Christian narrative as its latent compass. With the third couplet, I will enumerate and elaborate on the *human attitudes* exemplified by Dr. McWilliams as a psychoanalyst.

My Religious Tradition

I was only child to immigrant parents from the Middle East. My parents migrated from the Greek Orthodox Church, to Methodist, Baptist, Pentecostal, and independent churches. At home, mother, father, and I studied the Bible and prayed for others daily.

I attended a rigidly conservative Christian university. Together with my future husband, Lowell, we attended an off-campus church that provided a model of a more relational, authentic Christianity. After four years of marriage, with one child born and one on the way, Lowell and I studied at a community in Switzerland called L'Abri. There, in the context of loving relationship and scholarship, we were drawn toward a truly relational experience of our faith, and a career in psychology. Our religious orientation became Presbyterian, for we appreciated the doctrinal depth and the representative church governance.

Like Dr. McWilliams, Lowell and I have come to recognize the considerable resonance of our personal faith with our psychoanalytic theories. I first published my formulations of this resonance in 2004 and subsequently in 2008, 2011, and forthcoming in 2014. We value both our secular and religious communities, and appreciate them most when they propel us toward love and justice. Having presented my religious influences, I now turn to Dr. McWilliams' moving chapter.

Human Nature

In the final paragraph of Dr. McWilliams' chapter she distills the legacy of her Protestant background. The first two influences of her Protestant upbringing form a couplet that she lists as, "*an ethic of respect*, [and] *a sense of the presence of both good and evil (especially evil) in everyone*." This couplet aptly represents both Dr. McWilliams' and Christianity's perspectives on human nature and is my first focus.

Dr. McWilliams writes:

> As I consider my religious background and its effect on my work, I suspect its strongest influence has been on my overall moral sensibility. I loved Jesus's tendency to hang out with prostitutes and low-lifes. The Judeo-Christian emphasis on the dignity of every person rings true to me....The ethic of respect, the I-Thou, subject-to-subject connection that I hope characterizes my clinical work, derives directly from the Judeo-Christian tradition.

Supporting her stated values, Dr. McWilliams offers a panoply of experiences with patients that illuminate her view of their worth. She first describes her long treatment with a lesbian woman trapped in a heterosexual marriage. Dr. McWilliams narrates, "I watched her slowly feel seen and accepted as she was."

She then recounts the experiences of a man raised in a contemptuous, secular Jewish home where the only escape had been the young man's flight to Buddhist meditation. He feared that Dr. McWilliams would "assail his spiritual interests and devalue his Buddhist meditation." Like many spiritual people who grace our offices, he feared that her psychoanalysis would have no room for his spirituality. Dr. McWilliams relates, "He was surprised to learn that I *really* do not, like his parents, have contempt for faith, that my stance supporting his spiritual quest is not simply an assumed professional persona..." For Dr. McWilliams, her ethic of respect is based on the intrinsic worth of each individual, without regard to their unique sensibilities that may differ from hers.

Dr. McWilliams' third illustration is with a young man who "had the charm and manipulativeness of the psychopath." For an author of a book on psychoanalytic diagnosis, who facilely recognized the character issues involved, Dr. McWilliams' respect for the intrinsic worth of even this broken man allows her to work with hope.

Dr. McWilliams' belief in the real presence of evil, not just of good, gives contrast and potency to her ethic of respect. This respect in the face of human brokenness, she derives from her embrace of "The concept of grace: God loves us despite our not deserving this love…" It is perhaps her belief in the presence of both good and evil in human nature that also gives Dr. McWilliams her continued resilience. In each of these situations, the ruptures of the psychoanalytic hour are anticipated as manifestations of our broken human condition. She writes, "It seems that I am circling back to the topic of the sin of pride and the value of recognizing the futility of human efforts to be perfect or omnipotent. The notion that we are all, in Sullivan's words, 'more simply human than otherwise,' and, as Lacan noted, we are all 'broken' has a deep appeal to me."

I resonate with Dr. McWilliams' views on human nature, and would like to contemplate the theological narrative from which, I believe, these views emanate. That narrative begins with humans who were created perfect and whole, reflecting their Creator, and worthy of all respect. Into this idyllic state a rupture of cosmic proportions interposes between humans and God, between humans and other humans, as well as within each human being. Evil enters the world, and renders humans internally and externally broken. Though the reflection of the Creator would remain, it would be distorted by brokenness perpetuated generationally through identifications with parents. This narrative asserts that the longing of the Creator is for a reversal of this fractured condition, a renewal of shalom through the instrumentality of humans empowered by love. This longing echoes in the radical words that Jesus taught us to pray: "…Thy kingdom come, thy will be done on earth as it is in heaven."

In the thick theological construct of *imago dei*, humans are made in the image of God. Despite damage, deprivation, or lack of capacity, all are worthy of the greatest dignity and care; no one can be deemed unfit, unworthy, unnecessary. This ethic of respect directs our sight beyond our patient's shattered state, and kindles hope for a meaningful destiny, one inspired by grace and reflective of the redemptive nature of a loving God.

While immersed in the pathos of Dr. McWilliams' clinical work, my mind traversed to my work with a patient whose encounter with evil was of the darkest sort. At six, Mandy's mother was murdered and mutilated by her father who then turned his violence on her. Mandy lost her eye, and lacerations to her face and torso required over 150 stitches. Through her twenties and thirties, Mandy and I worked with the shared belief in a God who could restore beauty and meaning in spite of her catastrophic childhood. Today Mandy, married and mother of two, is studying to help others in the very areas of her trauma.

Human Experience

The second couplet from Dr. McWilliams' chapter is a *tolerance for painful emotional states*, and *a sense of awe*. I find in these two human experiences a cause and effect that I will later ponder in the context of Winnicott's writings. But I would first like to stay experience-near and relate this couplet of understandings to what I feel is most gripping and stunning in Dr. McWilliams' presentation—her own story.

Dr. McWilliams entrusts to us her personal journey which is marked by shattering losses: The loss of mother; the loss of father in his season of mourning; the loss of Anna, her beloved African-American housekeeper just months after losing her mother; the loss of the family home in Massachusetts and her circle of childhood friends; the loss of her second home in Connecticut and a farewell to the lovely New England white, steepled churches; the loss of the familiar Congregational Church; the loss of her kind-hearted stepmother, and more recently, the loss of her companion, colleague, and husband of many years, Carey McWilliams. I am inspired—and even awed—by how Dr. McWilliams relates all of her losses with no discernible tinge of bitterness, sense of injustice, or expectation of reparation.

Dr. McWilliams' acceptance of the thrown-ness of life was surely aided by a personal appropriation of her early, theologically grounded views of goodness and evil in a terribly broken world. Dr. McWilliams muses, "One lesson of my bereavement was the searing realization that life is capricious, that we can all die at any time, and that given the on-going possibility of sudden loss or change, we must live as well and fully as possible in the here-and-now."

I suspect that there is more here than a mere mental assent to the capriciousness of life. Dr. McWilliams' capacity to tolerate excruciatingly painful affect and her equanimity in sharing her story suggest a sense of surrender to something greater than herself, a sense of awe at "the presence of God—or whatever we call that which is unimaginably greater than ourselves." In surrender to that which is greater than herself, Dr. McWilliams becomes enabled as a psychotherapist to experience this sense of awe with her patients. She recounts:

> When a patient makes a surprising discovery, or has survived a traumatic background with more resilience than I would have thought possible, or in the mysteriously synchronistic moments when my client and I have a similar dream or find ourselves with the same mental image, or when I witness sudden growth after a stretch of mutual frustration and deadness, I feel awe.

The human relational experiences that structure mental life much more than memorized maxims, principles, and derivations of formal logic are painfully evident in Dr. McWilliams' path from bereavement to equanimity. Paul Ricoeur, French philosopher and Christian, once wrote, "I cannot conceive of a religious attitude that did not proceed from 'a feeling of absolute dependence.' And is this not the essential relation of humankind to the sacred, transmuted into speech…?"(1995, p. 65) Ricoeur links the ability to depend—that trusting surrender to a benevolent other—to the very essence of what it means to be religious.

This capacity for absolute dependence on, or surrender to, God or fellow humans was a principal investigation of Donald Winnicott. In his paper, "The Use of an Object" Winnicott (1968) details defensive processes that humans employ to control their experience of the world, such as clutching to feelings of omnipotence. In this state of omnipotence, a person cannot experience others as separate people, nor can he/she experience the joy of receiving since dependence cannot be acknowledged. Winnicott depicts the role of the analyst as surviving without retaliation the attacks that stem from the objectifying omnipotence of the patient. Dr. McWilliams, elaborating on Winnicott, writes: "The 45- or 50-minute session and the other conventional boundaries of treatment provide a container in which both patient and therapist can tolerate the pain that we must process in bits and pieces in order to heal from our psychic injuries..."

The bridge between mental assent to the need for surrender and its realization is the span of relational experiences that make the tolerance of painful emotions survivable. Safe passages across this bridge facilitate possibilities for trust and even awe.

Dr. McWilliams describes two experiences found in the facilitating environment of her own history and in her clinical work, which also have valency in the Christian narrative. The first is that of "witnessing." Though in years past "witnessing" was related to religious proselytism, the word when reconstructed conveys a most basic redemptive function—a function exemplified by Jesus with the agonized and humiliated Samaritan woman at the well. Dr. McWilliams, referring to her religious tradition, explains: "The language of my religious tradition captures this universal human need for honest engagement with suffering, as in Isaiah's 'man of sorrows…acquainted with grief.'" Dr. McWilliams continues: "Much of psychotherapy, at least as I see it, is simply bearing witness. Unbearable suffering and the inability to imagine anything better require a relationship in which grief can be tolerated and hope can emerge."

Dr. McWilliams' second experience is that of "comforting." In the Christian narrative, the Spirit of God sent to encourage, strengthen, and guide Jesus's disciples upon his ascension was called, "The Comforter." "When I was bereaved as a child," writes Dr. McWilliams, "I was comforted not by those who tried to distract me but by those who could bear my pain and tell me the truth." As painful affects are experienced and tolerated in the presence of another, the impulse to grasp at omnipotence begins to fade and the acceptance of necessary comfort from another becomes less mental assent and more lived experience. In the shared suffering of painful emotional states such as grief, mourning, powerlessness, despair, and fear, we can acknowledge our finiteness, find courage to receive, and discover a space for awe at that which is other than ourselves.

Human Attitude

In the final couplet—*a tilt toward gratitude* and *compassion in the face of suffering*—Dr. McWilliams describes attitudes that are the polar opposite of narcissism. She observes: "I have written about gratitude and remorse as the 'glue' that supports and repairs relationships, and I understand narcissistic psychopathology in terms of the absence of the capacities for genuine appreciation and apology."

The developmental achievements that contribute to the emergence of gratitude and compassion can be traced to a recognition of good as well as evil, and a relinquishing of omnipotence. Gratitude, which is only possible when omnipotence and entitlement are surrendered, gently flows through Dr. McWilliams' essay. She does not expect a perfect world, a perfect colleague, or a perfect patient. Dr. McWilliams traces this sense of gratitude from her childhood in its earliest form where life was lived by the Golden Rule, to her adult life in which she recognizes gratitude flowing from the experience of grace. Of her early life she writes, "A deep sense of gratitude for the things I still had (health, intelligence, people who loved me, the memory of a good mother), became a constant companion." Speaking of her current experience of gratitude, she comments,

> I am often possessed by gratitude. I find myself saying spontaneous prayers of thanks for my life, for my family, for friends, for bodily pleasures, for moments of joy, for natural beauty, for meaningful work, for all the people who have nurtured me. I am keenly aware that although I have worked hard to succeed as a therapist and teacher, I have had innumerable advantages of which I was no more deserving than anyone else.

The Christian narrative portrays the unmerited, unbidden seeking by a God who forgives, restores, and embraces even as persons struggle to retain their omnipotence. Surrender to this love transforms the tenaciously self-sufficient to the humbly grateful. But how does one express gratitude to God beyond mere words?

Paul Ricoeur offers help with this question that is based in his study of Mauss's (1989) work on gifting practices among tribal groups. In groups such as the Maori, the gift carries a magical power that binds the community together, a power that presses to be passed on. Ricoeur (2005) demystifies these practices and establishes that, in fact, Maori practice points to a universal desire to pass on the gift as part of the action of gratitude. The generative power of gift to which gratitude is a response, is also supported by research. In a 2006 study by Bartlett and DeSteno, findings demonstrated that prosocial behavior is augmented by gratitude. Prosocial behavior subsequent to an experience eliciting gratitude was found to occur totally independent of a motivation to reciprocate. Grateful recipients of care were motivated to offer care to complete strangers who bore no relationship to the initial gift.

The capacity to share in the suffering of another is developed in those who have themselves been recipients of compassion. The gift of compassion for the suffering of another is given through empathic identification. In empathic identification, the other is recognized as a separate person, unlike the defensive and narcissistic functions of projective identification that objectify the other. St. Paul describes the course of compassion as a redemptive dynamic that originates in God. He writes: "[God] comes alongside us when we go through hard times, and before you know it, he brings us alongside someone else who is going through hard times so that we can be there for that person just as God was there for us" (II Corinthians 3:5, *The Message*).

I understand Dr. McWilliams' gifts of comfort to her patients as an outpouring of comfort received. Her gratitude for comfort received regenerates with each expression of her gift of loving comfort. Her very sensitivities hewn during her own sufferings give rise to her empathic identifications and expressions of compassion. As she expresses her compassion, she simultaneously embodies the originary compassion of God's redemptive heart. Dr. McWilliams' personal and clinical practice of giving a grace received both reiterates and replicates the redemptive covenant of God with humankind which was so succinctly stated by St. Paul: "Where sin abounded, grace abounds more."

I have attempted in my response to Dr. McWilliams' chapter to describe three broad intersections where I find psychoanalysis and the Christian narrative meet. Her view of human nature that includes an ethic of respect and a sense of both good and evil corresponds to the Judaic and Christian cadences of being made in the image of God, yet being broken. Her descriptions of the human experience of bearing painful emotional states and being surprised by a sense of awe spring from her acceptance of finiteness and her achievement of surrendering to that which is greater than herself. Her capacity for gratitude brings to expression her compassion for the other who, like her, knows suffering.

For all who know Dr. McWilliams, and I count myself as one of the many who are blessed to know her, Dr. McWilliams embodies and shares a personal kindness and gracious humility that reflects the originary goodness of humanity, stained by the human condition, yet always believing in and hoping for all that is good in each person. Dr. McWilliams' commitment to witness and bear with another the radical evil that has befallen them, and her sense of awe when she experiences Other, reveals within her that which is greater than herself. Dr. McWilliams' contagion for gratitude has borne much fruit in the psychoanalytic community and beyond.

REFERENCES

Bartlett, M., & DeSteno, D. (2006). Gratitude and prosocial behavior: Helping when it costs you. *Psychological Science, 17*, 319–325.

Birtles, E., & Scharff, D. (1994). *From instinct to self, Vol. 1.* Northvale, NJ: Aronson.

Carveth, D. (2008). Erik Erikson and the American psyche: Ego, ethics, and evolution. *Canadian Journal of Psychoanalysis, 16*, 108–111.

Fairbairn, W. R. D. (1952). *Psychoanalytic studies of the personality.* London: Tavistock.

Ferenczi, S. (1952). *Further contributions to the theory and technique of psychoanalysis.* New York: Basic Books.

Freud, S. (1927). *The future of an illusion.* In J. Strachey (Ed. & Trans.), *The standard edition of the complete psychological works of Sigmund Freud.* Vol. 21, 3–56. London: Hogarth Press.

Goldman, D. (1993). *In search of the real: The origins and originality of D. W. Winnicott.* Northvale, NJ: Aronson.

Greenberg, J., & Mitchell, S. (1983). *Object relations in psychoanalytic theory.* Cambridge, MA: Harvard University Press.

Hazell, J. (1994). *Personal relations therapy: The collected papers of H. J. S. Guntrip.* Northvale, NJ: Jason Aronson.

Hoffman, L. (2014). *Relational Psychoanalysis.* In: Strawn, B. & Bland, E. (Eds.), Forthcoming, Downers Grove, IL: Intervarsity Press.

Hoffman, L. (unpublished). *The object relations origins of attachment theory.*

Hoffman, M. (2004). From enemy combatant to strange bedfellow: The role of religious narratives in the work of W. R. D. Fairbairn and D. W. Winnicott, *Psychoanalytic Dialogues, 14*(6) 769–804.

Hoffman, M. (2008). Fairbairn and Winnicott on my mind: Counterpoints, tensions, and oscillations in the clinical setting. *Contemporary Psychoanalysis, 44*(3), 454–475.

Hoffman, M. (2011). *Toward mutual recognition: Relational psychoanalysis and the Christian Narrative.* New York: Routledge.

Hoffman, M., & Hoffman, L. (2014). *Religion in the life and work of W. R. D. Fairbairn.* In: Clarke, G. & Scharff, D. (Eds.), *Fairbairn and the object relations tradition.* London: Karnac.

Mauss, M. (1989). *The gift: The form and reason for exchange in archaic societies.* New York: Norton.

McWilliams, N. (1994). *Psychoanalytic diagniosis: Understanding personality structure in the clinical process.* New York: Guilford Press.

McWilliams, N. (1999). *Psychoanalytic case formulation.* New York: Guilford Press.

McWilliams, N. (2004). *Psychoanalytic psychotherapy: A practitioner's guide.* New York: Guilford Press.

McWilliams, N. (2006). See: PDM Task Force.

McWilliams, N. (2011). *Psychoanalytic diagnosis: Understanding personality structure in the clinical process, second Edition.* New York: Guilford.

Mitchell, S. (1988). *Relational concepts in psychoanalysis: An integration.* Cambridge, MA: Harvard University Press.

Newcombe, N., & Lerner, J. (1981). Britian between the wars: The historical context of Bowlby's attachment theory. *Psychiatry: The Journal for the Study of Interpersonal Processes, 45*(1), 1–12.

Phillips, A. (1988). *Winnicott.* Cambridge, MA: Harvard University Press.

Pringle-Pattison, A. S. (1920). *The idea of God in the light of recent philosophy.* New York: Oxford University Press.

PDM Task Force. (2006). *Psychodynamic Diagnostic Manual.* Silver Spring, MD: Alliance of Psychoanalytic Organizations.

Rickman, J. (1957). Need for belief in God (1938), *The International Psycho-Analytic Library, 52*, 384–390.

Ricoeur, P. (1995). *Figuring the sacred.* Minneapolis, MN: Fortress.

Ricoeur, P. (2005). *The course of recognition.* Cambridge, MA: Harvard Univ. Press.

Roazen, P. (1993). The illusion of a future. *International Journal of Psycho-Analysis, 74*, 559–579.
Rodman, F. R. (2003). *Winnicott: Life and work.* Cambridge, MA: Perseus.
Sutherland, J. D. (1989). *Fairbairn's journey into the interior.* London: Free Association Books.
Suttie, I. (1988). *The origins of love and hate* (1935). London: Free Association Books.
Winnicott, D.W. (1968). The use of an object and relating through identifications. In C. Winnicott, R. Shepherd, & M. Davis (Eds.), *Psycho-Analytic Explorations*, 218–227, Cambridge, MA: Harvard University Press, 1989.

Chapter Four

Religion—"It's Complicated!"

The Convergence of Race, Class, and Sexuality in Clinicians' Reflection on Religious Experience

Phillis Isabella Sheppard

Eliezer Witztum and David Greenberg (2001), in their work on mental health treatment with ultra-orthodox Jews in Israel, noted, "going beneath the surface…has also meant going beneath our own surfaces, as physicians, as people, and particularly as Jews. No medical school prepared us for what we were to encounter" (p. 32). While religion and spirituality have increasingly become topics for clinical articles, psychological workshops, and psychoanalytic conferences, experiences of religion are still too frequently ignored in the clinical milieu, viewed with a lens of pathology, and when engaged, often broached primarily through the lens of patients' experiences. In other words, the world of religion in psychodynamic treatment has remained an inner world with little recognition of the social and cultural dynamics that come to bear on the clinical encounter. Furthermore, the religious and spiritual commitments and inclinations of the clinician, except with occasion, remain outside the discussion of clinical process. *The Spiritual Soul of the Psychotherapist*, as a project, makes an entirely different demand on the authors and respondents: to go beyond and, possibly, beneath the theoretical surface and to tell the story of one's life in religious and psychological terms and, from this vantage point, offer clinical commentary.

What is required of the analyst who considers her analyst self in the discourse on religion and spirituality? Susan Bodnar (2004), in her article "Remember Where You Come From: Dissociative Process in Multicultural Individuals," makes the claim that though analysts "participate in the internal constructs and the external exigencies of the people with whom they work, sitting where society and individuality cross paths" (p. 581), the writing of the analyst seldom gives voice to the pervasive expression of culture and cultural values that shape the analyst and her practice. This process of silencing by the analyst of her cultural roots, according to Bodnar, is a "dissociative process where self meets culture" (p. 582). Reporting on the 2009 "Class and Psychoanalysis" conference, Dewing (2010) identifies a central challenge as "whether we as a profession can, paradoxically, examine our tendency towards silence about the continuing significance of class as a large-scale oppressor, even as we remain complicit with both its articulation and oppressive activities" (p. 242).

While it is spirituality and religion, and to some degree, ethnicity and race, that, in recent psychoanalytic discourse, are more often examined, the convergence of these factors is underexplored in clinical writing, psychoanalytic training programs, or practice. Acting as a respondent to Dr. McWilliams' chapter affords me an opportunity to consider this convergence, in a preliminary way, and I thank her for her work.

INTERSECTIONALITY IN THE CONVERGENCE OF RACE, CLASS, AND SEXUALITY

> "For most whites, racism is like murder: the concept exists but someone has to commit it in order for it to happen." —Akintunde, 1999

Intersectionality, as a theory, is concerned with the convergence of the concurrently experienced position of marginalization and the power relations implicated in this "multidimensionality" of lived experience (Diouf, 2013). For example, for a brown-skinned Latina lesbian woman who is also a practicing Santeria, all five aspects of her self (color, ethnicity, sexuality, gender, and religion) are lived simultaneously even though she might be pressured (externally and as internalized) to privilege or hide one aspect of her self in some situations for a variety of reasons. In other words, there are social, political, and religious contexts that foster, maybe require, the kinds of splits that as clinicians we profess to aim to cure. At the same time, there can be a privileging of some aspects of who we are while subverting other aspects in ways that contribute to the splits we hope to lessen. Furthermore, in the clinical situation, the power of privilege on the part of the clinician (a power that may be part and parcel of race or gender or class or the status attributed to psychoanalysis' proximity to medicine, etc.) may be ignored or assumed by the clinician, as well as by the patient, without ever being fully engaged, analyzed, or challenged by the treatment.

Attending to the intersectionality of lived experience can offer psychoanalysis the opportunity to treat not only those who live mostly with the advantages of social privilege and bask in its ill-gotten gains (sustained and reproduced by the social structures that are taken for granted) but also those who live on the margins of the social fabric of power. Furthermore, making intersectionality integral to our work can enable psychoanalysis to become a force in the addressing of the social ills that are sustained by the power dynamics of privilege and the invisibility of one's place in relation to privilege. Evangelina Holvino (2006) asserts that most often we approach identity as if "differences are essential, innate, fixed, independent, and additive variables. These models of differences lead to what Joan Scott has termed the equality-differences dilemma: if people are inherently different, then how can we be equal?" (p. 1). For psychoanalysis to wrestle with this question and what it means for the practice and theory of psychoanalysis, a "simultaneity model" is required. Holvino's simultaneity framework for such a model is based on becoming aware that (1) differences are "relational and socially constructed"; (2) there is an asymmetrical distribution, and exercise, of power in social differences; (3) intersectionality sheds light on the multiple "identity groups" to which we each belong and to the subjective experience of the conflicting nature of the power we may hold in one identity as opposed to another; (4) these various identities are intertwined and inter-dynamic; (5) social identities are contextual, and different aspects of our identity are evident (and possibly experienced) based on context (pp. 1–2). For psychoanalysts to take into account the implications of intersectionality theorizing presumes the following: a desire on the part of the psychoanalyst to move beyond the confines of the four walls of the consultation office in order to bring about change; and, a willingness to appreciate the impact of social dynamics on the individual psyche and the social structures governing our relationships while remaining committed to a depth psychology. The movement toward an understanding of the intersectional begins with the self.

INTERSECTIONALITY: A PERSONAL NARRATIVE

> "I name myself lesbian because I want to be visible. I call myself Black too, because Black is my perspective." —Clarke, 2005, pp. 85–86

I am not sure where my mind would have naturally taken me in thinking about the links between my religious sensibility and clinical work, but in reading Dr. McWilliams' chapter and her description of her New England suburb and belonging to the First Congregational Church in Longmeadow, I was struck by the early smooth entrances into a family religious practice. As I read about the freedom from emphasis on religious education, the typical, white steeple New England Churches, something about the imagery led me to think that this setting welcomed, with little discord, her and her family.

My own memories surprised me: one of my earliest memories involved my first grade teacher handing out pictures we had colored and turned in for "grading" and Sister Marietta telling me that I had colored the picture of the baby Jesus (it was shortly before Christmas) the wrong color. Jesus, she explained, was not brown. I remember the shock I felt, especially since we had a brown Jesus at home, and the satisfaction I felt when my mother marched up to school to have a talk with the teacher and principal. And another memory involved Sister asking why my parents had not attended mass on a Sunday and, when I reported this question to my mother, her replying that it was none of Sister's damn business. Because I repeated my mother's response verbatim, I was made to stay after school over at the convent. I was both angry that my mother did not immediately come rescue me and intrigued by the community life of the convent. They were, it seemed to me, vibrant and talkative—and included me in their activities. I was there to be punished, unfairly I thought, but they also gave me an early inkling of the importance of community life that continues to be important to me.

Neither of my parents grew up Catholic. My mother was raised in the Free Methodist Church and my father in the Baptist Church. They converted shortly after they married, and as converts, they were sometimes adamant about what it meant to be Catholic, and it was not an infrequent occurrence to hear that the pope had said something or the other that had significance for our lives. Specifically, I distinctly recall when I was about eight years old that the pope said we, Catholics, could visit Protestant churches, and my great aunt invited me to the Free Methodist church for a visit. Unlike Our Lady of Lourdes, which only had a few black families as members, the Free Methodist church was filled with black, brown, tan, and pink individuals who were connected by years of membership and family ties. Whereas Holy Souls parish was north of the Mason Dixon line, in Philadelphia, and beautiful to me in its silence, candles, and sense of the still order, the worship and ethos at Dennison Free Methodist was southern, Atlanta southern, lively, responsive, and loud in comparison to Catholic worship life. And, unlike the role of the priest of my childhood parish, women held a decidedly different position at Dennison. While it was clear that the pastor, a man, was powerful, and the pulpit was completely his domain, I recognized that the women of the church made things happen. They brought to religion and the church a force not to be ignored. My great-grandmother, Hattie Booker Peterson, and great-grandfather, Joseph Peterson, were founding members. Both were former slaves and brought to their religion and faith an awareness of both the racial and gendered struggles of the southern context in which they lived. These dynamics were embedded in my family's religious experiences and gave religion a compelling but complicated place in my life. Religious experience was always understood as racial and cultural experience. Religion was a part of bringing about change—in one's self certainly but, more importantly, in the world where, according to my mother, God seemed absent. Our job was to be black and involved, to confront injustice, regardless.

The expectation to stand up and count, to have one's voice heard, was just part of the oxygen. I could experience deep disappointment in myself if I failed to confront any fear or anxiety about contributing my voice. I was to take a deeper breath of the oxygen, commit myself more fully, and give my heart and mind over to this work as if I were finding faith for the first time. This was all a part of how I understood what were acceptable black/religious ways of being. But I also recognized, even though I did not know what to do about it, that there were also parts of this oxygen that were not life giving, that the pressure to be this kind of moral, ethical, and justice-seeking good person demanded a great price. As a result I developed a deeper—observing—interest in black experience, in particular black women's experience of religion, self, culture, and embodiment: I guess my solution, given that I was not inclined to give religion up, was to begin to recognize it as a complicated facet of my experience, and as a clinician, in my patients' lives.

WHITENESS AND THE CONTOURS OF IDENTITY

I think Dr. McWilliams' chapter provides an occasion to engage some of these complicated features of religion, class, race, and sexuality as well. First, as is clear, as clinicians we bring our religion, spirituality, morality, etc. with us. Transformed or not, it enters where we enter. But we also bring race, gender, and sexuality into the clinical room with us.

My social location situates me toward a particular reading of Nancy's chapter: In my reading I notice that her chapter is filled with the fact of her whiteness, her Christianity, her heterosexuality, and her class. Her social location affords her a worldview and set of experiences. Throughout her chapter she both assumes the privileges, and also recognizes that she has inherited the benefits of these social privileges by virtue of her family, race, sexuality, class, and religious context. Listen to these juxtaposing images and intimations of awareness from her chapter:

- "I thought the church was beautiful. . . . spare, elegant, white, steepled New England house of worship"
- "My father. . .considered going into ministry but decided against it because he worried about the kind of life his wife would live as the spouse of a pastor"
- "I wanted to understand the role of men in conception. I asked why only women with husbands had babies. She replied God would not want a child to grow up without a father."
- "My mother's death . . .was a terrible loss . . .my sanity was saved by a loving African American woman my father hired. My father paid Anna $40 dollars a day."

- "I made a close and continuing friendship with an African American girl in the National Council for Christians and Jews."
- "I met my husband at Oberlin. We married…"
- "I have had innumerable advantages of which I was no more deserving than anyone else."

Obviously I have pulled these bullet points from McWilliams' chapter that were evocative for me, and that directed our attention in the direction of race, color, and religion: I am a black lesbian clinician and practical theologian. I wondered what difference our differences make in the clinical room and in our scholarship. Melanie Suchet's (2007) question "What does it mean to be white?" and her answer, "Whiteness is that which is not seen and not named. It is present everywhere but absent from discussion. It is the silent norm" (p. 877), speaks volumes to me. Whiteness then, is everywhere except where I stand. Whiteness as a lived ideology with implications for the practice of psychoanalysis has only recently been broached. Melanie Suchet's paper "Unraveling Whiteness" examines the failure of psychoanalysis fully to examine race. Race is more often examined ahistorically, and even though race is socially constructed, if pursued, it is regularly viewed as part of the non-white experience of self. "Discussions of race today remain largely limited to an investigation of otherness when someone of a different color enters the consulting room. Further, the burden of writing about race has until very recently fallen on those with darker skins who have been trying to tell us for decades that a racialized subjectivity is crucial" (p. 877). Furthermore, Suchet continues, "It is important to understand that whiteness is not only about race and racism. Whiteness is a lived experience. It is an ideology" (p. 877). Ideologies of race are also embedded in ideologies of religion and religious practices though, like psychoanalysis, very often outside of self awareness and invisible to the religious practitioner. I have found that race, gender, and sexuality are almost always a feature in my patients' concerns, dreams, or fantasies—in relation to me—and in fairly undisguised form.

CLINICAL VIGNETTES

"Karen," a white woman from Germany, is in a protestant seminary and is referred to me by her professor. When I enter the waiting room to get her, she looks up and begins to sob. When I inquire about her tears she says that her therapist back home was perfect: "she is white, small, and speaks perfect German." This woman was longing for her former therapist during this current crisis, so this is not only about race, size, and language—but my not being a slim white woman was a part of her pain in the moment. She is pursuing a ministry degree and plans to be ordained. She is confused by the tensions between the white women and the black women in her feminist theology class. She tells me, "We do not have this kind of tension at home."

"Ana," an Afro-Puerto Rican woman, a lesbian, is referred to me and is convinced that I too am Puerto Rican and a lesbian. She is so convinced that, early on, she would speak in Spanish to me. She is Roman Catholic, and no one, she tells me, knows that she is lesbian—though her mother repeatedly invites her girlfriend to family gatherings. My patient tells me of her split life—straight at home and church (where she is very involved) and "in the life" on the weekends. She is depressed, growing to hate going to church, and to family gatherings. When it finally occurs to her, outside of the treatment space, that I am not Puerto Rican she almost leaves treatment: she wonders if I am qualified to treat her, whether I attended a good school, and am I good enough—and Catholic.

After six months of treatment, "Claudia," an African American woman who is an associate pastor in a large black church, decides to stop straightening her hair and start wearing it in a short cut hairstyle. She proceeds with the change in hairstyle but also buys large earrings to "offset" her feeling that she might look too masculine. She takes up in the treatment her long-standing and ambivalent feelings about being black. She wants to "be comfortable in her black skin." How, she wonders, did I do this? She goes so far as to research me online, finds my dissertation on black women's experiences of embodiment in light of theological and psychoanalytic perspectives. The decision to cut her hair is met with surprise by members of the church and they let her know. She begins to hear subtle messages that she may not be "straight;" a teenager in the youth group begins to make negative remarks about queer people. Claudia reports that she has been sexual with men: a one-night experience with a friend in college and once with a colleague while at a conference. "I liked sex but because of my parents and religion, I think I am supposed to wait until I am married." My patient tells me she is not a lesbian, but she is afraid, she says, that people will begin to think that she is, and that she will be rejected as a result. She is in a double bind in which she feels pressured to "save" her sexual interest for marriage, and men, and to disavow any sexual attraction she feels for women. She participates in a self-identified black progressive protestant church where gender and sexuality are frequent topics in sermons and adult religious education. A year into her treatment, she becomes romantically involved with a woman but keeps it secret from almost everyone in her life, including lesbians who are friends or colleagues.

These kinds of splits that are operative in these patients, and clinicians alike, do not just reside in their individual intrapsychic lives; their social and religious contexts are implicated in the ways in which splitting one's private sexual life, feelings about race and gender, and views about sexuality out of awareness are fostered by religious communities and in psychoanalytic treatments. As a practical theologian who is also a psychoanalyst, I attempt to bring an awareness and critical reading of the ways in which institutions, communities of religious practices, and their theories establish boundaries, both spoken and unspoken, and censure through the use of religious and theoretical language, symbols, imagery, and interpersonal processes to shape and dictate ideologies of the self. These ideologies very often produce and sustain whiteness, heteronormativity, blackness, and the rules—and social practices—for embodying gender roles—McWilliams recalls that she met her "husband at Oberlin. We married…" and I think about how the environment at Oberlin supported this trajectory of dating and eventual marriage. Oberlin, I imagine, in very explicit and socially recognized ways, communicated approval of the heteronormative expression of their sexuality. I imagine that heterosexual couples could assume, without being aware of it, that their relationships would be reproduced in the public representations along with public images of heterosexual coupling, love, marriage, and a future life. In other words, the broader social milieu offered public practices, practices that shape expectations of normativity, to maintain and reproduce heterosexuality. Thus, "Heterosexuality—like masculinity and femininity—is taken for granted as a *natural occurrence* derived from biological sex. *Heterosexual expectations are embedded in social institutions"* (Schilt & Westbrook, 2009, p. 443) and "guarantee that some people will have more class status, power, and privilege than others" (Ingraham, 1994, p. 212).

RELIGION, THE HIERARCHY OF NORMALITY, AND MOURNING

> "To decenter heteronormativity, the rules of culture must be suspended—particularly the constraints attached to binary definitions of gender, family and sexual orientation." —Hudak & Giammattei, 2009

It seems obvious that religion is implicated in the construction and maintenance of heteronormativity, and most obviously through religious institutions' rituals and practices. Religion and religious experience are active and intentional in the reproduction of what are considered normative expressions of sexuality. And the psychological experience, and conscious and unconscious meaning, of religion is intertwined in relation to these practices of heterosexuality: "we married." The implication is that all of us are implicated in heteronormativity via practices, relationships, imagination, longings, and resistance. Therefore religion, in the context of psychoanalytic treatment, must be analyzed not only in terms of what it does for the individual practitioner, but also must be examined in terms of how it situates the individual in relation to social practices related to race, gender, class, and sexuality. Pursuing a depth psychological understanding of religion links the private and social, and reveals its place in the hierarchy of normality.

In each of the vignettes I presented earlier, a subtle dynamic emerged during treatment: the need for a process of mourning. While each woman presented with different concerns related to the intersection of ethnicity, race, gender, sexuality, and religion, there were elements of loss as these features of their lives were examined. Claudia's sense of loss was in terms of her sense of place in the black church, even in one that professed to be open and affirming of diverse expressions of sexuality and emphasized the importance of black identity. Karen was mourning the loss of her white, small, and German-speaking therapist, especially as she is experiencing the discourse around race and religion, and conflict among white and black feminists, in a theology class in the United States. And Ana expressed a longing for a Puerto Rican, lesbian, Catholic therapist and almost left treatment because her fantasy about me "fitting the bill" was shattered. Each mourns the loss of her proximity to the benefits of privilege of race, sexuality, and religion. As women, they are removed from the center of privilege but in differing degrees: Karen was a white exchange student suddenly in a class where black women interrogated whiteness, and she was sent to a black therapist. Karen was thrust into the painful analysis of her assumptions about her whiteness, German nationality, size, and language. In addition, she needed to plumb the depths of meaning intersectionally—points that converge in her experience in this new setting—and therefore, intersubjectively and relationally. Karen quickly realized that her religion heretofore had been German and white. The presence of black women who also identified as feminist disrupted her religious self. Claudia, on the other hand, was terrorized by her black sexuality and gender in her black religious context: as a single ordained woman she felt pressured to be "feminine" (as evidenced by longer hair) and asexual or, if married, heterosexual. Her focus on my short natural hair brought her conflict about herself to the surface. In the end, her temporary solution was to "leave the church." Ana initially thought she would be able to firm up her Puerto Rican, Catholic, lesbian identity because she experienced me in twinship transference. The discovery, because of information shared by the referral source, that I was not Puerto Rican and (no longer) Catholic (but lesbian) was a break in empathy and a disruption of the twinship transference. Ana's identity as Puerto Rican was not disrupted, but her struggle to remain Catholic (as were most of her family and neighborhood) was challenged when she slowly revealed that she was a lesbian. Her priest stated that he could not serve her communion, and her mother, who knew she was a lesbian, though they had not explicitly discussed sexuality, ultimately expressed her disappointment with Ana's "lifestyle" on religious grounds but accepted Ana's relationship. For Ana, religion was inextricably interwoven into sexuality, ethnicity, and family. Her mourning has been a long period of ferreting out whether she can remain Catholic and lesbian.

The psychoanalyst Esther Menaker (1995) is instructive: While giving a lecture for a public, non-psychoanalytic, audience, Menaker noted her difference with Freud with regard to sexuality, stating that "love was primary, innate human capacity to relate to others in a positive way . . . This is akin to religious feeling—a spiritual awareness of a love of life" (p. 187). A participant took issue with her "description of the human appreciation for participation in the life of the universe and calling it religious . . .[and] when the meeting was opened up for questions" a man responded, "Religion is not about love. It is about suffering. This is the whole meaning of Christ on the cross" (p. 187). McWilliams' reflections suggest otherwise. She does not deny suffering but, instead, takes up some kinds of suffering as evidence that "life is capricious, that we can all die at any time, and that given the ongoing possibility of sudden loss or change, we must live as well and as fully as possible in the here and now . . . [feeling] A deep sense of gratitude . . ." Religion for McWilliams became the backdrop for an ethical compass that shaped her development and treatment of others. These vignettes suggest that analyzing the hierarchy of normality, and its demanding nature on the psyche and self, are important elements to a psychodynamic understanding of the psychology of religion.

Another psychoanalyst, without the psychic reward reaped through a shared self-reflection such as offered by McWilliams, profited from the trappings of whiteness, protestant Christianity, gender, and heterosexuality but did so, likely at great psychological cost, through a lifelong strategy of disavowal and denial (Strozier, 2001). It is by now well known that Heinz Kohut stressed, in his development of Self Psychology, the continuity of the self. Many are also familiar with the complicated relationship he had to his own Jewish ethnicity and religious history. We now believe that Kohut's famous case of Mr. Z. is actually based on Kohut's self-analysis (something he denied for years). When Kohut immigrated to the United States from Vienna, he essentially reinvented himself. After arriving in the United States in 1941, Kohut described himself as a Christian Unitarian Universalist and denied his relationship to Judaism and its religious practices. How and why this discontinuity existed for Kohut cannot be fully known. Constance Goldberg (2003) offers a reflection on implications for his theory:

> Let me just suggest one idea about why Heinz took the stand that he did about the importance of a sense of continuity in one's life. I believe that Heinz did not live out the continuity that he so ardently stressed to others because, for reasons best known only to him, he could not do so . . . he knew what constituted health, *not* by the way in which he had lived his life, but by what he had learned from making the choices he had made; the price that he paid was the recognition of the psychic cost of these discontinuities (p. 355).

An under-explored Kohutian concept that I have previously employed for discussing black experience (Sheppard, 2011), and one that remains somewhat removed from clinical conceptualizations, is that of the cultural selfobject. I think this concept is apropos to a discussion of Kohut's experience of religion. In brief, the concept of cultural selfobject is an aspect of Kohut's theory to link the self and cultural imagoes. Cultural selfobjects give shape to the social productions that meet the selfobject needs of individuals and the groups to which they belong. In other words, the needs for mirroring, idealization, and kinship might conceivably be met in the experience of art, literature, politics, and religion. This construction of the cultural selfobject, as Kohut conceptualized it, assumes a cultural and societal milieu where what is reflected in cultural productions is obviously self-sustaining. This assumption is a fantasy in direct contrast to Kohut's life.

It can be said that Kohut, in varying degrees, suffered from something similar to the "colonization of the psyche." Central to the process of colonization, as developed in Franz Fanon's (2008) *Black Skin, White Masks,* "is the colonization of the psyche such that 'natives' identify with the colonizer and come to view their own 'mother tongue' as negative because it is associated with being black. However, the identification with the colonizer fails to relieve the psyche of the painful effect of being colonized" (Sheppard, 2011, p. 92). "Identifying with the white ego ideal, however, is doomed . . .(and) unattainable" (Haskins & Butts, 1973, p. 79). Kohut distanced himself from the religious, ethnic, and cultural aspects he associated with Jewishness—aspects that in his original context, and in his U.S. context in its own variation, were "demonized." He not only fled to bodily safety, he fled to whiteness, and this included religion. Thus, for Kohut, religion was complicated. It is, in fact, complicated for most people, and left unexamined in the clinical milieu, can have insidious and even traumatic effect (Root, 1992).

When I began my psychoanalytic training program in 1998, a consultant I had been working with for my private practice advised me: "be careful how you talk religion up there (at the institute for psychoanalysis) because they are a little strange when it comes to religion." It was not until five years after I graduated, in the year 2010, that the same institute offered a class on culture and psychoanalysis (and I was co-teacher). It has not been offered since, and, to my knowledge, the institute has not offered a full class on religion or spirituality in psychoanalysis. Without ever having to acknowledge it, religious institutions and psychoanalytic bodies can reproduce, in the area of religion, race, gender, and sexualities, the very same problems that bring people to our offices—splitting, silences, and/or identifying with the values and ideologies that actually render one invisible or silent.

Dr. McWilliams thinks of psychoanalysis as "a kind of religion . . . in the sense of offering a worldview and an ethic of honesty," and in good psychoanalytic fashion reminds us that much of "our behavior is unconsciously motivated." Unconscious motivations ignored produce blind spots. In my view, we are just beginning to take up the complexity of psychological and social meaning of religious experiences *or* the psychological content in religious productions, that is, the materials to which black women and men are exposed and which are ultimately an aspect of what is expressed in their words, behaviors, and spiritualties. The question in need of exploration is whether psychoanalysis can hold the social-cultural dimensions of religious experience while simultaneously examining the psychological action between individual intrapsychic dynamics and unconscious processes and the social aspects of religious experience. In other words, we need to be able to grapple with how religious experiences also form—shape and misshape—the self and self-experience in religious contexts. Moreover, can psychoanalysis put itself to the hard self-analysis that is required to reveal and transform the habitus in which psychoanalytic theories and approaches participate in practices that reproduce normativities of privileged positions?

This is where Dr. McWilliams' chapter directs us when she recounts her case where an African American woman is told by her faith community that God will not give her more than she can bear, or that of the gay and lesbian clients trying to live up to their faith communities' convictions regarding the necessity for celibacy. McWilliams' chapter reminds us that religious experience is multifaceted and complex, and confronting this should help us deepen our understanding of religious experience in our own lives and in the lives of those who seek assistance from us.

My intention, and the conversation I have sought to establish between Nancy's work and my concerns, has centered around the intersectional nature of religious experience, the psychodynamic forces that make some aspects of religious experience material available for examination while rendering other aspects as split off from awareness, and the societal practices that define and produce normativity of acceptance and exclusion. The examination of these forces illustrates the complexity of psychologies of religion and, hopefully, contributes to the conversations concerning gender and sexuality, race and ethnicity, and whiteness, which currently are approached as separate and discrete factors of the self, in psychoanalytic dialogue.

REFERENCES

Akintunde, O. (1999). White Racism, White Supremacy, White Privilege, and the Social Construction of Race: Moving from Modernist to Postmodernist Multiculturalism. *Multicultural Education, 7*:2–8.

Bodnar, S. (2004). Remember Where You Come From: Dissociative Process in Multicultural Individuals. *Psychoanalytic Dialogues, 14*: 581–603.

Clarke, C. (2005). New Notes on Lesbianism. *The Days of Good Looks: The Prose and Poetry of Cheryl Clarke, 1980–2005*. New York: Carroll and Graf Publishers.

Dewing, H. (2010). Conference Reflection: Class and Psychoanalysis. *British Journal of Psychotherapy, (26)*2, 242–244.

Diouf, E. (2013). Kimberle Crenshaw and Patricia Hill-Collins. https://www.msu.edu/~aaas/newsletter/article6.html. accessed 11/13/13.

Fanon, F. (2008). *Black Skin, White Masks* (translated by Richard Philcox). New York: Grove Press.

Goldberg, C. (2003). A Reminiscence of Heinz Kohut. *Explorations in Self Psychology, Vol. 19,* edited Mark J. Gehrie. Hillside, New Jersey: The Analytic Press.

Greenberg, D., and Witztum, E. (2001). *Sanity and Sanctity: Mental Health Work Among the Ultra-Orthodox in Jerusalem.* New Haven, CT: Yale University Press).

Haskins, J., and Butts, H. (1973). *Psychology of Black Language.* New York: Hippocrene Books.

Holvino, E. (2006). Tired of Choosing: Working with the Simultaneity of Race, Gender, and Class in Organizations. *CGO Insights.* Briefing Note Number 24: 1–4.

Hudak, J., and Giammattei, S (2009). Doing Family: Decentering Heteronormativity in 'Marriage' and 'Family' Therapy. http://www.psychologytoday.com/files/attachments/45260/hudak-and-giammattei-doing-family-12-09.pdf. Accessed 2/10/10.

Ingraham, C. (1994). The heterosexual imaginary: Feminist Sociology and theories of gender. *Sociological Theory 12*:203–219. Quoted in Schilt, K. & Westbrook, L. (2009). Doing Gender, Doing Heteronormativity: 'Gender Normals,' Transgender People, and the Social Maintenance of Heterosexuality. *Gender & Society, 23*: 440–464.

Menaker, E. (1995). More on Masochism. *The Freedom to Inquire: Self Psychological Perspectives on Women's Issues, Masochism, and the Therapeutic Relationship.* New Jersey: Jason Aronson, Inc.

Root, M. (1992). Reconstructing the impact of trauma on personality. In L.S. Brown & M. Ballou (eds.) *Personality and Psychopathology: Feminist Reappraisals.* New York: Guilford Press.

Schilt, K. & Westbrook, L. (2009). Doing Gender, Doing Heteronormativity: 'Gender Normals,' Transgender People, and the Social Maintenance of Heterosexuality. *Gender & Society, 23*: 440–464.

Sheppard, Phillis Isabella. (2011) *Self, Culture, and Others in Womanist Practical Theology* (New York: Palgrave Macmillan).

Strozier, C. (2001), *Heinz Kohut: The Making of a Psychoanalyst.* New York: Farrar, Straus, & Giroux.

Suchet, M. (2007). Unraveling Whiteness. *Psychoanalytic Dialogues, 17*: 877–886.

Chapter Five

A Therapist's Psycho-Spiritual Autobiography with Clinical Implications

David J. Wallin

Kenneth Pargament's (2011) book, *Spiritually Integrated Psychotherapy,* visible to my patients as it sat on the table beside my chair in the office, proved an initially unexpected catalyst for a number of conversations. One patient inquired about the source of my interest in the book, which eventually led me to let her in on the conference that was the occasion for both my reading and the writing I was about to do. She asked for details: "What's the conference called, you know, if I wanted to find it on the Internet?" When I told her—*The Skillful Soul of the Psychotherapist*—she paused for a second, looking at me quizzically, and, then with a barely suppressed but friendly laugh half-asked, half-exclaimed, "Wow, isn't that kind of a tall order for the shrink?"

Nancy and Salman and I were asked to write spiritual autobiographies to illuminate how our sense of the extraordinary informs our work with the ordinary. Searching for the form of my own account—which involves Buddhist mindfulness practice grafted onto a Jewish identity—I'm aware of my internal conflict between the writer who wants to tell stories and the scholar who wants to refer to books like Pargament's. Put differently, I'm struggling with the legacy of growing up in my particular Jewish family in which the psychic inheritance could be summed up in three words: *suffer, study, succeed.* I'll have more to say about this maxim later, but because today's assignment is explicitly personal I will begin with a story.

GROWING UP JEWISH

I was six or seven, and we had arrived the day before on a trip from California to Canada to visit my father's father, whom we called Zaide. It was dinnertime now and my parents, my twin brother, and I were seated with various relatives around a large table at one end of which sat Zaide—stern and intimidating, a patriarch's patriarch, whom I never recall seeing without a yarmulke on his head. An Orthodox Jew who spoke with a pronounced Eastern European accent, he had an exacting set of rules and expectations related to being Jewish—but their precise nature was a mystery to me, and thus I was always afraid I might say the wrong thing. At dinner that night, Zaide broke the ice by asking me what I had eaten for lunch when we were out with Auntie Lena—the family's designation for the handsome and dignified woman he had married after my father's mother died. My nervousness in Zaide's presence clouded my memory: I could picture the restaurant where we'd had lunch, but what *had* I eaten? Then happily an image arose in my mind's eye and with relief I was able to recall and announce that for lunch I'd had...a bacon, lettuce, and tomato sandwich. Of course, at this moment the room went silent and the earth stood still as a dark cloud of incredulous rage formed around Zaide's head. Then he spoke: "*WHAT* did you say, David?" I was speechless, but Auntie Lena calmly answered for me: "Dear, he said he had a bagel, lettuce, and tomato sandwich." With these words, life as we had previously known it could resume.

The fact is that life as a child in Zaide's presence was entirely discontinuous with life as I ordinarily knew it. When with Zaide, life was a minefield of potential missteps related to being Jewish in the Orthodox religious sense; it was all about going to *shul*, learning to *daven*, keeping kosher, keeping the rules. By contrast, my ordinary life meant growing up with parents who had largely left the *religion* of the Jews behind them (except when with Zaide where I sensed we were expected to pretend that at home too we hewed to an Orthodox way of life). All the while my parents held on to what it meant to be Jewish in the cultural sense that suggested answers to questions like these: *What is ultimately important? Who are you in the world? What does it mean to be part of a people (like many others) that has been the object of vicious, in fact, murderous persecution? And what in a life well-lived is the place of suffering, study, and success?*

Maybe study and success are the *solutions* to suffering. That and Jewish humor. The injunction to *succeed* seems built in to the culture, as in "my son/daughter, the doctor," and what I'm tempted to call the tyranny of *nachas*—the parents' self-referential satisfaction at the success of their children. As for study, that too seems virtually inherent in the culture. My own father's bookshelves were lined with Freud and Marx, Havelock Ellis, and Margaret Mead. He told me proudly that when in college he and a group of intellectually ambitious friends tried to produce (or maybe they just imagined producing) their own encyclopedia of all the relevant knowledge of their time. Had they not been rebellious they might have been students of the Talmud and the Mishnah. Not tangentially, a psychiatrist friend once said to me "the body is for the *goyim*."

But let's cut to the chase: Suffering. Two anecdotes: After dinner with a Jewish friend in Boston with whom I shared the three S's, I received her email in which she agreed with my formulation but suggested that after the injunction to suffer I needed to add in parentheses *but not silently.* A couple of days later I was teaching in Minneapolis and a therapist in attendance also endorsed it, noting that his mother shared my understanding. A Holocaust survivor, her own maxim was "life is war."

I'm sure the centrality of suffering in my own life, psyche, and career choice has roots that are primarily psychological. Yet the psychological and religious/cultural influences can intertwine and reinforce each other. Or maybe the latter provide metaphors through which some of the meanings of formative psychological experiences are expressed.

The year I was to be Bar Mitzvah'ed, my father's sabbatical from Stanford brought our family to London. In Zaide's geography, this was next door to Israel, and so he arranged for my twin brother and me to have our Bar Mitzvah at an Orthodox *shul* in Jerusalem. The year was 1961. This was Israel's Bar Mitzvah as well as our own; it was also the year of the trial of Adolf Eichmann. For ten days we stayed at the King David Hotel, along with journalists from around the world. And every day over breakfast, as I recall, I would read the *Jerusalem Post* which seemed filled, front to back, with highly detailed first-person accounts of horrific suffering. Documenting Eichmann's role in the "final solution" were stories from survivors of Auschwitz, Dachau, Bergen-Belsen, and Treblinka who told of systematic torture and starvation, scientifically engineered extermination, and "medical" experimentation. I didn't want to read what I was reading, but couldn't or wouldn't stop. I wanted to withdraw from the horror but felt compelled to know it. This was what the survivors had endured. I somehow felt I owed it to them to register their suffering in my mind, in myself.

For many years thereafter I was regularly visited by unbidden and unwanted images of this suffering, often imagining that I too was a helpless victim of excruciating torture. Though these dreaded waking nightmares had to have been in some sense self-generated, I felt I had no alternative but to submit to them, to suffer. When I described this compulsive suffering to the therapist whom I saw when I was in graduate school, he suggested that I needed to become more comfortable in the role of the torturers, the guards, rather than always "agree" to play the part of victim, prisoner, concentration camp inmate. He suggested too that the horrific reality of the concentration camp was also, for me, a metaphor representing the most disturbing aspects of my experience of my family.

As I write this, it occurs to me that the analyst Stephen Seligman (1999) has proposed that our fantasies provide one more royal road to our "implicit relational knowing"—our non-conscious, procedural sense of ourselves in relation to others. I'll have more to say about this later, but my "masochistic" fantasies did indeed reflect an aspect of my sense of myself in relation to others: Specifically, I felt that I could bear to suffer in a way that other family members could not, and that my suffering served or protected them. And somehow this dovetailed with my sense of myself as a Jewish boy and young man.

As a teenager I experienced a frightening (and grandiose) identification with the character at the center of Andre Schwartz-Bart's overwhelming novel of the Holocaust, *The Last of the Just* (1960)—a book I found too painful to finish. The novel's premise has a long history in Judaism: God has arranged the world so that there exist among the Jews in each generation thirty-six "just men" or *lamed vovniks*. So named because *lamed* and *vov* are the Hebrew letters corresponding to the number thirty-six, their role is to take on the suffering and pain of all. The young character with whom in a very disturbing way I identified was one of these *lamed vovniks* whose nobility and compassion in the face of suffering, whose acceptance of the most *extreme* suffering, somehow keeps the world in moral balance.

This idea that my suffering was a necessary service to others was entirely consistent with my parents' (secular) Judaism that was really a kind of religion of humankind. It was the social justice form of Judaism—in my father's case, the communist version. This take on the religion was expressed in my political activism (and theirs), as well as the fact that Passover—a holiday celebrating liberation from slavery—was my favorite Jewish holiday.

That my parents were secular Jews is probably one reason I could never "believe in God." More importantly, perhaps, because my mother was frightening to me and (I believe) because she found my (infantile) need for her disgusting, I grew up without a sense that I could depend on another, that I could cry for help, that there was someone who would see, hear, and helpfully respond. So how could I believe in God? I never could. I heard a somewhat different story from a friend of mine who grew up in Argentina where he attended a boarding school with other Jewish kids whose parents had escaped the Holocaust but also the kids of Nazis who had fled Germany after Hitler's defeat. My friend had doubts about the existence of a God who would allow such monumental suffering to be imposed upon his own (or any other) people. But he still had a shred of belief—or hope—that compelled him of a midnight to sneak out of his own room and into a room that held the Ark that held the Torah—and to piss on it as a provocation so that God might show him a sign. But God did not and that, my friend told me, was the end of that, putting his quest to rest, sealing his disbelief.

My own story of growing up Jewish "magnetized" suffering—both my sense of being beleaguered and besieged myself, and my compulsion to experience through identification, and thus to somehow assuage, the suffering of others. Doubtless much of this history is strictly personal. But for God's "chosen people"—chosen for an exceptional dose of suffering?—there are probably elements also of a culture-wide PTSD, a centuries' long intergenerational transmission of trauma that predisposes many of us to identify too readily with the role of victim (as well, perhaps, as the roles of victimizer and rescuer). As I will shortly explain, such identifications have both complicated and facilitated my work as a therapist—in particular, my efforts to be of help to my patients through allowing, understanding, and thus, eventually, diminishing their suffering. But first, the second chapter of my spiritual autobiography.

WAKING UP TO MINDFULNESS

Counter-posed to my own (personal/psychological and/or cultural/religious) Jewish drift toward suffering is the suggestion of the Vietnamese Buddhist teacher Thich Nhat Hanh to "enjoy" (2001). The latter is part of a developing spiritual orientation of mine which grew out of a single transformative experience that is easier to talk about than it is to write about. Talking makes more room for the informality and humorously ironic distance that can keep an account of (what feels like) an extraordinary and moving experience from seeming self-aggrandizing or crazy. In any case, the experience in question arose unbidden and unexpectedly during a period in which I was writing a book on attachment theory and psychotherapy (2007). More specifically I was thinking about the ideas of Peter Fonagy, one of the giants in the attachment field. I was sitting on the deck of my home in Berkeley on a warm and sunny afternoon when a visual image came to mind that seemed to capture some of Fonagy's key ideas.

The image consisted of three concentric circles. The outermost circle represented external reality—what happens to us. A second circle represented the internal world of mental models through which we take in, as through a filter, what happens to us. And within the two outer circles was a third which represented what Fonagy calls the "reflective self"—that part of the personality which is capable of reflecting on the relationship between our internal world and external reality. As I considered this image of three concentric circles, it occurred to me to ask what seemed the logical—even inevitable—question: *Exactly who is it who is doing the reflecting here?*

And as I asked myself the question I did indeed get an answer, not in words or concepts, but in the form of an utterly compelling experience: I felt my ordinary sense of self implode, collapse, reduce to virtually nothing at all but a spark of consciousness. A moment before, the subjective center of me had been my usual *self*—a dense construct of history, identity, feeling, purpose taking up a lot of mental space. Now at the center was simply *awareness* that seemed to take up no space at all. Suddenly it seemed obvious and undeniable that the answer to my question was *no one*—that is, no personal self but only impersonal awareness.

Along with this newly discovered sense of self (or "no self") came profound feelings of well-being and gratitude. For a couple of weeks or so I could call up this new state of mind and the feelings associated with it virtually at will. During this time, I experienced diminished defensiveness, a heightened capacity for empathy and acceptance, and a much intensified connection to others on the basis of what I felt we all shared at the core of ourselves. There was also the sense that I'd accidentally bumped up against something of great importance. And having stumbled upon what seemed a crucial fact of life of which I'd previously been completely ignorant, I couldn't stop talking about it—this altogether compelling *awareness of awareness itself,* rather than the internal or external objects of which we're ordinarily aware.

I remember sitting in a café down the street from my office, conversing with a psychologist friend who told me that my account of my experience on the deck called to mind the views of his own spiritual teacher. In the world according to Ramana Maharshi, he said, what I was talking about was God (!)—the universal Self (or non-self) that is one with the divine. No scholar of Hindu mysticism, I couldn't even tentatively vouch for this interpretation until I went online and found a phrase that described how, in the Vedantic tradition, God (Brahman) and the self (atman) are one: this identity is understood as an "*objectless consciousness, awareness nondualistically self-aware*" (Craig, 1998, p. 476; italics mine). And didn't that describe my experience to a T?! Short of discussions of God, I repeatedly found that the friends and colleagues who resonated with what I was trying to put into words were those who meditated or had a "spiritual path" of one sort or another.

Through conversations like these—and dismayed that my transformative experience, once effortlessly accessible to be re-lived was now gradually fading into memory—I came to the whole matter of "mindfulness" and to meditation. Mindfulness, like psychotherapy, must be experienced to be known. And meditation, I came to understand, is a practice that exercises the "muscle" that allows us to be mindful—that is, deliberately and fully present for, and aware of, whatever arises in the immediacy of the moment. As for my own experience of "no self" it was one I can't resist describing as "mindfulness on steroids."

And so I began to meditate, initially with the hope of bringing back that experience which had first shown up like an uninvited guest—a guest who turned out to be a beloved friend, who soon departed, and for whose return I deeply longed. To set out to re-find such a valued experience is usually a mistake, though an understandable one. Or so I was advised by a meditation teacher I knew. Better, it would seem, is to approach meditation and our spiritual aspirations in general very much as the British psychoanalyst Wilfrid Bion recommended we approach our patients—that is, "without memory, desire, or understanding." For memory involves the past, desire involves the future, and understanding (in Bion's framework) involves ideas—while mindfulness aims for a quality of attention that is non-conceptual and focused as much as possible on the here and now. In my own practice of meditation that is anchored in a focus on the breath, I have found it useful to cultivate a stance I describe as "waiting in the silence" or "listening in the silence." Such a stance allows me (intermittently) to rest in awareness, to "be" awareness rather than the thoughts, feelings, sensations that come and go as the objects of awareness. In such a stance I am often at the edge of the unknown—ready to notice whatever next arises, and then to attend once more to the breath, to awareness, to the waiting.

Like much of the rest of my life, the book I'd been writing on attachment and psychotherapy was changed by my experience on the deck which compelled me to attend to the whole matter of mindfulness. The book had been organized around three key findings of attachment research. These findings highlighted the centrality of the relationship, the nonverbal dimension, and the stance of the self toward experience. With regard to the latter, it was the capacity for a "mentalizing" (or reflective) stance that was seen to be significant. Such a stance allows us to interpret—to make sense—of our own (and others') behavior and experience in light of underlying mental states (such as feelings, beliefs, desires). This ability to "read minds" is an invaluable resource—for all of us, but especially parents and therapists—because it helps us to regulate our emotions and to experience both insight into ourselves and empathy for others. No less valuable, however, is the ability to be mindful, for mindfulness, too, promotes affect-regulation, insight, and empathy. In the book I would eventually describe mentalizing and mindfulness as the "double helix of psychological liberation": the first frees us through understanding, the second through acceptance, presence, and awareness. To which I would now add that the mindful dimension—which I initially came to through my "awareness of awareness" and my experience of "no self"—can be a spiritual, as well as a psychological dimension. For it does seem to connect us, at least potentially, to a mysterious something that is (to borrow

Pargament's three descriptors of the sacred) "transcendent, boundless, and ultimate."

Suffering and the urge to heal it is threaded through my own Jewish experience and the history of the Jews; in Buddhism, suffering is regarded as the primary fact and challenge of life. Perhaps for therapists, in particular, suffering is the heart of the matter. It is what brings our patients to therapy. And from the other side of the couch, it is usually our own suffering that brings us to the work of therapy, as a calling and as a hope.

It's my theory, but not mine alone (see Sussman, 2007), that therapists are "called" rather than made. In other words, it is who we are—and who we *hope* to become—that draws us to the work. Moreover, it is who we are—and who we *can* become— that ultimately determines our capacity to create relationships with our patients that are genuinely therapeutic. Very much as the psychology of parents determines their capacity to raise secure kids, it is our own psychology that shapes our ability to "raise" secure patients. This psychology is originally shaped, of course, in the context of our first attachment relationships. But therapists are also shaped by religious and spiritual experiences and values. These experiences and values can support adaptive, progressive, and reparative trends in the personality and conduct of the therapist—but they can also reinforce trends that are problematic. My own personality and my conduct as a therapist were shaped most profoundly in the context of my relationship with my mother. Sketched in broad strokes, the influence of this relationship was reinforced by my "Jewishness" and softened by my "Buddhism."

"IF IT'S NOT ONE THING, IT'S YER MOTHER"

When my mother was in her early eighties, I tried to tape record an interview with her, an oral history. I thought this would have meaning for her, for me, and for my children. I began by asking her to tell me something about her growing up in Chicago. She broke a very long silence by speaking—in an odd and unfamiliar, halting and disorganized way—about the stink of urine in the halls of the tenement where her family lived and about the chaos there, the noise and the crazy people. Then she became tearful and unable to speak. I quickly backed off, in the face of what I intuitively recognized as her history of unresolved trauma.

Perhaps this history had roots in the trauma of my grandmother who as a teenager in 1905 had fled the murderous anti-Jewish pogroms of Czarist Russia. Per my mother, her own mother was a tyrannical "monster" who drove her mercilessly to succeed. I only know that my mother was once a brilliant, beautiful, and vivid woman who had been a child prodigy pianist under her mother's thumb who stopped playing the moment she left home to attend the University of Chicago on a scholarship.

Our relationship had multiple facets—many of them positive—but most influential, perhaps, was my mother's vicious (alcoholic) rage and my need to manage it. I did so in various ways: I took on her view of *me* as a monster; I apologized abjectly for whatever triggered her rage; most of all, I tried to *read* her so as to be able to behave in ways that might somehow avert or diminish the rage. Mainly what I read in her was a need never to feel abandoned (so I suppressed every sign of my separateness) and never to feel the shame of her own neediness (so I tried always to satisfy her needs before they could be shamefully exposed—while internalizing the shame she disowned). In the role of her confidant, I empathized with her experience and provided the attuned emotional responsiveness of which I felt my father was incapable. When I wasn't her victim, I was her perfect son, her surrogate husband, her idealized object. I felt I was the "chosen" one but also viciously persecuted. My father watched all this unfold without a word. Appearing cowed by her and passive, he modeled a certain kind of victimhood. On the other hand, he was also a profoundly decent man who, according to my mother, raised me until I could talk to her.

THE JEWISH STRAND (OR, MY FIRST CLINICAL PLACEMENT)

Therapists-to-be usually receive their earliest clinical training in the context of relationships not dissimilar from the one I've just described with my mother. Often, it seems to me, our history involves trauma at the hands of traumatized parents to whom we adapt with what attachment researchers (Main, 1995) call a "controlling-caregiving strategy." That is, we learn to take control of scary parents by taking care of them. This provides an education in many essential clinical skills (interactive affect regulation, reading nonverbal cues, and the like) while also building-in certain countertransference vulnerabilities. What I took from the family "practicum" described above was reinforced, both for better and for worse, by growing up Jewish.

On the plus side, Jews are interpreters, or in the contemporary parlance, we "mentalize." Psychoanalysis has been called "the Jewish science" partly because Freud and most of the pioneering analysts were Jewish but more meaningfully, I believe, because Freud's essentially *interpretive* method can be seen to extend a centuries-long Jewish tradition of interpreting holy texts. Rabbis and their students, rather than taking the Talmud's words at face value, enlisted multiple interpretive "technologies" to discern God's intent *beyond* the literal meaning of the text. Similarly, Freud treated his patients' symptoms and dreams as "texts" to be interpreted. And because problematic mental phenomena were "over-determined," multiple interpretations were required to free patients from the grip of their internal world.

Mentalizing, per Fonagy, essentially involves the generating of *multiple* perspectives on experience and behavior—rather than being trapped in the "reality" of one view. This is why mentalizing—especially the two-person mentalizing that occurs in therapy—can be affect-regulating, can create mental space, can liberate. I like to think that my own mentalizing capability, my own interpretive imagination, arose, at least partly, in the relationship I had with each of my parents. For at their best, both conveyed the sense that behavior (mine, that of their friends, that of characters in novels—but rarely their own) had meaning and was the product of motivations that could only be inferred or interpreted. Early on I absorbed the idea that what one saw on the surface was often merely appearance; the essential reality was complex and lay within. In keeping with Jewish culture, my parents also conveyed to me that feelings mattered a lot. In keeping with the religion *and* the culture, they conveyed that other people mattered and that we were called upon to consider the well-being of all. In the words of the Old Testament prophet Micah: *Act justly. Love mercy. Walk humbly with your God.*

Not so positively, my impressions of Jewish history, and especially my early exposure to the Eichmann trial and to Holocaust literature, converged with the most painful features of my family experience in a way that reinforced my original sense that my role was to suffer. This suffering seemed a legacy and a burden, but also a source of good feeling about myself. It strengthened a sense of moral superiority and, because I had the ability to endure what I felt would destroy others, it supported what a friend of mine referred to as a kind of "Jewish macho." Obviously all this contributed to my disturbing identification with the *lamed vovnik* in the novel, *The Last of the Just.* And it was all too consistent with my role in relation to my mother, which was to absorb and thus manage her anger—out of my fear of her no doubt, but also out of a sense that I could tolerate suffering better than she and that my own anger would destroy her.

The grip of this identification with suffering—and the fear of imposing suffering on others—has diminished as I've come to understand and work with it in my own therapy and analysis. Nonetheless it has been and remains, intermittently, a vulnerability. I recognize it in my tendency at times simply to experience vicariously and endure the pain of my patients, when the alternative might be to explore, confront, deepen, or attempt to bring my own understanding to that pain. Particularly in the past, I have noticed myself stopping myself out of fear that my "intervention" would be too painful for a particular patient to bear. Or as if I then might experience myself as the victimizer, rather than the rescuer or the victim. Of course, inhibiting myself to "protect" the patient diminished my capacity to help. And on occasion this surplus inhibition eventuated in an explosion of anger that was destructive in a couple of instances and unexpectedly productive in a number of others.

Perhaps needless to say, what I'm describing here is my idiosyncratic drift toward particular kinds of "enactments"—those mini-psychodramas that constantly unfold where the attachment patterns and core vulnerabilities of the therapist interact with those of the patient. Unrecognized, these enactments function like an invisible straitjacket. Once recognized, they can become the single most powerful means for transforming obstacles in the therapeutic relationship into opportunities for insight, inspiration, and change. As I'm about to explain, a stance of mindfulness is extraordinarily well-suited to recognizing our participation in enactments—because mindfulness involves *being aware of what we're doing while we're doing it.* The Jewish poet, Bob Dylan, puts it this way: "Some people feel the rain. Others just get wet."

THE "BUDDHIST" STRAND

(Or, to quote the Jewish poet again, "There Must Be Some Way Out of Here")

When I put quotation marks around the word "Buddhist," it is because I'm using that word in an informal, descriptive, and very personal way to suggest the nature of my own experience of spirituality which is exactly that—*my own.* And my spirituality—my sense of a mysterious *something* that is "transcendent, boundless, and ultimate"—mainly goes back to three related matters. The first is my *awareness of the impersonal awareness* that seems to lie at the very center of all sentient beings and that seems to go on being—"within you and without you" (as the George Harrison song puts it). Second is my experience of *connection* to and *compassion* for others rooted in the fact that all of us sentient and suffering beings are, in the sense I've just alluded to, essentially one and the same. Third is my understanding of the vital importance of *the present moment* that Thich Nhat Hanh identifies as the doorway to Heaven on Earth.

Just as growing up Jewish conferred both strengths and vulnerabilities, waking up to mindfulness has strengthened my work as a therapist in many ways but doubtless created an additional vulnerability or two as well. In the plus column—and this is by far the more significant—mindfulness exercised in meditation and elsewhere has vastly heightened my ability to be present and my conviction that this matter of presence is at the very heart of a life well-lived.

Sitting with a patient yesterday I felt a sadness in myself that turned out to be an arrow pointing in the direction of *his* buried sadness in realizing that he was just "going through the motions"—absent rather than present for the living of his own life. Mindfulness and meditation have deepened my sense of the ways in which the mind mediates our experience of the world, either creating surplus suffering or diminishing it. Of vital importance for me is the understanding borne of experience that suffering is intensified to the extent that we identify exclusively with the suffering itself, rather than with the *awareness* through which we know the suffering. When we are aware of *awareness*—when we can locate our awareness and rest there—we often find a world of unexpected calm to which we may potentially have access. I have also come to recognize, in meditation and elsewhere, how suffering can be amplified by our efforts to avoid it. Paul Fulton writes, "Mindfulness offers a way to change our relationship to suffering by surrendering our need to reject it. This is an act of kindness to oneself" (Fulton, 2005, p. 63). Together, these developments have loosened the grip of my own identification with suffering and my attachment to the "controlling-caregiving" strategy I initially adopted to protect myself from my mother's rage—but later tended to repeat in other relationships, including those with my patients.

Feeling more present now means that the past I "know" and the future I imagine can be more easily "sheared away" so that in the moment I can relate to my patients with greater freedom. Specifically I don't feel compelled, as I did with my mother, to do anything and everything possible to help them to *avoid* their suffering. Similarly liberating is my understanding that their suffering has a lot to do with automatic, history-driven patterns of thinking, feeling, and doing that can neither be illuminated nor transformed so long as I meet them with my own automatic, history-driven pattern of compulsive care-giving.

As for the minus side (what's not to like about mindfulness?) I've noticed a few things. First, there's my tendency at times to collude with patients who are themselves on a "spiritual path" that parallels my own. How might this look? "Cheerleading" is one descriptor that comes to mind here; "mutual admiration society" is another. Second, I can be guilty on rare occasions of a kind of "spiritual bypass" (Welwood, 2000) in which my own (no doubt over-determined) *dis*-identification with suffering has me encouraging the patient to somehow dis-identify with her own suffering rather than feel it, share it, make sense of it, and thus begin to work it through. Third, I have annoyed at least one patient by too enthusiastically advocating meditation, which struck her as my confusing a personal with a universal solution, assuming that what's worked for me would necessarily work as well for her.

CLINICAL ILLUSTRATION

For a number of years I have worked with a delightful but anxious and easily overwhelmed woman patient in her early fifties whom I will call Leslie. The treatment was initiated by Leslie's mother who felt that her daughter, now facing the stress of caring for two ailing parents, could use the support of a therapist. My own sense was that despite Leslie's acute and deeply thoughtful sensibility, she was not in full possession of her own rather eloquent "voice." She seemed, in fact, uncertain about her right to a life of her own. In summarizing my work with this patient, my aim is to illustrate by example how our conduct as therapists can be affected, both for better and for worse, by our personal history, including the history of our religious and spiritual experiences.

As I've emphasized, my own experiences growing up Jewish (with an Orthodox grandfather, secular parents, and a profoundly disturbing early exposure to the details of the Holocaust) converged with traumatic aspects of my relationship with my mother to generate not only a commitment to healing but also an identification with the role of the sufferer and a dread of imposing suffering. Years of analysis and therapy, and a good marriage, have softened this identification and diminished the dread. But perhaps in addition I also needed what I got: the grace of the profoundly transformative experience I've described, and the meditative practice and perspective on mindfulness for which it was the catalyst.

Like my own history, Leslie's bore the scars of trauma. She was raised in the shadow of a brilliant and charismatic father who was also profoundly narcissistic, controlling, denigrating, and sexually intrusive. As a child, he had been a musical prodigy. As a parent, he expected no less of his daughter, going so far as to contemplate a surgery upon Leslie's hands when they seemed too small for her to succeed as a concert pianist. Recently she wrote me the following in an email:

> Yesterday in session you gave me the answer to the puzzle which has confounded me all my life about my relationship with my father. You said that with extreme narcissists, there is often an impersonal quality even when they are being generous. This exactly named the quality I had been searching to express or even formulate in my mind. It encompasses all the paradoxes: while providing for my material needs, I felt little sympathy and more often his anger at me for falling short of his expectations; his mentally turning the tables so quickly that my efforts to express myself were seen as rank disloyalties to him and I would simply become confused and fall silent; his wit often masking a lack of connection and warmth; his anger and impatience resulting in my self-doubt and insecurity about my own motives and worth. I had suspected the narcissism but the word "impersonal" was what opened my eyes. A parent who demands unquestioning loyalty but dispenses impersonal affection or sympathy forever relegates the child to a dependent and inferior role. That is the mindfuck children don't understand; instead they think they are the deficient ones.

Leslie saw her father as almost a force of nature, against whose cruelties her mother was helpless to protect her. The oasis in this emotional desert was

Leslie's younger brother with whom she feels she shared a bond of nearly perfect trust and understanding. Early in our therapy, she told me in an oddly matter-of-fact way that when she was in her early twenties her beloved brother had been killed in an automobile accident in which the driver of the car—who had fallen asleep at the wheel—escaped unscathed. When I inquired about the details, she was reticent, and I quickly understood that I was being warned away from the memories of a loss too traumatic to address.

Over the course of a couple of years, we dealt with a variety of stresses in Leslie's current life and re-visited many aspects of her history. You might say, and I wouldn't disagree, that we were "building a relationship." I'm sure that Leslie felt supported by my efforts to know, understand, and be of help to her as we explored her marriage, her relationship—past and present—with her mother and father, her truncated career as an artist, and the suicide some years before of her closest friend. From my side, I was for the most part deeply engaged by Leslie's efforts to make sense of her experience; I also recognized the overlap in our experiences growing up and a connection between us grounded in, among other things, the passion we shared for music and books. At a certain point, however, I began to feel vaguely discontented with our work.

With the benefit of hindsight, I can now see that we were at an impasse. To put it much too simply, I was playing out with Leslie a familiar pattern, in a certain sense a memory, in which I felt I was taking care of someone by helping to diminish their suffering—not by confronting the suffering at its source, but rather by providing the balm of a soothing (if only superficially healing) relationship. From another angle, I was refusing to be the one to impose suffering—referring to my own religious identity, it was as if I were refusing to be the Nazi, the monster, preferring instead to be, if you will, a nice Jewish boy. And this, of course, suited Leslie who was, I believe, convinced that she was utterly incapable of confronting the double trauma of her father's abuse and her brother's death.

When dealing with traumatized patients, therapists with their own history of trauma are both burdened and blessed. We are blessed because we have the potential for deep understanding based on our partial identification with our patients. We are burdened because our history and our adaptation to trauma through a "controlling-caregiving" strategy can function like an invisible straitjacket constraining our ability to "move" in ways that might be therapeutic.

My freedom of movement with Leslie was restored—as it has been with many other patients of mine—through what might be called "mindfulness in action." The aim here is to bring to the interaction with the patient the same "bare attention" that we bring to our experience when we meditate. There the aim is simply to be aware of—and to label—our experience in the present moment. The way I operationalize this in the treatment setting is simply to ask myself, "What am I actually doing now with this particular patient?" Sitting with Leslie in the session in question I became aware that I was doing a number of things.

I was aware that I was enjoying looking at her. Then, listening to her talk about feeling overwhelmed and taking some medication, I was aware that I was staying on the surface, automatically conveying my "empathy" and "understanding" but making no attempt to have her deepen her experience or elaborate upon it. I was aware of feeling that I was going through the motions. Looking more searchingly at my moment-to-moment experience with Leslie, I was disturbed to recognize the sense in myself that I was giving up on her, as if I'd become convinced she was simply incapable of feeling or thinking more deeply.

Mindfulness of this kind *makes room* for the therapist's experience; then we need to enlist our mentalizing capacity in order to *make sense* of that experience. Beyond the key question—"What am I actually doing with this patient?"—we need to ask two others aimed at deepening our understanding: "What is the implicit relational meaning of what I'm doing?" and "What might be my motivations for doing what I'm doing?"

As for the implicit meaning of my conduct with Leslie, I could see it from several angles. Closest to consciousness was my sense that I was "protecting" her from the impact of experience I too readily assumed she could not bear. At a deeper level I saw that I was inadvertently ratifying her sense of her own fragility by colluding with her *fear* that should she confront her trauma it would sink her. As for my motivations, I was aware of at least two. First, to "push" her to address her trauma would raise the specter of seeing myself and/or being seen by her as the monster who imposes, rather than relieves, dreadful and irredeemable suffering. Second, and relatedly, I was fearful of the shame in her (and in me) that might be exposed were we to explore the details of her trauma. For it seems virtually inevitable to me that among the many unlovely consequences of being on the receiving end of trauma is the experience of nearly unbearable shame—the feeling not that one has *done* something bad, but that one *is* bad.

No coincidence, I presume, but in the session following the one I've just touched on, Leslie gave me an opening to begin to resolve the impasse that had gripped us. In reading the neuroscientist Joseph LeDoux, she told me, she had come across the idea that emotions can trump reason but that emotions can be controlled with a poker face. It's a paradox of her own experience, she says, that she studiously avoids stuff like scary movies that might evoke strong feelings but that she's still very "mercurial" as a friend put it in describing her: small stuff evokes big feelings. I say to her that to me these things really seem to go together: When people have suffered trauma, they're vulnerable. They have an exaggerated startle reaction and they deal with their vulnerability in different ways—she by staying away from stuff, like scary movies. I also say that staying away from scary movies is a low-cost solution, but she's needed to make use of this pattern of staying away from scary stuff more broadly, and maybe the costs here are higher. Leslie says, "Like with my husband? Where I didn't let myself feel my anger and hurt? "Yeah," I reply, "but also more broadly…I guess I'm thinking about how we've stayed away from stuff here." Looking a little deer-in-the-headlights-ish she says, "I'm not sure what you mean." "Well, your brother's death…your experiences with your dad…." Leslie adds, "Maybe Joseph's suicide?" "I think so…But it takes two to tango and I think I've sort of gone along with the idea that maybe this stuff is just too big and painful to approach."

Leslie responds that she's been in lots of therapy and thinks she's decided that she simply *can't* approach this stuff. She tells me that one of her previous therapists had quoted Freud to the effect that we never want to take away what's allowed people to maintain their equilibrium. "Of course," I respond. "You don't want and I don't want you to drown in your painful feelings. But I think people are often capable of knowing more and feeling more than they think they are. And I think I've sort of gone along with this idea—which I'm feeling more and more may not be true or useful—that you *can't* do any more here than you're doing, that you can't and we can't…and maybe that doesn't serve you." And now I tell her our session is nearly over, but add that I'm guessing we're beginning a conversation here, not ending one. Apparently she agrees: Not long after the session I get an email from her asking if it might be possible to meet again later in the day. She writes, "Somehow a chord was struck in the course of our conversation which has returned that old sensation of having a stone on my heart which I can't seem to wish away."

When we met later that afternoon, she told me with barely suppressed tears that for more than thirty years she had sustained herself with the belief that her brother was not actually dead, but was residing on the East coast. Twice she had in fact seen him after his death, an "apparition" standing tall at 18 years old, looking forbidding and even angry. Why these should have been the emotions on his face she couldn't understand, but it grieved her. Much later, she told me that when feeling completely distraught at his death, she had cried, "It should have been me!" But apparently her grief and guilt had all been kept, as she put it, in "cold storage," so long as she had been able to believe that her brother was still alive.

As an update on this still ongoing therapy I will offer an email that Leslie sent to me in June. She wrote:

> As a patient of yours, I think I can say that I have progressed in ways I never could have anticipated when I started—I think this has to do with the feeling I have that I can finally express myself freely—you've certainly encouraged that—and that much of what I say you understand intuitively, having a similar

> family history in important ways. In my case, it seems that the therapeutic value has stemmed from my desire to think of you as a friend and brother; the hard part was giving up the illusion that my own brother and I would somehow meet again someday; he was gone so suddenly that I simply couldn't embrace that reality. When I was forced (albeit gently) to recognize that, I felt such pain that I thought it would be better for me to stop therapy, though I didn't tell you this because I wasn't sure what to do. Just as I relied on my brother's support and our shared history, I seem to have relied on you to keep alive that shared relationship which was so important to me while enduring my father's abuse.

Leslie was one of the patients who saw Pargament's book on psychotherapy and spirituality sitting on a table beside my chair in the office where I work. Seeing the book sparked a conversation in which she told me that her own belief in God had instantly been extinguished when she learned that her brother had been killed. She simply could not sustain faith in a deity who would allow such tragedy and suffering to occur. But she was aware of the comfort and meaning that her mother and some of her friends derived from their faith, and she wished that somehow she too could believe.

For myself, an unbeliever in a conventional personal God, I am sustained by my participation in the culture and traditions of the Jewish people—these are my roots—and by my more newly acquired "Buddhist" spirituality. And I very much appreciate the fact that this spirituality is grounded in experience rather than belief, in practice rather than faith. As a modestly scholarly, always questioning, Jewish therapist, that's a spirituality that suits me.

REFERENCES

Craig, E. (1998). *Routledge encyclopedia of philosophy.* London and New York: Routledge.

Fulton, P. R. (2005). Mindfulness in clinical training. In C. K. Germer, R. D. Siegel, & P. R. Fulton (Eds.), *Mindfulness and psychotherapy* (pp. 55–72). New York: Guilford Press.

Hanh, T. N. (2001). *Essential writings*. Maryknoll, NY: Orbis Books.

Main, M. (1995). Recent studies in attachment: Overview, with selected implications for clinical work. In S. Goldberg, R. Muir & J. Kerr (Eds.), *Attachment theory: Social, developmental and clinical Perspectives*. Hillsdale, NJ: Analytic Press, Inc.

Pargament, K. I. (2011). *Spiritually integrated psychotherapy: Understanding and addressing the Sacred.* New York: Guilford Press.

Schwarz-Bart, A. (1960). *The last of the just.* New York: Atheneum.

Seligman, S. (1999). Integrating Kleinian theory and intersubjective infant research: Observing projective identification. *Psychoanalytic Dialogues, 9,* 129–159.

Sussman, S. B. (2007). *A curious calling: Unconscious motivations for practicing psychotherapy.* Northfield, NJ: Jason Aronson.

Wallin, D. J. (2007). *Attachment in psychotherapy.* New York: Guilford Press.

Welwood, J. (2000). *Toward a psychology of awakening: Buddhism, psychotherapy, and the path of personal and spiritual transformation.* Boston: Shambhala.

Chapter Six

Immanence and Intersubjectivity

Daniel Shaw

Spirituality and psychoanalysis were not always, and are still not always, thought of as compatible. But to me, based on what I think of and experience as "spiritual," they are inseparable. I have been asked to discuss Dr. Wallin's chapter, and I have also been asked to speak of my own spirituality in relation to my work. What I have chosen to focus on first are some of the similarities in our backgrounds, and the common themes that have influenced us both as psychotherapists. One similarity I recognize immediately is that David and I both bring to our work a desire for and a belief in freedom: freedom as a human right, freedom for ourselves as therapists in terms of the creativity we are capable of in our efforts to help—and freedom for our patients, from the tyranny of trauma and the fragmenting dissociation that is the result of trauma. The theme of freedom has run through psychoanalysis from the beginning. For Freud, freedom from misery meant becoming able to experience ordinary human unhappiness (Breuer & Freud, 1955). For Ferenczi, freedom meant healing traumatic experience (Dupont, 1995). For Erich Fromm (1941), freedom meant finding faith in oneself rather than in false idols. Hans Loewald (1979) saw freedom as the self-authorization one achieves when the individual recognizes she must cease to be simply the child of her parents and take on the authority of an adult. In my work and in my reading of David's work, I see all these kinds of freedoms as an integral part of what the analyst hopes the patient will be able to discover.

In terms of how I might differ in my approach from David's, that's a bit harder to get at. As I understand it, the mystical experience David shared with us involved a direct connection to something transcendent, an exquisite, profoundly moving broadening of his perspective accompanied by an immensity of well-being and gratitude. Since then, he has been able to offer something of this broader perspective to his patients in a way that is deeply meaningful and healing.

For me, Spirit is immanent in the *human* spirit, as it can be experienced in the intersubjective intimacy that we call love—and as it can potentially be known in the therapeutic relationship. So yes, I am using the old transcendence/immanence debate as a means of speaking to what may in fact be some very subtle differences in our perspectives. More on that later. For now, back to the similarities.

Like David, I too was raised in a secular Jewish home, with parents who were politically to the left. Though the religious aspect of being Jewish was never given importance or emphasis in my family, the ethical and moral values of Judaism, conveyed mainly through my parents' cultural and political leanings, moved and inspired me. A memory of childhood Passover Seders comes to mind. While my dad's parents were still alive and well enough, we had the traditional Passover dinners with them, and as the story of the Jewish slaves escaping Egyptian oppression is told, my family always sang the Negro spiritual, "Go Down Moses —Let My People Go." My father would sing it very loudly, and when I was a bit older, I realized that he was trying to sound like Paul Robeson. That spiritual as sung by Robeson was a civil rights anthem in the years of Martin Luther King's activism. This was the best part of the seder for me—the song that cried out for freedom. Freedom from subjugation is a theme I have been drawn to again and again, in my life and in my work.

David speaks of developing a "masochistic" relationship to suffering, a compulsion to assuage the suffering of others, referencing not only his particular family situation, but a culture-wide PTSD for Jews, "a centuries' long intergenerational transmission of trauma." I think this is exactly right. A significant trauma in my family was my mother's undiagnosed and untreated OCD, which took the form of hoarding. Her problem grew progressively worse as I got older and was the source of endless rages and tears if any of us ever tried to throw anything out. As a child, I was deeply identified with her as the victim of my older sister and my father, and I was her staunch ally, her rescuer. Later, I came to a much more conflicted position, as I realized how trapped and destructive my mother had become, and how much my father too had suffered.

But it wasn't until after both parents had passed away that I understood the intergenerational trauma that haunted us more deeply. I saw a Broadway production of *Fiddler on the Roof* in 2004. Watching the scene where the Cossacks shoot up Tevye's village, suddenly I remembered the story my mother had told long ago: she was three years old, and she and her mother had run to a barn in their Ukrainian village. The Cossacks had swept in, looking for Jews, shooting and killing. The cow my grandmother and my mother were hiding behind took the bullet, and my mother and her whole family escaped shortly thereafter. Arriving in New York Harbor on July 4th, 1918, fireworks were going off as the ship pulled in, and my three-year-old, terrified mother screamed "The Cossacks, the Cossacks" in Russian. In retrospect, her hoarding in later life became comprehensible, given how much unspoken, unprocessed loss, grief, and terror she and all her family members had known and had always sought to forget. Escaping persecution, poverty, and starvation by coming to America was fortunate for many, but at the same time, traumatic.

So very much like David, the masochistic streak I developed early on was linked to Jewish themes of oppression and to my mother's depressive suffering and the sense that I should be able to save her.

Now to the spirituality. David describes the numinous, transcendent experience of mindfulness he has had as a profound sense of "impersonal awareness," a variety of spiritual experience, not unlike one that William James might have described (James, 1902) in his classic study of religious experience, that is free of the "dense construct of history, identity, feeling, purpose." Beyond the capacity for mentalization that David describes as a key to the possibility of finding freedom from the constraints of an internalized past, David recognizes "mindfulness" as a further possibility for freedom—an experience of knowing and being that transcends the personal, that links all being to the pure consciousness that is the ground from which all individual consciousness springs.

David's experience of mindfulness has led him to a greater awareness and understanding of his involvement in enactments with his patients. He perceives that his Buddhist strand, an awakening to mindfulness, has blended with his Jewish strand, his identification with suffering, in such a way as to help him recognize when he might be overidentified with suffering, too immersed in the patient's suffering to allow either of them to imagine the possibility of transcendence. As I hear it, David's mindfulness experience supports his ability deeply to recognize his patients' suffering, at the same time that it allows him to step back, and give his patients a chance to step back, to recognize something transcendent, something that might help to restore faith in life and evoke compassion for self and others. This awareness David describes seems to have been freeing, emboldening, and imbued with healing compassion. This is what I think psychotherapy can and should do—free, embolden, and, ultimately, awaken compassion.

For many who have grown up knowing depressive suffering, an experience of transcendence, or even the idea of it, can be deeply appealing. No surprise then, that by the time I got to high school, Thoreau and Emerson were among my idols, though Walden Pond and Concord seemed a million miles from my Bronx apartment. So I was not entirely unprepared for my first extraordinary spiritual experience, but it certainly came as a surprise. As a struggling actor in New York in my 20s, I struggled a good deal more than

I acted. There were some awfully low points: the short version is rejection, poverty, and loneliness. There was one day of despair when I just started walking, out of my tiny apartment and up Riverside Drive, until I found myself at Riverside Church. I was cold, and I walked in to sit down. This was one of the few times in my life I had ever been inside a church. Alone in one of NY's most beautiful landmarks, the autumn sun streaming through the stained glass, a few things were suddenly happening all at once: I felt warm; my tears were falling; and I felt a strong firm hand clasping my right hand, telling me it would be alright. Not a real hand, not audible words—but then again, as real and as audible as could be. When I got up to leave, I was restored, for a while at least. And as I read the New Testament in the days that followed, I knew that The Comforter, spoken of in the Gospel of John, had come to be with me that day. I was amazed and moved, and I was very tempted to consider becoming a Christian. I got as far as reading a bit of Thomas Merton, and listening with rapture to Mahalia Jackson records and the Bach Cantatas. And over the years I have read a great many of the writings of the Christian mystics—but where I ultimately went in terms of religion was not what I would have expected. Here's what happened.

Not so long after my experience in the church, my luck changed, or so it seemed. I was cast in a show, an exciting workshop with some well-known people involved, where I got to sing and act and dance. It was a show, of all things, about an Indian guru, about his spiritual journey and his teachings, like a Hindu version of the musical *Godspell.* It was all some crazy cult nonsense, as far as I was concerned, and the show went nowhere, along with my acting career. But a few years later, at the end of another long bout of despair, I learned that the guru we sang and danced about in the show was in residence upstate, at his ashram, and that he was giving spiritual initiation. This was around 1980. I had by then sought help from two analytic therapists, candidates in training, I later understood. I left the one who was almost completely silent; I stayed for a while with the second one, and when I succeeded in getting a romantic relationship off the ground, she declared that therapy was over. So therapy ended, the girl soon broke up with me, I heard that the guru was upstate, and I decided to go.

I spent 13 years in all, calling first this man, and then after he died his female successor, my guru. My initial meditation experiences were literally electrifying, indescribably ecstatic, the most intense love and oneness I have ever known. It was only a few months before I sold my possessions and took off to follow the guru. For many years as a full-time worker for the guru, on her world tours and in her ashrams in the United States and in India, I meditated and chanted daily, served in many managerial and teaching positions within the organization, travelled the world as a teacher and spokesperson for the guru, and worked my way up, closer and closer to the guru—the person I believed to be God incarnate.

When I left, and fortunately my wife left when I did as well, I was in shock for quite a while, as I came to realize more and more fully how abjectly I had submitted myself to this abusive, corrupt guru. Sadly, if I am really honest with myself, I knew the truth early on, but I didn't want to know that I knew. There were a great many kinds of dishonest and abusive behaviors practiced by the guru, of which I heard some whispers and saw some hints. But what I did see plainly was the cruelty—for months before I moved out of the ashram, I had been on the receiving end of it from my ex-guru and her appointed surrogates—the scathing public criticism and taunting, the public shaming and humiliation. It was treatment I had witnessed many before me receiving, and I always believed it reflected the guru's determination to help us along the spiritual path. Eventually, I was able to reflect on my own experience, and I came to realize that there was no genuine purpose to the public humiliation—it was simply an excuse for sadistic cruelty.

When I finally severed my ties with this group, I could feel myself coming out of dissociation, like coming back to life. I had tried so hard to murder my subjectivity and make myself the kind of object the guru would approve of and pay attention to. In this kind of relational system, only the leader is perfect, and no one else is, and to make sure that this is clear, the leader must continually bring followers up, raise their hopes of being favored, and then put them down (see Shaw, 2014). Initially, having experienced an indisputably ecstatic mystical experience connected to my ex-guru, I was at my most vulnerable. But it was a bait and switch. My pre-existing idealism and tendencies toward self-sacrifice, and the unhappiness in my personal life at the time, made me all too susceptible to exploitation. The leader I chose to follow led me to idolatry and masochism, perversions of idealism and self-sacrifice, and the opposite of what I now can thankfully think of as spiritual. This perversion of the experience of surrender into compulsive, masochistic submission was brilliantly identified by Emmanuel Ghent (1990). Surrender in this sense would mean the opening of oneself to the sublime, spiritually and interpersonally; submission is a closing down, a negation of self.

As powerful and as beautiful as my experience in the church was, and as my experience of spiritual initiation in meditation was, for me, what has been the most meaningful and enduring change and growth I've known is the experience of finding, claiming, and knowing myself as subject—and working out the difference between feeling like a subject, or feeling like I have to be the right kind of object for someone—a guru, a spouse, a patient, a friend, colleague—in order to feel like I am not alone. Bach (1985, 1994, 2006) has written extensively of this narcissistic problem—he describes the inflated narcissist who is fixed in his own subjectivity, and the deflated narcissist who self-objectifies, and automatically finds himself striving to be a gratifying object for another. The deflated narcissist is also hoping that the approval of others will quell his sense of unworthiness and unlovableness. Confused and unconscious about my own attachment narrative and family history, searching for a way to feel that I had a self I could feel good about, I ended up drastically objectifying myself in the hopes of being certified as good by my ex-guru, in whom I invested all goodness. I have discovered that many others behave similarly, with bosses and colleagues, parents, lovers, siblings. Many who enter psychotherapy know they are depressed, or anxious, but do not know the extent to which they have forsaken their subjectivity and submitted to objectification as though that would be a way to finally feel good enough.

The many years of self-subjugation I experienced under the influence of an abusive guru have led me to ponder deeply the nature of being an authority figure, a teacher, a therapist. Based on my understanding of the trauma of objectification, I want to construct with each patient a way of being in our process so that neither of us has to feel negated or subjugated as a condition of being in the relationship. In the psychotherapy context, I view the construction of intersubjective relatedness as necessary for therapeutic change and psychological growth. I am referencing Jessica Benjamin's (1988, 1995, 1998, 1999, 2004, 2009a, 2009b) use of the term, in which intersubjectively constructed relationships reflect what she terms the lawfulness of the moral third. Benjamin speaks here of mutual recognition, the effort we make in relating such that we resist the pull toward becoming a dominator or a submitter, the pull toward falling into a mode of relating where one person must be the object of the other. Lawfulness in relating means that each person's value as a human being is recognized and respected and that relating as two separate people, mutually recognizing their shared humanity, is what both emanates from and creates the space of the moral third. In this realm, the experience of being two opens to the thirdness of mutuality, because relating has not been forced into collapse, by one negating the other.

In one of Jessica Benjamin's earliest, seminal writings on the subject of recognition, she offers a list of near synonyms that capture what she means by the term:

> to affirm, validate, acknowledge, know, accept, understand, empathize, take in, tolerate, appreciate, see, identify with, find familiar, . . . love. . . What I call *mutual recognition* includes a number of experiences commonly described in the research on mother-infant interaction: emotional attunement, mutual influence, affective mutuality, sharing states of mind (1988, pp.15–16).

Benjamin (1998) asks, in her elaboration of concepts drawn in part from Hegel and Winnicott, how do two people "make known their own subjectivity and recognize the other's?" (p. xii). Bringing the importance of this deceptively simple question into sharper focus, Benjamin (p. 100) cites philosopher Richard Bernstein:

> Reciprocity must . . . be preserved as a condition of conceiving the ethical relationship, in which, as Bernstein (1992) says, both self and other "stand under the reciprocal obligation to seek to transcend their narcissistic egoism." For "without a *mutual* recognition of the *Aufgabe* [task/obligation] of searching for the commonalities and precise points of difference, without a self-conscious sensitivity of the need always to do justice to the other's *singularity*. . . we are in danger of obliterating the radical plurality of the human condition" (p. 75).

In this model of mutuality, there is an understanding that both parties are supported and enhanced when they consciously attend to striking a reciprocal balance between giving and taking. But mutuality is not a simple achievement, nor is it easy to sustain without effort. As Benjamin shows, the "shadow" of intersubjective recognition and relating is complementarity: the sadomasochistic, domination-submission dynamic of "doer-done to" (Benjamin, 2004). Relating in this mode, each person fears the loss of superior power, and insists on the supremacy of their own subjectivity. Each becomes locked in to the conviction that they are the victim of the other, each feeling they must negate the other, or be negated. One dominates, the other submits, then the other one dominates, and the other one submits… ad nauseaum. Giving and taking is now based not on goodwill and gratitude, but on strategic calculations aimed at maintaining dominance, and at the deepest level, aimed at preventing being destroyed by the other—being the destroyer, not the destroyed. Failure of mutual recognition represents a collapse of intersubjectivity that Benjamin likens to a kind of death. "Just as Freud posited an inherent conflict in intrapsychic life between eros and death," Benjamin (1999) wrote,

> so [we can] posit an inherent conflict in intersubjective life between eros and narcissism, recognition and omnipotence. The tension that we ideally imagine between these continually breaks down and has to be accomplished over and over (p. 202)… It is the constantly renewed commitment to restoring … intersubjectivity that allows us to get beyond a struggle of your meaning versus my meaning, to a sense of working together to transcend complementarity in favor of mutual recognition (p. 208).

Benjamin is careful to highlight here that we cannot perfect an ideally intersubjective position and then live happily ever after in a Utopian relational world. Recognition is a "constantly renewed commitment" we make, working together, creating a dialogue with our others—parents with children, spouses, siblings, colleagues, teachers with students, analysts with patients—that moves us toward mutual liberation from the tendency to seek power and control through negation of the other, out of fear of otherness.

So to bring this around to David's work, the essential teaching of Buddhism as I understand it is that wisdom and compassion for suffering are inseparable and are the goal of being human. I hear that David's experience of a transcendent spiritual wisdom has opened up for him ways of being compassionate that had previously been foreclosed. Identifying with and witnessing suffering are crucial ways of being compassionate—but sometimes, compassion will mean helping our patient to recognize a stuckness in his victimization, or perhaps a tendency to negate the alive aspects of himself so as not to lose sight of the parts of himself that have suffered unbearably. It is as though being alive betrays and abandons the traumatized child in him. Perhaps our compassion can extend to the various parts of this patient—his suffering, of course, but also his aliveness, creativity, resilience, and so on. We are not merely what has happened to us, I hear David saying; trauma can cause our victimization to be dissociated, but conversely it can cause our strong, healthy, and vital self-states to be dissociated as well.

For David, the capacity to become the witness of one's own emotional states links to the sublime experience of transcendence he describes. For me, the way toward spiritual and psychological health need not be based on a connection to something that transcends the mind and the body. When we are relating to the Other—stranger, friend, patient—as a subject in his own right, we are expressing the human spirit immanent within us and all beings. For me, intersubjective relatedness in the analytic dyad is a powerful force, mutative for both analyst and patient. Finding a way out of transferential impasses and reaching intersubjective connectedness is a kind of spiritual quest in psychoanalytic work. Succeeding can produce a profound, revelatory experience for analyst and patient.

An example of this kind of experience took place recently in my work with Elliot. I have seen Elliott for a three-year period, followed by a one-year hiatus, and now resumed for a year so far. Elliott grew up in a wealthy family, with his father almost constantly away on business. His mother was very charismatic, and Elliott became what we eventually recognized was a kind of surrogate husband to her—but one that she could powerfully influence and control, unlike her actual husband. Elliot's father died of brain cancer rather suddenly just after Elliott graduated from college, and not too long after, his mother developed a form of cancer which slowly, over a ten-year period, took her life. When I first saw Elliot, his adult life had all but ground to a halt because he had been attending to his mother throughout her illness, as she pursued dozens of quack remedies, healers, and other New Age practitioners.

Elliott and I had reached a point in our work where we had a coherent and persuasive narrative of his attachment and developmental experience. But our work was not leading Elliott to the kind of change he wanted. He was stuck in a dead-end relationship with a woman he was not happy with; he came late to sessions, changed times often, sometimes forgot. He often began sessions in an annoyed, out-of-it state. It took me a while, but I went ahead one day and confronted him about this behavior.

He was immediately angry, and shouted, "Why don't you tell me what I'm supposed to do? Why don't you help me remember where we left off the last time? Why am I spending all this time and money, for what?"

I thought for a moment, and said, "what about my time? The time I spend waiting for you when you're late; the time I spend rearranging your appointments. The time I've put in to help you understand all that's happened to you? The time I've spent caring?"

Of course, I did exactly what critics of the idea of mutual recognition as part of the therapeutic process (Teicholz, 2000) would point to as a clinical error. I directly asked Elliott to consider me from my point of view, not just his. In retrospect, I understood that speaking to Elliott this way was unique in his developmental experience, where any expression of his anger would be met not with acceptance and a willingness to negotiate relationally, but with complete withdrawal. I hoped that what I said would be experienced by Elliott as my willingness to be real with him, and to stay in the relationship without withdrawal.

Elliott was quiet for a short time. He then said, calmly now,

> I'm making you into my father. I'm angry at you for not advising me and teaching me—but he's the one I'm really angry at, because he never tried, he never tried to connect with me. I got him to drive cross country with me, and he had the radio on constantly. If the station went out of range, and all we heard was static, he'd leave it on and listen to that rather than talk to me.

Elliott was crying softly, acknowledging the anger and grief he felt about his father more deeply and fully than he ever had before. As we continued to work through Elliott's pain, and to sort out the enactment we had been in, we continued in a very fresh, new way for both of us. We were connecting, each of us taking the other in more deeply, in a way that was moving and real for us both. No longer the objects of our frustration with each other, we were intersubjectively connected in a way that now allowed Elliott to feel my care and my attention and for me to feel able to respond more freely to Elliott. Elliott's new ability to use me led to his becoming more self-reflective, and more connected with himself.

Our experience was not, as I perceived it, one of transcendence as a means of gaining a broader, more nuanced perspective about what was happening for Elliott and for me. Rather, we collided (Bromberg); we hung in there through the mess (Bromberg) of our collapsed intersubjective relatedness. Out of our effort to be real with each other, we found ourselves with each other. I could be an analyst; Elliott could be an analysand; and our work opened up and became alive.

I bring my personal biases and beliefs about spirituality to my work, and David brings his. The inevitable personal biases of the analyst cannot be denied, and in fact can be a source of deep trust between analyst and analysand if openly acknowledged (Orange, 1994). The fruit of David's transcendent experience is that he has deepened his empathy and compassion, as he has shown us in his work today. The transcendent aspect of consciousness can illuminate a way that we are more than merely our particular selves, our unfree selves. This kind of experience of oneness, of the interconnectedness of all being, can be deeply healing. But for me and others like myself, the transcendent experience ultimately became a way of feeling separate: as I chased after my concept of transcendence, I lost myself. The dark side of "enlightenment" is duality—in which the transcendent is viewed as the only reality, supposedly superior to the mundane, illusory, petty, material world. Getting my feet back on the ground for me has meant working from the immanence side of the dialectic. As a psychoanalyst and in my personal life, the experience of intersubjective relatedness—a form of relating that is always seeking freedom from the domination and submission agenda, that allows us to experience ourselves as subjects in our own right, free of objectification, and free of the need to objectify others—has turned out to be my most valuable spiritual experience. When David speaks of the "caregiving/controlling" strategy from which he has worked to free himself, I know just what he means. From that place, the patient subtly becomes our object, the one we need to show us that we have been helpful, so that we ourselves can overcome the feeling of helplessness. Freed of that need to control, David and his patient broke through, from impasse to revelation. David and his patient each became free, more alive, more fully and truly themselves, subject to subject.

What David has helped me think about is how I have reconciled within myself the transcendent, mystical experiences of my 20s and 30s, with the disillusionment of my post-cult life and my subsequent embrace of the healing potential of relational psychoanalysis. My bias is on the side of immanence, a belief that intersubjective relatedness is a nurturing and healing human capacity. But whether through awareness of transcendence, or awareness of immanence, the goal I think is the same: the deep recognition of our common humanity, recognition that lifts the burdens of shame, fear, and aloneness that are the universal psychic wounds of the human subject.

A long time ago, I stopped wondering if I believe in God or not. The intimate, subject-to-subject experience, in which the human spirit in each of us can be most fully expressed, is sublime enough for me, for now.

REFERENCES

Bach, S. (1985). *Narcissistic states and the therapeutic process*. Lanham, MD: Jason Aronson.

Bach, S. (1994). *The language of perversion and the language of love*. Lanham, MD: Jason Aronson.

Bach, S. (2006). *Getting from here to there: Analytic love, analytic process*. New York: Routledge.

Benjamin, J. (1988). *The bonds of love: Psychoanalysis, feminism and the problem of domination*. New York: Pantheon.

Benjamin, J. (1995). *Like subjects, Love objects: Recognition and sexual difference*. New Haven, CT: Yale University Press.

Benjamin, J. (1998). *Shadow of the other: Intersubjectivity and gender in psychoanalysis*. New York: Routledge.

Benjamin, J. (1999). Recognition and destruction: An outline of intersubjectivity (1990). In L. Aron & S. A. Mitchell (Eds.), *Relational psychoanalysis: The emergence of a tradition* (pp. 181–210). Hillsdale, NJ: The Analytic Press.

Benjamin, J. (2004). Beyond doer and done to: An intersubjective view of thirdness. *Psychoanalytic Quarterly, 73*, 5–46.

Benjamin, J. (2009a). A relational psychoanalysis perspective on the necessity of acknowledging failure in order to restore the facilitating and containing features of the intersubjective relationship the shared third. *International Journal of Psychoanalysis, 90*, 441–450.

Benjamin, J. (2009b). Response. *International Journal of Psychoanalysis, 90*, 457–462.

Bernstein, R. (1992). *The new constellation*. Cambridge, MA: MIT Press.

Breuer, J., & Freud, S. (1955). Studies on hysteria (J. Strachey, trans.). In S. Freud & J. Strachey (Eds.), *The standard edition of the complete psychological works of Sigmund Freud* (vol. 2). London: Hogarth Press.

Bromberg, P. (2011). *The shadow of the Tsunami and the growth of the relational mind.* New York: Routledge.

Dupont, J. (Ed.) (1995).*The clinical diary of Sándor Ferenczi, by Sándor Ferenczi* (J. Dupont, Ed., M. Balint & N.Z. Jackson, trans.). Cambridge, MA: Harvard University Press.

Fromm, E. (1941). *Escape from freedom*. New York: Farrar and Rinehart.

Ghent, E. (1990). Masochism, submission, surrender: Masochism as a perversion of surrender. *Contemporary Psychoanalysis, 26*, 108–136.

James, W. (1902). *The varieties of religious experience*. New York: Longmans, Green and Co.

Loewald, H.W. (1979). The waning of the Oedipus Complex. *Journal of the American Psychoanalytic. Association, 27*, 751–775.

Orange, D. (1994). Countertransference, empathy, and the hermeneutical circle. In R.D. Stolorow, G.E. Atwood, & B. Brandchaft (Eds), *The intersubjective perspective* (pp. 177–186). Northvale, NJ: Jason Aronson, Inc.

Orange, D. (2010). Recognition as: Intersubjective vulnerability in the psychoanalytic dialogue. *International Journal Psychoanalytic Self Psychololog*y, *5*, 178–194.

Shaw, D. (2014). *Traumatic narcissism: Relational systems of subjugation*. New York: Routledge.

Teicholz, J. G. (2000). The analyst's empathy, subjectivity, and authenticity: Affect as the common denominator. In A. Goldberg (Ed), *Progress in self psychology* (vol. 16) (pp. 33–53). Mahwah, NJ: The Analytic Press.

Chapter Seven

Shared Histories, Emerging Horizons

The Jewish Search for Spirituality and the Psychoanalytic Ethos

Celia Brickman

In the conference from which the essays in this book originated, I encountered an unexpected interpersonal conjunction. Of the three panels convened, each were comprised of one "master clinician" who was invited to discuss the role that spirituality had played in his or her personal and professional development, and two other clinicians who were invited as respondents. When I learned about the panel on which I was invited to talk, I realized that alone amongst the other panels and quite unbeknownst to the organizers of the conference, the three of us were all clinicians from Jewish backgrounds working and writing within a contemporary psychoanalytic framework; and all were presently and/or formerly involved to a significant degree in the practices of eastern religions. David Wallin (2007), the author of *Attachment in Psychotherapy,* his remarkable synthesis of psychoanalysis, attachment theory, and Buddhist mindfulness technique, was the master clinician to whom I had been invited to respond, as had Daniel Shaw, whose book *Traumatic Narcissism* (2014), was just about to appear in print.

SHARED JEWISH HISTORY

At first I thought the commonality of our backgrounds and trajectories was a striking coincidence; but upon further reflection I realized that underlying cultural, historical, and sociological forces contributed to make this seeming coincidence actually quite predictable, if not inevitable. The three of us shared our similarities because we are emblematic of major trends among third-generation North American assimilated Jews; and further, these similarities run parallel to major developments in contemporary American psychoanalysis. Rather than what seemed at first glance to be an anomalous group within a conference where all the other presenters, writing and speaking from within a psychoanalytic perspective, were non-Jews with no particular interest in eastern religious practices, the religious, social, and cultural backgrounds and trajectories of those on our panel combined to make us perhaps the most prototypical group of psychoanalytic thinkers at this conference. In this chapter I will account for these similarities by tracing their social histories, and I will end by demonstrating the ways in which David Wallin's work exemplifies the integration of the three streams of thought—Jewish, psychoanalytic, and Buddhist—which are so prominent within our generation of psychoanalytically-oriented clinicians.

Each element of the biographical narrative that David Wallin presents to us—growing up in an American Judaism that was transmitted not as religious belief, but as a communal identity that stressed suffering, study, and success, as well as the resolution of these themes that he has arrived at through psychoanalysis and Buddhist mindfulness—can be seen as representative of his (and our) particular generation within our particular social, ethnic, and religious location, stages shared, as I will show, by psychoanalysis itself. The search for meaning and identity amongst our generation of (North)[1] American Jews, whose grandparents immigrated at the turn of the nineteenth century, has frequently led its members to draw from the insights of eastern religious thought as well as from those of psychoanalysis, and often, from some combination of both.

Toward the end of the nineteenth century, there was a large wave of immigration of Jews from eastern Europe to North America, Jews who were fleeing the pogroms and persecutions that had been a regularly recurring feature of their eastern European lives. Often risking life and limb and travelling in steerage in ships, they left behind their village or urban lives, or perhaps forced conscription in the Russian army, to take up a new life in these lands of opportunity. Because they fled countries inhospitable to them, they had little nostalgia concerning what they had left behind, and they looked forward to becoming Americans and Canadians. Once here, they worked at whatever trade they could; they aimed for assimilation, but they also kept up their practice of Judaism. In turn, their children, our parents, negotiated a meteoric social rise in a single generation: born to immigrants who had arrived with very little in their pockets (one of my relatives gave his occupation on his citizenship papers as "rag-picker"), our parents attended colleges and universities and became well-established across the professions.

With the exception of certain orthodox communities, many in our parents' generation diluted their parents' religious observance significantly, becoming less strict in their religious practices, attending Conservative or Reform synagogues that were more accommodating to the changing realities of life in mid-century America, or turning their backs entirely on religious observance and belief. Many families, like Wallin's, retained only a modicum of Jewish religious observance, but nonetheless retained a strong sense of cultural and ethnic identity as Jewish.

When the news of the Holocaust reached North America, the shock of this immensely tragic and traumatic event served to shore up our families' sense of Jewish identity, out of a sense of solidarity with those who had been annihilated ("this could have been us!") and a fear of the seemingly limitless violence to which anti-Semitism could now be seen to extend. This traumatizing knowledge also strengthened a Jewish antipathy to racism of any kind, since it was due to their race that Hitler wanted to exterminate the Jews. This abhorrence of racism led leaders of the Jewish community, most notably Abraham Joshua Heschel, to join in the civil rights movement and march with Martin Luther King. Sadly, at the same time, the upward mobility and the trappings of white privilege which this generation assumed rather easily contributed to a strained dimension of the relationship between American Jews and African Americans.

The story of Jewish immigration to North America, drawn in broad strokes to which there are bound to be several exceptions, is largely one of successful assimilation to the middle and upper middle classes, with many families retaining diminishing degrees of religious observance as they attained increasing degrees of social and professional success. Diminishing degrees of religious observance, however, did not mean a diminishing sense of belonging to the Jewish community. Like Wallin's family (and my own), Jewish families remained strongly identified as Jews regardless of their lack of belief and minimal observance of religious practices. They represented the rank and file of those whose emblematic figure had been described by Isaac Deutscher a generation earlier as "the non-Jewish Jew." Deutscher coined this phrase to describe a lineage of great thinkers and activists from Spinoza to Marx, Einstein, and Freud, who rejected the religious traditions of the Jews yet held onto its message of "universal human emancipation." He astutely pointed out that these non-Jewish or secular Jews understood universalism as a form of solidarity with all of humankind, rather than as the uniformity with which it is currently often conflated. Deutscher argued that living in the diaspora, always "on the margins" of other cultures and "amid historic cross-currents," led these Jews to identify with those strands of Jewish thought that stressed the universality of God and of the Jewish message, rather than God's dedication to a particular "chosen people" (Deutscher, 1968, pp. 26–30).

JEWISH IDENTITY AND RELIGION

Indeed, the question of what Judaism actually *is*—a religion, a race, an ethnic identity, a civilization, a culture, a community, or a nation—and, therefore, who counts as a Jew, has vexed and continues to vex Jews of all stripes for well over a hundred years. The category of "religion" itself is to a great extent a modern, European creation, born out of Europe's attempts to grapple with and distinguish itself from the often baffling customs of the inhabitants of the lands it conquered and colonized from the Age of Exploration onwards. Being neither completely unrelated to Christianity, nor sufficiently assimilated to it, Judaism has had a complex and ever-shifting relationship to this term.[2] At one end of the spectrum the definition of a Jew circles around those who define themselves by descent from other Jews via the maternal line and concomitantly by their regular observance of religious practices handed down by tradition. At the other end are the non-Jewish Jews described by Deutscher, including both those who, in the words of Israeli writer Amos Oz, understand the community of Jews as a "textline" rather than a bloodline or a community of belief (Oz & Oz-Salzberger, 2012, pp. 1, 56, 203) and secular Jews who identify with some part of their cultural heritage but have no interest in the texts that have been tied to that heritage. Thus the sense of Jewish identity has persisted across a wide range of belief and nonbelief. Although our parents had little observance of Jewish tradition and even less belief, if they had been asked "what is there left to you that is Jewish?" they probably would have answered, as Freud himself did, "A very great deal, and probably its very essence" (Freud, 1913/1959, p. xxxi).

As we, the third generation of North American Jewish children, grew up, we did not find it so easy to sustain even this degree of clarity about the essence of Judaism. More assimilated into the North American mainstream than even our parents, less vulnerable to anti-Semitism than perhaps any previous Jewish community, steeped in the values of religious and racial tolerance, we found that our Jewish identity often became less of a given. Values of "study, suffering, and success" as in Wallin's family were passed along, but without much if any theological or religious anchor. For secular assimilated Jews, what it meant to be Jewish was a question without an easy answer.

This challenge posed by the meaning of Judaism was shared—probably unknown to most of us at the time—by Jewish theologians, who struggled mightily with the possible meaning, if any, of God after the Auschwitz.[3] Some of them, as well as several Christian theologians, faced with the theological challenge of the Holocaust together with the increasing secularism of mainstream culture, declared that God was dead.[4] In this sense, we might say that all of us in the post-Holocaust west were born in the wake of the death of

God, prophesied a century earlier by Nietzsche and made palpable by the genocidal realities of the twentieth century.

Nonetheless—or perhaps because of this—a significant segment of this third generation of North American Jews made up a disproportionate number of those seekers who from the sixties onward found their way to ashrams and meditation centers in India and around the world, as well as to university departments of south Asian culture and religion. Not finding God at home, as much as we may have taken for granted a degree of Jewish identity and a certain amount of Jewish ritual, we went in search of something other than what we had learned of Judaism. Perhaps many of us had learned of the Holocaust so early in our lives that coming of age meant searching for meaning outside of the onerous burden of history within which we had been brought up and with which Judaism had become identified. The counterculture of the sixties, with its psychedelic emphasis on ecstatic experience and its questioning of authority, together with the exposure to cultures overseas made possible by the Peace Corps and a healthy postwar economy, contributed to an interest in eastern, non-monotheistic religions and cultures (Taylor, 1998, p. 11); suddenly it was economically feasible for middle-class American youth to travel to India to study with traditional gurus. Many of these teachers of Buddhism and Hinduism offered their students practices of prayer and meditation that did not require the belief in an omnipotent God whose existence would have posed the intractable questions of theodicy after the Holocaust. Although the practice of mindfulness is traced back to the teachings of the Buddha, one does not have to (although of course one may) believe in the Buddha as a god in order to practice and benefit from meditation. In addition to these reasons, perhaps the attraction of meditation and yoga to third-generation Jewish Americans has been a response to an intergenerational, inherited, unconscious "postmemory"[5] of a sense of the transcendent: a response to a haunting by a spiritual past that was all but unknown to this third generation, and which took the guise of a longing for an as-yet undiscovered form of connection with something beyond our everyday lives. Eastern religions provided a response to this longing and an antidote to the increasing blandness of assimilated Jewish American life, yet without a demand for conversion out of Judaism and/or a belief in yet another monotheistic god.

SPIRITUAL SEEKING

Many who searched out ashrams in India brought back the teachings they had received there to a popular culture that was interested in both sampling and commodifying the sacred practices of the east. Fast-forward to the growth industry of yoga schools, meditation centers, and gurus of dubious ethical standards surrounded by sexual scandal, as well as the sincere seekers, teachers and students, who managed to hold on to their ethical integrity as they translated what had until recently been thought of as the obscure mysticism of the inscrutable east into the now-familiar lingua franca of the un-churched spirituality of the North American public.

When the American seekers of the sixties and seventies flocked to ashrams around India and elsewhere in the east or attended workshops given by eastern teachers in the west, and then brought what they had learned to centers around North America, none were so prominent as those from Jewish families (Kamenetz, 1994). Whether it was Ram Dass, making the once exotic gods and theologies of Hinduism familiar and meaningful to his psychedelicized audience in *Be Here Now;* Joseph Goldstein, Jack Kornfield, and Suzanne Goldstein setting up the first Insight Meditation Center in Massachusetts in 1975; or Dr. Jon Kabat-Zinn introducing Buddhist Mindfulness techniques at the Stress Reduction Clinic at the University of Massachusetts Medical School, in these and many other places Jews were represented disproportionately.[6] Having searched and found, for better or for worse, alternative forms of religiosity and/or alternative ways of understanding the human condition in its religious expressions, a number of differing paths were taken. Some remain to this day adept in their adopted eastern practices; some have taken their new-found passion for religiosity and have returned to the religion of their birth to infuse it with religious ardor (the Baalei Teshuva, those who have "returned" to Judaism, usually in a much more demanding orthodoxy than required by the branch of Judaism in which they had been brought up (Shapiro 2012); some, burdened by the dishonorable and interpersonally destructive conduct that has often lurked behind the high-minded teachings of eastern spiritual guides, have turned away from them and/or sought to expose them; while some have become outstanding academic scholars of Hinduism and of Buddhism. Many, however, have felt the need to understand these experiences and perspectives in an idiom closer to home, and to integrate them with features from the inner landscapes of their backgrounds. For Wallin, as for many others, it was psychoanalysis that provided the language with which to reckon with the similarities and contradictions between religious ideologies from far away and the more familiar, psychoanalytic idiom and ethos that had become, by the time we were children, part and parcel of the North American scene.[7]

AMERICAN PSYCHOANALYSIS AND RELIGION

The fact that a segment of these grandchildren of nineteenth-century Jewish immigrants turned to psychoanalysis to mediate a new-found religiosity fits hand in glove with the social history of American psychoanalysis. Psychoanalysis, like our grandparents, was once a Jewish immigrant to North America. As Lew Aron and Karen Starr have provocatively suggested, American psychoanalysis itself can be seen as "a Holocaust survivor," imported to a large degree by a generation of émigré analysts who fled Nazism in the 1930s (Aron & Starr, 2013, p. 111).[8] These émigrés contributed to the rising importance of American psychoanalysis in the mid-twentieth century, founding psychoanalytic institutes, teaching in psychiatry departments, and exerting considerable influence on popular culture (Zaretsky, 2004). Although they were largely Jewish, they were not only secular but often actively antagonistic toward religion, and their theory and practice codified this antagonism by considering religious belief either reason enough to disqualify someone from analysis altogether, or as something that would be cured through a successful analysis.[9] Either way, they saw religion and psychoanalysis as incompatible. This was a viewpoint they had inherited from Freud, and one that had been written into the foundations of psychoanalysis.

Even before the arrival of psychoanalysis in the United States, Freud, like many in our parents' generation, had left behind the religious observance of his upbringing. Peter Homans has persuasively argued that the psychological and sociological conditions for the emergence of psychoanalysis were created by a rupture with the religious past within the first and subsequent generations of psychoanalysts and by the resulting disintegration of the overarching system of religious symbols that had previously helped organize the structure of the religious psyche (Homans 1989). The early psychoanalysts were Jews and others who had left their traditional religious practices behind; even those who weren't Jewish, such as Carl Jung and Ernest Jones, had broken with their religious pasts prior to becoming involved with psychoanalysis. Repudiation of the past, a key movement in the creation of "the modern," found one of its most striking expressions in the psychoanalytic repudiation of religion.

Much ink has been spilt on the question of whether, how, and to what degree psychoanalysis has been influenced by Judaism (Aron & Starr, 2013, pp. 328–356; Brickman, 2010). Freud famously called himself a "godless Jew" and disavowed religion even as he remained faithful to his non-religious identity as a Jew. Freud's antipathy toward religion was well-known, even though his explanations for it changed somewhat throughout the development of his work: Religion was a universal obsessive neurosis; a wish-fulfillment; a slavish following of authority instead of thinking for oneself; a developmental arrest of a society or a re-instatement in that society of a preoedipal level as a compensation for the rigors of civilization; at most, religion was a community's way of working through the primal crime through which it had cemented its origins. Freud's aversion to religion combined Enlightenment disdain with a distaste for an often antisemitic Christianity,[10] and with a desire to be rid of the denigration that was the burden of being Jewish in his time.[11] For Freud as for other European Jewish intellectuals of his generation, secularism and science promised to offer a way out of a persecuted Judaism and into a universal solidarity with all of humankind. Freud hoped that psychoanalysis would take the place of religion and would make evident the secular truths of the human condition, and he, like the American ego psychologists who followed in his steps, correlated psychological maturity not only with the resolution of the Oedipus complex, but also with the rejection of religion in favor of the scientific outlook (Freud, 1913/1959, p. 90).

Like Freud, the analysts who fled Nazism and landed in the United States had for the most part already left behind the world of strict Jewish observance and had adopted Freud's enmity to religion. They presented psychoanalysis as a medical science with no overt links to Judaism, and psychoanalysis became, for its practitioners, a passport to assimilation into one of the more prestigious ranks of American society (Aron & Starr, 2013, pp. 110–123). These newly American psychoanalysts created ego psychology, positing the ego as a potentially "conflict-free sphere" in the psyche, and affirming the positive role of adaptation to society. Adaptation, rather than Freud's view of the psyche as fundamentally in conflict, and the ego as a "conflict-free zone" rather than as envisioned by Freud as an undependable mediator between the clashing impulses of id and superego, were theoretical correlates to the drive to adapt to and assimilate without conflict into mainstream America. Their commitment to a psychoanalysis devoted exclusively to the intrapsychic origins of psychopathology dismissed the social and cultural contexts of their patients as irrelevant, interpreting disaffection with the status quo as pathology (e.g., women unhappy with their limited roles as housewives were diagnosed with penis envy, while African Americans whose family structures and modes of interaction differed from the white American norm were assessed as not having enough "ego strength" to undergo psychoanalytic treatment at all[12]). Convinced as they were of the neutrality and universality of their scientific endeavor, their theories rendered invisible the conflictual inequalities of race, gender, and social class. There were of course notable exceptions, such as Erich Fromm and Karen Horney, but because of their views they suffered a kind of marginalization from the mainstream of psychoanalysis.

By the time our generation, the third generation of Jews descended from that large migration in the late nineteenth century, came of age, the hidden exclusionary premises of universalism were coming under siege. The civil rights movement, the anti-war and student movements of the sixties, and the women's movement and gay rights movement that followed, began to make evident the differences of race, gender, and sexual orientation that had been repressed in order to create the presumed universalism to which our families—and psychoanalysis—had aspired. And some decades after these concerns had surfaced in the culture at large, they found their way into the psychoanalytic institutes.

One of the major changes that allowed this to happen was the de-medicalization of psychoanalytic institutes in 1988. Until then, and against Freud's will (Freud, 1926/1959), the practice of North American psychoanalysis had been limited to medical doctors, an arrangement which facilitated the conception and dissemination of psychoanalysis as a medical science whose focus was solely on the intrapsychic life of the patient. Once the doors to the analytic institutes were opened to psychologists, social workers, and students of the humanities, the newly admitted generation, which included a much larger proportion of women, brought its social preoccupations along, inevitably expanding the concerns and thus eventually the scope of psychoanalysis. Leading the way, feminist critiques saw in psychoanalysis both a way to analyze the reproduction of women's inferiority within patriarchal society, as well as a path toward a more encompassing understanding of the psychodynamics of human subjectivity, gender, and interrelationship. The work of Juliet Mitchell, Nancy Chodorow, and Jessica Benjamin, together with French feminist psychoanalysts such as Luce Irigaray and Julia Kristeva, forever changed the way gender could be thought about and through psychoanalysis.[13] Others posed similar critiques about the exclusion of African Americans in psychoanalysis, both in practice and as dictated by the classical theory itself.[14] The hitherto accepted psychoanalytic orthodoxy that cultural, gender, racial, and social issues were irrelevant and external to the work of psychoanalysis came under challenge, and new theories accounted for the significance of the relational and even social contexts in which the individual psyche developed. The ignored or excluded "others" of psychoanalysis were slowly but surely finding their way into the psychoanalytic framework. And among these excluded others, significantly, lay the realm of religion.

Of course, hidden behind the orthodoxy of the psychoanalytic repudiation of religion, there had already been a centuries-long conversation between psychoanalysis and religion that had never quite surfaced into the mainstream of psychoanalytic thought, one which sought to correlate various religious traits with particular psychological needs and/or dynamics. From Freud's early correspondence with his friend the Protestant pastor Oskar Pfister to the taking up of ego psychology by the pastoral counseling movement in the mid-twentieth century, there have been repeated attempts to reconcile what Freud himself thought of as irreconcilable. Christian writers by and large have attempted to reconcile their faith with a psychoanalytic perspective, while Jewish writers have focused on the construction of religious identity and the continuity between religious and psychoanalytic as forms of interpretation (Brickman 2010). More recently, these conversations have been joined by a discussion between Buddhism and psychoanalysis. Erich Fromm's pioneering conversations with D. T. Suzuki in 1957 constituted a first, lone foray into this field, but a more robust dialogue has emerged from the final decade of the twentieth century onwards, led by such psychoanalysts as Mark Epstein, Barry Magid, Jeffrey Rubin, and Jeremy Safran.

PSYCHOANALYSIS AND BUDDHISM

New developments in Anglo-American psychoanalysis had begun to open up avenues of connection with Buddhist perspectives. The ego psychology that had dominated American psychoanalysis during the mid-twentieth century had championed the expansion of an autonomous ego as a standard of mental health; nothing could have been further from the teachings of Hinduism and Buddhism, which saw the ego as an obstacle to mental health, peace of mind, and oneness with the environmental and spiritual surround. British psychoanalysis after Melanie Klein was hospitable to works that addressed mystical themes directly (e.g., Wilfred Bion and Marion Milner) or that made room somewhat more indirectly for bridges between psychoanalysis and insights gleaned from the practice of meditation. For example, Winnicott's notion of the importance of "unintegration" and "unknowing," a necessary if temporary relaxation of the mental structures that hold us together, provided a counter-balance to American psychoanalysis' ideals of ego strength and the cohesiveness of the self, and paved the way for interconnections with eastern doctrines which aim to deconstruct the centrality of the self.[15] The psychoanalytic view found in nascent form in Freud and more fully developed in contemporary theories of intersubjectivity, relationality, and psychoanalytic constructivism, according to which selves are brought into being through intimate interaction with others, along with the related view that subjective experience is constructed out of the multiple contexts of interaction in which two or more people find themselves, form bridges to the Buddhist doctrine of dependent origination, which sees the self as coming into being moment after moment as a result of multiple contingent causes and conditions.

Once again, this development, of which David Wallin's work is a notable example, has been spearheaded largely by members of the third-generation North American Jewish community, who have been students and/or teachers of Buddhist meditation at the same time as practicing psychoanalysts. Different authors stress differing strands of psychoanalytic thought (self psychology, British object relations, relational psychoanalysis with specific reference to Peter Fonagy) to form bridges with a variety of insights from Buddhist teachings. This combination has been both reciprocally illuminating and reciprocally self-critical: the psychological shortcomings of meditation teachers and teachings have been critiqued, explained, and complemented by psychoanalytic understandings of interpersonal dynamics, while the spiritual shortcomings of psychoanalysis have been critiqued, explained, and complemented by the insights and practices of meditation.

Because North American psychoanalysis shares a social and cultural ancestry with many members of the third generation of the North American Jewish community, it inevitably shares a similar set of concerns with them. Because of this shared heritage, psychoanalysis has provided a framework that could mediate between Jewish heritage, psychological-mindedness, and the meditation practices of Buddhist traditions. It has done this by providing a kind of "going home" without quite going home: it has given us a language with which to reckon with both our heritage and new horizons of meaning, but, in Wallin's words, it has allowed us to do this without remaining solely or completely "embedded" in them. The challenge, as Wallin has charted out so well in psychodynamic fashion, is not only to *en*act, but to *inter*act with these inheritances, addressing shortcomings critically, and working with what remains to open up new horizons of value. The language of psychoanalysis is familiar to us because of our shared ancestry and cultural trajectories, but it allows us a degree of distance or flexibility from these shared domains because of its analytic distance. It mediates a dialectical movement between the immediacy of lived experience and the critical remove of remembrance in language. Otherwise said, psychoanalysis has allowed us to reflect upon heritage and horizon with both insider and outsider status, providing a framework with which to integrate new modes of reflection, such as mindfulness, as part of the psychoanalytic work of self-knowledge that we are engaged in for ourselves and our patients.

In *Attachment in Psychotherapy*, David Wallin (2007) has beautifully brought together a number of different bodies of research—attachment theory, neurobiology, relational psychoanalysis, and Buddhist mindfulness technique—to produce a clear and coherent synthesis. He demonstrates how each of these dimensions is interwoven with the others, clarifying the neurobiology of attachment, the relevancy of attachment theory to clinical work seen from a relational perspective, and the ways in which mindfulness can work within and emerge from a relational perspective. His (remarkably readable) study of the neurobiology of attachment allows him to bring into the conversation the salience of the non-verbal experiences of the body as the underpinning of our emotional experience. Breathing new life into Freud's dictum that "the ego is first and foremost a bodily ego," Wallin demonstrates the vital connection between dissociation (repression or disconnection from one's emotional states) and disembodiment (disconnection from one's bodily sensations). Based on this research, he has skillfully mapped a developmental and therapeutic movement from insecure to secure attachment, from avoidance or preoccupation to authentic relationship, from dissociation to mentalization, and from mentalization to mindfulness. In a clinical world where mindfulness techniques have often largely been thought of as the province of cognitive behavioral therapy, he demonstrates how organically mindfulness can arise out of and alongside the processes of mentalization that are the hallmark of psychoanalytic reflection. Building on the work of attachment theorists John Bowlby and Mary Main and the psychoanalyst Peter Fonagy, his model opens up the possibility of a non-authoritarian, non-religious language in which to talk about the enfoldment within psychoanalytic practice of the mindfulness that is at the center of Buddhist practice. Wallin's autobiography alerts us to the religious dimensions of the breakthrough that led him to this synthesis; in turn, his work is a careful but psychological mapping of the transformative psychodynamics of mindfulness practice onto a rich integration of attachment theory and relational psychoanalytic theory.

In his theorization of the relationship between body, emotions, embeddedness, mentalizing, and mindfulness, Wallin has helped to clarify some important distinctions between embeddedness and mindfulness. The immersion in the "going-on-being" of life of which Winnicott speaks, or the immediacy of breath and bodily sensations attended to in meditation, sound very similar to a kind of embeddedness in experience. But Wallin characterizes embeddedness as the way in which we are gripped by strong emotional turmoil, and he characterizes mentalization as a reflection upon this embeddedness, granting us a degree of flexibility with it. Mentalization itself is in turn accompanied by mindfulness, yet another level of attention to body, breath, and mind that follows from, rather than precedes, reflection upon emotional reactions, and allows for an even greater degree of freedom from emotional turmoil (through acceptance rather than disavowal). As most if not all those who have written on these topics have pointed out, spirituality can function as a defense against our emotional blindspots, while psychoanalysis can fall short of the transformative potential found in spiritual practice. In Wallin's terminology, mindfulness without mentalization can too easily allow us to escape the painful knots we are tied up in, while mentalization without mindfulness may alert us to those knots without fully helping us in untying them.

For Wallin, mindfulness helps "loosen the grip of the internalized past and the imagined future." His Jewish heritage is part and parcel of the grip he is trying to loosen through the insights of attachment and psychoanalytic theory, and it is Buddhist mindfulness practice that opens up the horizon of something more. This is one, very effective, way of negotiating the spiritual losses, discoveries, and recoveries of our generation. Yet we can find similar negotiations of the same existential/religious challenges in other contemporary archives, both theological and psychoanalytic. Michael Fishbane's (2008) recent work of Jewish theology, *Sacred Attunement,* seems from the outset to share certain premises that we find in Wallin's work. Fishbane's work is an elaboration on the themes he announces early on: "without the hidden call to attention, and the rehabilitation of awareness, we are all but dead in the midst of life," and "task of theology is…to attune the self to the unfolding occurrence of things in all their particularities and conjunctions…" (pp. 22, 34). Similarly, Eric Santner (2001) has written a treatise on the theological implications within Freud's psychoanalysis itself, and elsewhere has used his complex, philosophically-inflected psychoanalytic thought to contend that, in our day and in our age, "Miracles Happen" (Santner, 2005).

Wallin's work, too, demonstrates how a certain religious stance—the *nunc stans,* the everlasting *now* of the church fathers, alluded to by Walter Benjamin as "time filled by the presence of the now" (Benjamin, 1968, p. 261)—is something we can discover and cultivate in our psychological work with our patients as in our daily lives. Wallin spells out the psychodynamics of this stance which, while it may seem to have nothing explicitly to do with faith, God, or religion, may nonetheless be expressive of a clinician's deepest spiritual commitments. The end of the capacity to believe in a deity or transcendental entity does not necessarily mean the end of faith. Rather, the "death of God" that we have inherited can come to indicate the end of locating holiness in an "elsewhere," or a "beyond," and can point instead to the possibility of attuning ourselves in the here and now to encounters with the ordinary extraordinariness of life.

NOTES

1. As a Canadian who grew up in Montreal, I generalize the shared social and cultural conditions of Jewish immigration to and life in the "new world."
2. See Batnitzky, 2011 for a discussion of the different positions taken by early modern Jewish thinkers on this question.
3. e.g., Rubenstein, 1966/1992; Fackenheim, 1982; Cohen, 1981.
4. e.g., Rubenstein, 1966/1992; Moltmann, 1974; Vahanian, 1961; Altizer and Hamilton, 1966; Haynes and Roth, 1999.
5. I have borrowed this evocative term from Marianne Hirsch, at www.postmemory.net (retrieved 2/16/14). While Hirsch, like theorists of the intergenerational transmission of trauma, uses this term to refer to experiences that have been heard about and otherwise vicariously experienced second-hand, I am suggesting here an intergenerational transmission of unconscious data, of loss that has not been, or has barely been, consciously heard about or seen; the inheriting generation experiences this loss only as a lacuna that has no name, no description, and no—or very few—conscious referents.
6. See Kamenetz, 1994, for a discussion of the surprisingly large proportion of Jews studying Buddhist and Hindu practices, as well as for the tale of a meeting over several days between the Dalai Lama and eight Jewish rabbis and scholars in 1991.
7. For an account of the extensive interpenetration and mutual influence of psychoanalysis and (North) American culture over the course of the twentieth century, see Zaretksy, 2004.
8. Aron and Starr are quoting R. Prince, 2009.
9. See, for example, Fenichel, 1939, p. 111; or Sandor Rado quoted in Lawrence-Lightfoot, 1988, p. 179.
10. *Group Psychology and the Analysis of the Ego* can be read, among other interpretations, as a critique of the forces at work in the popular mass anti-Semitism of the era, epitomized by the Catholic church. See Brickman 2003, pp. 90–102.
11. See my discussion in Brickman 2003, pp. 145–153 and 162–170.

12. This American psychoanalytic view of women's "problem that has no name" was documented in the now iconic books of Betty Friedan, Germaine Greer, Phillis Chesler, and others. For the treatment of African Americans in psychoanalytically-oriented mental-health agencies, see Altman, 2010.

13. For somewhat later interventions into psychoanalysis and homosexuality, see Dean and Lane, 2001; and of course, the ground-breaking works of Judith Butler.

14. Altman, 2010; Brickman, 2003.

15. Epstein (2007 and other works) in particular emphasizes the interconnections between Winnicott's work and Buddhist meditation.

REFERENCES

Altizer, T. J. J., & Hamilton, W. (1966). *Radical theology and the death of God.* Indianapolis: Bobbs-Merrill.

Altman, N. (2010). *The analyst in the inner city : Race, class, and culture through a psychoanalytic lens* (2nd ed). New York: Routledge.

Aron, L., & Starr, K. (2013). *A psychotherapy for the people: Towards a progressive psychoanalysis.* New York and London: Routledge.

Batnitzky, L. (2011). *How Judaism became a religion: An introduction to modern Jewish thought.* Princeton, NJ: Princeton University Press.

Benjamin, W. (1968). Theses on the philosophy of history. In W. Benjamin, H. Arendt, & H. Zohn (Eds.), *Illuminations: Essays and reflections* (253–264). New York: Schocken Books/ Harcourt Brace Jovanovich.

Brickman, C. (2003). *Aboriginal populations in the mind: Race and primitivity in psychoanalysis.* New York: Columbia University Press.

Brickman, C. (2010). Psychoanalysis and Judaism in context. In L. Aron & L. Henik (Eds.), *Answering a question with a question: Contemporary psychoanalysis and Jewish thought.* Boston: Academic Studies Press.

Cohen, A. (1981). *The tremendum: A theological interpretation of the Holocaust.* New York: Crossroad.

Dean, T., & Lane, C. (Eds.). (2001). *Homosexuality and psychoanalysis.* Chicago: University of Chicago Press.

Deutscher, I. (1968). *The Non-Jewish Jew and other essays.* London: Oxford University Press.

Epstein, M. (2007). *Psychotherapy without the self.* New Haven: Yale University Press.

Fackenheim, E. (1982). *To mend the world: Foundations of future Jewish thought.* New York: Schocken Books.

Fenichel, O. (1939). Problems of psychoanalytic technique. *Psychoanalytic Quarterly, 8,* 303–324.

Fishbane, M. (2008). *Sacred Attunement: A Jewish Theology.* Chicago: University of Chicago Press.

Freud, S. (1959). Totem and taboo. In S. Freud & J. Strachey (Eds.), *The standard edition of the complete psychological works of Sigmund Freud* (vol. 13). London: Hogarth Press. (Original work published 1913)

Freud, S. (1959). The Question of lay analysis. In S. Freud & J. Strachey (Eds.), *The standard edition of the complete psychological works of Sigmund Freud* (vol. 20). London: Hogarth Press. (Original work published 1926)

Fromm, E., Suzuki. D. T., & Martino R. (1960). *Zen Buddhism and psychoanalysis.* New York: Harper Press.

Gay, P. (1987). *A Godless Jew: Freud, atheism, and the making of psychoanalysis.* New Haven: Yale University Press.

Haynes, S. R., & Roth, J. K. (Eds.). (1999). *The Death of God movement and the Holocaust: Radical theology encounters the Shoah.* Westport, CT: Greenwood Press.

Homans, P. (1989). *The ability to mourn: Disillusionment and the social origins of the psychoanalytic movement.* Chicago: University of Chicago Press.

Kamenetz, R. (1994). *The Jew in the lotus: A poet's rediscovery of Jewish identity in Buddhist India*. San Francisco: Harper Books.
Lawrence-Lightfoot, S. (1988). *Balm in Gilead: Journey of a healer*. New York: Penguin Books.
Magid, B., & Beck, C. J. (2005). *Ordinary mind: Exploring the common ground of Zen & psychotherapy*. Somerville, MA: Wisdom Publications.
Moltmann, J. (1974). *The Crucified God*. London : SCM Press.
Oz, A., & Oz-Salzberger, F. (2012). *Jews and words*. New Haven: Yale University Press.
Prince, R. (2009). Psychoanalysis traumatized: The legacy of the Holocaust. *American Journal of Psychoanalysis*, *69*, 179–194.
Rubenstein, R. (1992). *After Auschwitz: History, theology, and contemporary Judaism* (2nd ed.). Baltimore: Johns Hopkins University Press.
Rubin, J. (1996). *Psychotherapy and Buddhism: Toward an integration*. New York: Plenum Press.
Safran, J. (Ed.). (2003). *Psychoanalysis and Buddhism: An unfolding dialogue*. Boston: Wisdom Publications.
Santner, E. (2001). *On the psychotheology of everyday life: Reflections on Freud and Rosenzweig*. Chicago: University of Chicago Press.
Santner, E. (2005). Miracles happen: Benjamin, Rosenzweig, Freud, and the matter of the neighbor. In S. Žižek, E.L. Santner, & K. Reinhard (Eds.), *The neighbor: Three inquiries in political theology* (pp. 76–133). Chicago: University of Chicago Press.
Shapiro, L. (2012). *Driven to Orthodoxy: Jewish identity and narratives of exceptionalism, essentialism, and the family in American Jewish culture as motivations for "conversion" to Orthodox Judaism*. Dissertation Abstracts International, Volume: 74-05(E), Section: A. School code: 0330.
Shaw, D. (2014). *Traumatic narcissism: Relational systems of subjugation*. New York: Routledge.
Taylor, M. C. (1998). Introduction. In M. C. Taylor (Ed.), *Critical terms for religious studies* (pp. 1–20). Chicago: University of Chicago Press.
Vahanian, G. (1961). *The Death of God*. New York: George Braziller.
Wallin, D. (2007). *Attachment in psychotherapy*. New York: The Guilford Press.
Zaretksy, E. (2004). *Secrets of the soul: A social and cultural history of psychoanalysis*. New York: Alfred A. Knopf.

Chapter Eight

Three Pillars of Therapeutic Attitude

Salman Akhtar

> "If God is a projection, even so is there a God who created me in such a way that I have the material in me for such a projection? Aetiologically, if I may use a word here that usually refers to disease, the paradox must be accepted, not resolved." —Donald Winnicott (1968, p. 205)

Psychoanalytic work is not only about activities. It is also about attitudes. The latter, it is my contention, have received inoptimal attention. Modell's (1976), my own (Akhtar, 1992, pp. 343–346), and Lewin and Schulz's (1992) explications of "holding" (Winnicott 1960) functions of the analyst notwithstanding, a fuller understanding of the analytic attitude still eludes us. This contribution constitutes one, relatively modest, attempt to accomplish just this task. In it, I will identify three facets of the analytic attitude, namely survival, vision, and faith. Vis-à-vis each of them, I will offer a metaphoric emblem, some hypotheses regarding developmental origins of the attitude, its technical implications, and a clinical vignette or two illustrating the particular attitude in action. Following these three sections, I will conclude with some synthesizing remarks and hint at some broader applications of the notions outlined here. Before starting, however, I would like to note the potential pitfalls and limitations of the ideas I have to offer here.

SOME CAVEATS

First and foremost, the three facets of analytic attitude (namely survival, vision, and faith) are not meant to provide an exhaustive list of all that is sustained under such an attitude. Devotion readily comes to mind, but it seems to be included under "survival." Benevolence stakes its claim but seems to be included, at least the way I see things, under the category of "vision." Similarly, hopefulness appears to be a metaconstituent of "faith." This, however, does not mean that there might not be aspects of analytic attitude that lie outside the phenomenological domain of the three upon which I have chosen to focus. It only indicates what has caught my attention over some twenty years of busy analytic practice. Second, it must be emphasized that by the virtue of being "attitudes," these three facets do not manifest themselves directly in our clinical work. They silently but forcefully guide our listening and talking activities. Their presence or absence is deductively inferred rather than empirically observed. Third, while I am describing these in the context of a human relationship, these attitudes might have phylogenetic bases and evolutionary advantages. The discussion of animal prototypes in my paper on forgiveness (Akhtar, 2002) and Seelig and Rosof's (2001) essay on altruism offer a parallel, corroborative support to such speculation, though more work is certainly needed to flesh out the issues involved here. Finally, as we tackle the powerful, even if silent, role of survival, vision, and faith in the conduct of our work, the question whether these attributes can be taught (to our trainees) surfaces in the mind. However tempting it might be to respond with a resounding "yes" or "no," the fact is that we do not know the answer to this question. The deep anchor of these capacities in early childhood development makes one think that their presence or absence must be so well-ingrained by adulthood that the hope of generating them afresh later in life might be foolhardy. On the other hand, such pessimism might be unwarranted, especially in the light of contemporary psychoanalytic understanding of adult development and assumption of hitherto thwarted ego functions by conflict-analysis, strengthened "mentalization" (Fonagy and Target, 1997), and selective identification with one's mentors, supervisors, and analysts. It is with such caveats in mind that I now proceed to address the first of three facets of the analytic attitude.

SURVIVAL

Visual Icon

As an aid to elucidating what I mean by "survival" as an aspect of psychotherapeutic attitude, I will offer a visual image that captures the essence of my proposal. I suggest that the reader bring to his mind the children's toy called Weeble. For those unfamiliar with it, let me explain that Weeble is a plastic balloon filled with air and has a solid lead base. As a result, upon being knocked in this or that direction, it also restabilizes its position. It does not fall. It bounces back and its unflappability gives children great pleasure. I suggest that a practicing psychotherapist (or psychoanalyst) is a human equivalent of the Weeble. He receives and absorbs "shocks" from the patient's emotional outpouring, revelations, and attacks, but he steadfastly maintains his analytic posture. Any movements away from it are largely private, momentary, and subtle. Even when these are more overt—as in the case of intensely hateful patients (Kernberg, 1992), for instance—the analyst soon returns to his non-judgmental position of patience and curiosity. He is a Weeble par excellence.

Developmental Prototype

The analyst's capacity for "survival" seems derived from two types of sources. The first category can be called sources from above and includes his commitment to "technical neutrality" (Freud, 1914; Kernberg, 1976), "holding" (Winnicott, 1960), containing (Bion, 1962), and maintaining an "analytic persona" (Levine, 2007). Identification with his supervisors and training analyst buttresses this foundation. The second category is constituted by sources from below and rests upon characterological factors derived from childhood experience. Among such ontogenetic building blocks, two seem to be most important.[1] The first involves the child's interaction with the mother, and the second involves his interaction with the father. Vis-à-vis the mother, the situation is essentially this: the child has destructive impulses toward the mother, born out of frustration; however, whether these impulses actually end up being destructive or not depends upon whether the mother retains her maternal attitude (e.g., devotion, empathy, providing nourishment, offering support, remaining available) or reacts in a retaliatory manner. If she remains the mother, so to speak, then there is no destruction in reality. Her "survival" makes her an object that the child can now use. In Winnicott's (1968) words, "A new feature thus arrives in the theory of object-relating. The subject says to the object: 'I destroyed you,' and the object is there to receive the communication. From now on the subject says: 'Hullo object!' 'I destroyed you.' 'I love you.' 'You have value for me because of your survival of my destruction to you.' 'While I am loving you all the time destroying you in (unconscious) fantasy.' Here fantasy begins for the individual. The subject can now use the object that has survived." (p. 89). Over the course of time, the child also internalizes this capacity of the mother and, later, as an adult, himself becomes able to survive others' attacks upon him.

Other childhood experiences also add to the development of this capacity. Prominent among these is the child's experience with his father. Pruett (1988, 2000) has noted that a child uses the father's body primarily for enlarging his receptive or motoric expanse regarding external reality, horseplay, and testing his strength. The last mentioned function is involved in observing the father's "survival" capacity. The child notes that his father can withstand his "attacks" and incorporates this attribute into his own psyche. Working in unison, the infantile destructive impulses toward the mother and the toddlerhood-latency rough housing with the father permit the child to observe the parental "survival," and it is this that, through identification, lays down the groundwork for his own capacity to survive as an adult. To be sure, the pseudo-intellectual parent-child struggles of adolescence also contribute to this capacity. The psychoanalyst has all this in his background. However, his capacity for "survival" also comes from a myriad other adulthood experiences. His identification with his training analyst (who maintained the analytic attitude despite his analysand's transference distortions and ego regressions) and his clinical supervisors (who patiently helped him develop as an analyst without wincing at his early clumsiness) further refine this attribute of his ego functioning.

Technical Implications

The role played by the analyst's capacity for "survival" in clinical work is evident on many levels. Grossly speaking, the very fact that analytic treatment spans over many years attests to the analyst's capacity to "survive." Month after month and year after year, he accommodates the patient's transference distortions of him, bears strong affects from the patient's side and within himself (Coen, 2002), resists temptations to retaliate or seduce, avoids major departures from neutrality, and safeguards therapeutic boundaries. These forces tax and, from time to time, sway his "psychoanalytic work ego" (Olinick, Poland, Griggs, & Granatir, 1973), but he does not drown in the sea of sentimentality or dissipate in the desert of indifference. He remains steadfast in his analytic identity and commitment. On a more subtle level, "survival" is evident in the analyst's moment-to-moment recapturing of analytic position in the face of transference-countertransference pulls to act out this or that relational scenario; his "role-responsiveness" (Sandler, 1976) is transient, aim-inhibited, and readily subject to scrutiny by his observing ego. Even when he is the subject of sharp sarcasm from the patient, he does not give in to the temptation to retaliate.

Clinical Vignette: 1

As she entered my office, Joan Stein, a young borderline patient in psychotherapy, looked at me with piercing eyes and said "pissed again?," implying that I appeared angry to her. I, who had been quite peaceful till the moment of this seemingly innocuous inquiry, actually began feeling annoyed. No, let me be honest: I started feeling quite angry. The patient briskly moved toward her chair. Closing the door, I turned and took the two to three steps toward my chair. But in those few moments, I felt the impulse to say something sarcastic and nasty back to her. I suppressed the impulse, thought about it, and soon realized that I had become fully identified with what she had projected into me. My rage diminished. It was replaced by the usual stance of analytic containment and inquiry. My work ego, assaulted by the patient's evident projection, had survived. The attitude of "survival" is however not restricted to how one responds to the patient's hostility (and the counter-aggression that this might mobilize within the analyst). Intense emotions of all sorts can have a potentially destabilizing impact upon the analyst's work ego and thus necessitate the analyst to "survive" the internal crisis. The same is true of the erotic overtures of the patient as well.

Clinical Vignette: 2

Lisa Martinez, an extremely attractive analysand heard me give the paper I had recently written on "Someday . . . " and "If only . . . " fantasies. While I was elucidating the potentially narcissistic and masochistic deployment of such fantasies, which fuel relentless ambition or reduce all effort to waiting for wunderglauben, I also noted that the mere existence of these fantasies is not pathological. Indeed, their existence is ubiquitous and consonant with mental health if the fantasy is not taken literally and is used largely as a transitional object (Winnicott, 1953). With characteristic humor and self-disclosure, I told the audience that I have a "Someday . . . " fantasy of my own: "Someday all the books I have will be arranged in alphabetical order." Now, I knew that this would never actually happen, for I am neither driven enough to do it nor disciplined enough to maintain such an order (should someone else do it for me, which too is unlikely). The audience laughed knowingly. Approvingly, I moved on to more serious aspects of the topic. The next day Lisa came to her session. As she was about to lie down on the couch, she flipped her hair, tilted her neck just a little, and said in a soft, almost little girl voice: "If you like, I can come over to your office this weekend and we can together arrange all the books alphabetically." I found the comment intensely seductive. The scene of us alone in my office over the weekend, working together on a chore of mundane sweetness, flashed though my mind. I was instantly aroused. I wanted to grab her in my arms and plant a warm, eager, and wet kiss on her mouth. The impulse was almost painful, but I restrained myself, said nothing, and let the moment pass. Soon I found myself wondering about all sorts of questions: Why did I find this comment so sensually charged? Did Lisa mean it to be that way or was it of my own (wishful?) attribution? Should I have revealed my own "Someday . . . " fantasy in the previous evening's lecture when I knew that my analysand was in attendance? Was I being seductive by doing so? And, so on. In other words, I was back to being an analyst. My analytic ego had emerged from the transient drowning in erotic countertransference. It had survived.

In both the clinical vignettes cited above, the important point to note is that it is my capacity to have regained the analytic posture, after a brief "meltdown," that facilitated the patients' finding me transferentially "usable," in the Winnicottian (1968) sense of the word. Had I reacted to them with a hostile remark or a seductive overture, respectively, I (as a fantasy object) would have been "destroyed" and replaced by an actual object for which, in the end, they had little use.

VISION

Visual Icon

A sculptor who "sees" the contours of the statue he is yet to carve as already existing in the piece of rock in front of him is the best emblem for this aspect of therapeutic attitude. Just the way the sculptor feels that all he has to do is to remove the unnecessary parts of the stone to let the statue emerge, the therapist can also envision, with more or less clarity, how the patient would be were their work to succeed in dissolving his neurotic structures. Moreover, he keeps his eyes on the potential strengths of the patient and not only his psychopathology.

Developmental Prototype

While the overall parental attitude of expecting age-appropriate growth implies that they have a "vision" for their children's development, certain specific epochs help elucidate this idea more clearly. Take, for instance, the parental choice of a name for their offspring. It not only contains echoes from their past but also subtle messages for the child's future. And such "vision" on the parent's part gives the child's name its "determining power" (Abraham, 1911). Also pertinent in this context is the following observation by Lichtenstein (1961).

> The mother does not convey a sense of identity to the infant but an *identity*; the child is the organ, the instrument for the fulfillment of the mother's unconscious needs. Out of the *infinite potentials within the human infant, the specific stimulus combination emanating from the individual mother "releases" one, and not only one, concrete way of being this organ, this instrument.* It would, however, be a mistake to see this "organ" or "instrumental" identity as too narrowly defined. The mother imprints upon the infant not *an* identity, but an *"identity theme."* This *theme* is irreversible, but it is capable of variations, variations that spell the difference between human creativity and "a destiny neurosis" (p. 208, italics in the original).

Yet another illustration of how a mother's "vision" affects the unfolding psychomotor functions of the child is evident in the following scene. A toddler is walking around a coffee table holding on to its edges, ever so slightly afraid of letting go of their support. He wants to venture out on his own but seems hesitant. A few feet away stands his mother who spreads her arms and with a gleam in her eye says "come on; come on to mommy; you can do it; yes, sweetheart, you can." And, the toddler leaves the table's edge and takes his first unsupported steps toward his mother. It is as if the mother's gaze and encouraging voice have together created an invisible bridge of safety, walking on which the child crosses the distance between himself and his mother. Still later, the parental anticipation that the child can bear the pain of exclusion and "inferiority" during the oedipal phase illustrates their "vision." The same applies to the encouragement and auxiliary ego support they offer a latency-age child in his attempts at mastering difficult tasks in external reality and the gradual renunciation of control during their offspring's adolescence. Together all these parental qualities convey to the child that they can see ahead of him. They can therefore warn him of the oncoming risks and recognize that he will come out more or less unscathed, if not triumphant, in the end.

During his own childhood, the therapist has been the beneficiary of such parental vision. He has also identified with this capacity on his parents' part. His experience with his training analyst and with his supervisors has subtly replicated the process insofar as his transference distortions and his technical "mistakes" were tolerated as phase-appropriate, and he was seen to have the potential to overcome them. The combined result of all such experiences is the development of the capacity to have a "vision."

Technical Implications

"Vision" on the analyst's part implies his expectations that the patient is capable of better functioning. Commenting on Loewald's (1960) seminal contribution on technique, Cooper notes that the model analyst for Loewald works by being an "emotionally related object," with an important gradient of organizational maturity between him and his patient, "mindful of the patient's core of potential being, which he senses as a parent does, oriented towards the future, offering the patient opportunities to create new integrations on the armature of maturity that the analyst provides; his task is empathic communication, uncovering, and guidance towards new synthesis." (p. 26)

While such a future-oriented attitude pervades the course of treatment, there are junctures where it becomes quite explicit. One such point is during the assessment of "analyzability"[2] (i.e., of whether or not the patient will be able to go through the rigors of psychoanalysis). In recommending analysis, the analyst is implying that he expects that the patient can work through his problems to a very large extent. This is "vision" indeed.

On the other end of their long-term work, too, the analyst's "vision" plays an important part. Here I am referring to the termination of an analysis. This is well-captured in the following passage by Pulver (1991).

> One of the determinants of the analyst's intuition that termination is near seems to be an awakening of feelings analogous to those that a parent feels during separation-individuation. These feelings are twofold in nature. The parent feels a lessening of the demand for attention and libidinal gratification from the child who has successfully negotiated rapprochement; the analyst of the termination-ready patient feels a decrease in the transference demands. The analyst is less likely to be drawn into transference-countertransference enactments and feels less pressure to behave in ways foreign to himself. In addition to this direct response, the parent, by identification, senses the child's readiness to do more on his own; he can, for example, envision the child's spending the afternoon with a friend with the excitement that he himself feels about such activities rather than anxiety. Similarly, the analyst can picture the autonomous activities the patient describes with pleasure rather than with the feeling that this is a defensive retreat from the relationship (pp. 402–403).

The words "envision" and "picture" in the foregoing passage are tell-tale clues to the attitude of "vision." However, the impact of such "vision" of the patient's readiness for termination is not restricted to a certain ego-relaxation on the analyst's part. It also guides the flavor of his interpretation. His comments not only take the patient's concerns about the future to a greater extent, but they might also even be couched in a somewhat different term.

Clinical Vignette: 3

Ann Schwab, an internist at a hospital near my office, had been in analysis with me for quite some time and we were now approaching termination. Two traumatic events from her earlier years had played the organizing role in the transferences she developed toward me. The first pertained to her father who suddenly disappeared from her life when she was six years old, never to be seen or heard from again. The second involved her otherwise kind and loving step-father (who appeared in her life when she was nine) kissing her on her lips while drunk. She did inform her mother who arranged a family meeting where the step-father cried and apologized. This behavior never happened again, but it left an indelible mark on Ann's psyche. During her analysis, she would alternately fear abandonment and seduction by me. Interpretive work (about the wish-defense constellation underlying these "expectations") and reconstructive interventions (tracing the current distress back to its ontogenetic antecedents) worked well most of the time. Gradually, she mastered the fear and in her outside life became able to enter into a satisfying romantic relationship with a man. As termination approached, however, the two transference anxieties appeared afresh. Now that she would not be my patient anymore, running into me, in either of her hospitals, seemed truly dangerous to her. What if she approached me warmly and I ignored her? After all, we would have no relationship then. Or, worse still, what if I seduced her? Familiar though the fears were, the usual approach to them did not seem to work any longer. Then I could "see" the problem and its solution. I said to her, "I think you want me to reassure you, somehow, that if I run into you I will not act as if I were your analyst, but also to reassure you that I would always remember that I had been your analyst." The patient nodded in relieved agreement. The role of analyst's "vision" is also important in his capacity to conduct "developmental work" (Pine, 1997) which includes recognizing psychic development to be lifelong and understanding that the analytic process, like good parenting, includes both the provision of safety and the expectation of autonomous function.

FAITH

Visual Icon

The best way I can conceptualize a visual metaphor for faith is to encourage the reader to undertake a thought experiment. Here it goes. Imagine yourself to be in a circus. Looking upward, near the top of the tent, you notice a man on a trapeze. He swings back and forth, building confidence or courage for a while. It is as if he is figuring something out, not on the level of overt cognition but somewhere deep in his muscles, in his spirit. And then, just as you are about to give up on his seemingly futile rumination, the magic happens. The man leaves the trapeze and, for a shining moment or two, is in mid-air, and then catches a second trapeze that was coming his way from the opposite end of the tent. It is all over in the blink of an eye. But let us suppose you had a high power camera and the necessary skill to use it, and you shot a photograph of the man while he was mid-way between the two trapezes. Now print out a large size glossy copy and look at it. What you see there is a man of faith. Visibly captured. Pure and simple.

Developmental Prototype

Freud's (1927) tormented ambivalence about matters of religious belief (Akhtar, 2008) notwithstanding, the idea of "faith" has resisted demolition by the axe of psychoanalytic reductionism. Indeed, it is my sense that three different conceptualizations of "faith" exist within the corpus of our literature. The progenitors of these "models" are Erikson (1950, 1959), Winnicott (1953), and Bion (1967, 1970). According to Erikson (1950, 1959) a predictable rhythm of need gratification during infancy lays down the foundation of "basic trust." This implies the firm and, under ordinary circumstances, unshakeable conviction that the world is largely a "good" place (i.e., will, for the most part, gratify instinctual wishes and support developmental needs) and that one has the strength to withstand occasional disappointments, hurts, and betrayals. An air of "confident expectation" (Benedek, 1938) prevails. This strengthens one's ties to fellow human beings and to the world-at-large. Projection of "basic trust" into the future creates hope; conscious hope is for the fulfillment of wishes and "unconscious hope" (Casement, 1991) for finding development-sustaining opportunities.

Extending this Eriksonian premise further yields one particular psychoanalytic perspective on faith. Trust and hope, as conceptualized so far, involve the self as recipient of "goodness" and others (beginning of course, with the mother) as providers of it. However, if one were to replace oneself by everyone as the recipient and other humans by nature (e.g., rain, fertile land) and the institutions created by civilization (e.g., democracy, justice, education, science, poetry, athletics), then one can begin to grasp the essence of faith. Trust and hope tell the individual, "do not worry, there will always be people who will help you, and you have the strength to survive when such supplies seem scarce." Faith declares: "do not worry. All of us, including the generations that are yet to come, will be taken care of by the bounties of nature and by civilized institutions we have created (and will continue creating)." Faith is not about a single individual finding protection and love from fellow human beings. It is about fellow human beings finding nourishment (both literal and figurative) through natural resources and through the collective instruments of sublimation. While this view of "faith" depends upon a generous extrapolation of stated thought, the next view, namely that of Winnicott (1953), needs less embellishment. Indeed many of his ideas are subtly imbued with the notion of faith. The concept of "true self," for instance, has a pristine and wholesome quality, the beholding of which evokes wonder and humility. This has connection to the origins of faith. As articulated by Eigen (1981), in Winnicott's metapsychology:

> Truth and falsehood vie in the human soul. For Winnicott the essential battle is over one's sense of realness: does one feel real to oneself or merely a phantom or splinter self? The main problem that pervades his clinical writings is depersonalization and the profound self-splitting and self-anaesthesia that underwrite it. Both he and Bion link authentic wholling processes with trueness. This may be viewed as an assumption, a faith (p. 426).

On a more explicit basis, the concept of faith appears in relation to Winnicott's (1953) description of the "intermediate area of experience," where the customary distinctions between real and unreal, true and false, and actual and imaginary are set aside. There is a gentleman's agreement, as it were, of not bringing up the contents of this area for reality testing. This is the world of paradox. Play, metaphor, and creativity reside in this realm and so does religious belief. These are matters not to be argued about. One simply has to take them or leave them.

Finally, there is Bion's (1967, 1970) perspective on faith. His views on "O" or the ultimate truth, supremely coherent reality, or the thing-in-itself, are especially pertinent in this context. According to Bion, "O" represents the truth of the moment which is out there and waiting to be found by a receptive mind that has emptied itself of preconception, memory, and desire. Acquired knowledge can prepare the platform from which a leap of faith might be taken, but it is leaving knowledge and experience behind that actually constitutes a movement toward "O." Take, for instance, the Oedipus complex or, for that matter, the mathematical equation $E=mc^2$. These truths existed long before their discovery by Sophocles, Freud, and Einstein. In other words, "O" is the absolute truth and the supreme godhead of pure veracity.[3] It exists as a given and is only to be found. Unlike the "Eriksonian faith" which is ontogenetically earned or "Winnicottian faith" which is the dignified gift of others' restraint, "Bionian faith" is an external given. It is not created by the mind, though the mind can certainly experience it. Needless to say that all three models have relevance to the work of psychotherapy and psychoanalysis.

Technical Implications

The silent creation (and, in turn, operation) of "Eriksonian faith" occurs as a result of the analyst's reliability and patience. His punctual and unperturbed appearance, day after day and month after month, buttresses the patient's "basic trust." More importantly, his commitment to the analytic framework and theory, as well as his maintaining optimism over long periods of time, when the patient himself feels little hope, imparts to the latter a sense that scientific knowledge and accrued experience of man is on his side. The type of "faith" implicit in Winnicott's (1953) work becomes evident when the intervention the analyst makes is chiefly aimed at creating or strengthening the "intermediate area of experience."

Clinical Vignette: 4

Sarah Green, a fifty-five-year-old librarian, bought a parakeet to keep as a pet as she was coming out of the mourning over the loss of a profoundly significant romantic relationship. The bird, whom she named Dino, diminished her sense of aloneness, gave some order to her life after working hours, and, over the course of many months, became her confidante, "friend," if not the raison d'etre to live. She would talk about Dino as if he was a full grown human being with in-depth subjectivity, moods, and motivations. I avoided the interpretations that doing dot-to-dot psychoanalysis would have readily offered. I followed Winnicott (1953), who says that there is a gentlemen's agreement between the child and his parents regarding the child's transitional object that no one will ask him whether someone gave him that teddy bear (or blanket) or he "found" it himself. True to this spirit, I let things be. It was all in the spirit of play. Then one day Dino died, leaving Sarah devastated. Over the subsequent weeks—no, months—she grieved this loss. The earlier loss of the lover also got reactivated. Sessions were filled with wails and tears.

Around this time, Sarah reported the following incident. She had returned to her apartment after work and was sitting near the window watching the scenery outside. Then she caught a glimpse, from the corner of her eye, of a dark little spider on the windowsill. She was taken by the spider's quiet beauty and kept looking at him intently. A thought occurred to her: "Could it be that Dino has reincarnated as a spider and come to see me?" As Sarah related this, she emphatically said that she knows that there is no such thing as reincarnation, and she knows that birds do not transform themselves into spiders. She paused and murmured "Who knows?" After this, she turned, looked intently at me and said, "You do not think I am crazy, do you?" Guided by an unknown inner prompter, I spontaneously uttered the following: "No, I do not think you are crazy at all. In fact, I think this spider is actually a poem." Sarah broke into a big and very knowing grin which, however, lasted but a few seconds. Somber again, even a bit puzzled, she then said, "What do you mean by that?" I responded by saying that I thought she had immediately grasped my meaning but somehow lost that insight, and we should be curious about why that happened. But, I added, I would be glad to explain what I meant (which I was only now beginning to know myself).[4] Here my rejoinder that "the spider is actually a poem" constitutes a Zen Koan-like invitation to put reality-testing aside and allow for the creative elegance and sustaining power of the moment to take hold. In other words, this comment says to the patient "do not worry about whether birds can in reality become spiders or whether there is such a thing as reincarnation; just let the idea that your bird has come back as a spider to meet you, regale you." This is not to say that the defensive functions of this idea against the pain of loss can and might not be interpreted. But what would be the point of doing so? And, what is the loss in letting the patient treat the idea as a playful fantasy (as long as there is no loss of reality testing here)? That this goes against the usual and customary ways of working is not enough reason, at least for me, to suspect the veracity of the way I have suggested of working with such clinical material. The unconventionality of interventions arising from an attitude of "faith" is even more marked in the following vignette.

Clinical Vignette: 5

Olga Bokor, an East European patient, once reported what she called a "peculiar" phenomenon. She said that whenever she sees a patch of black-eyed Susans (the yellow flower with a black center) she feels a powerful impulse to lie down and put her head on the flowers; she feels convinced that it would bring her great emotional peace. If this happens while she is driving on a highway, she gets tempted to pull the car off to the shoulder and go lie down among the flowers. In describing this, Olga especially emphasized the "putting my head" on the flower patch, demonstrating it with a gentle tilt of her head. She found the whole thing puzzling because she had grown up in a downtown apartment building and had no memories of being in a garden as a child. Just as she was speculating what this impulse might mean, like a bolt from the blue a thought occurred to me. In fact, I became instantly convinced that I knew what this was all about. I said "You know what, I think your mother had a silk dress with such flowers on it and you, as a little girl, would put your head in her lap when you were tired or afraid of something." The patient was stunned, could immediately recall such a dress, and found my reconstruction to be astonishingly accurate. She then went on to talk more about that dress and her childhood feelings about it and about her mother.

This vignette exemplifies the workings of "Bionian faith." Knowledge (that the patient had grown up in a concrete jungle) and experience (that one does not offer an interpretation with little data to substantiate its genesis) are both left behind here. In making the remark about the patient's mother having a particular kind of dress, I was the man who has left one trapeze and is yet to catch the other. I was in clinical "mid-air," so to speak. This is what Bion (1970) refers to as the "act of faith." According to him, such an act, or "F," does not represent the system "K," or the register of knowledge. It represents the absolute truth, or "O."

In this contribution, I have highlighted the fact that the activities of talking and listening, while profoundly important, emanate from the bedrock of analytic attitude. This, I have asserted, consists of three facets, namely survival, vision, and faith. Taking one of these topics at a time and after entering some caveats, I have elucidated the developmental origins of these meta-attitudes and also their technical significance. I have also offered clinical vignettes to illustrate the attitudes of survival, vision, and faith. My hope has been to extend, however modestly, our understanding of how and why psychoanalysis and psychoanalytic psychotherapy work.

While concern about ameliorating mental suffering is central to my contribution, it also sheds light on two other matters. It is as if by shining a flashlight at the center, the periphery is also lifted from darkness. One of these "peripheral" matters is human development. The attitudes of survival, vision, and faith are not only necessary for the conduct of therapy and analysis, but are also important ingredients of good parenting. This is confirmed via the elucidation of the developmental origins of these attitudes offered in this contribution.

The second realm is a larger, existential one. In the strife-riddled, prejudice-infected, and war-torn world we live in today, the triad of survival, vision, and faith is a life-saving companion. As bombs fall on Hiroshima, Cambodia, Vietnam, and Iraq, we come back with renewed vigor for strengthening international understanding via formed and informed diplomacy and transcultural dialogue. Our concern is toward the world, and especially toward the poor and disenfranchised survivors. As Hitler, Stalin, Mao, Pinochet, and Pol Pot strangulate our conscience and murder our humanity, we create memorials, overthrow totalitarian regimes, and spread education; we retain a vision of better days to come. And, when we are struck by the narrow-minded and violent mentality of George W. Bush and Osama bin Laden, we remind ourselves that the same world has given birth to Mahatma Gandhi, Martin Luther King, and Nelson Mandela. In other words, we maintain faith. Working in unison, the three factors of survival, vision, and faith sustain us through the existential hardship of the contemporary era. They are like three well-lit candles in a dark night of the soul!

NOTES

1. In the emphasis upon experience with the two parents here, it should not be overlooked that the metabolism of aggression within the sibling relationship might also contribute to the genesis of the ego capacity for "survival."

2. Parenthetically it should be added that the enthusiasm for finding the ideal personality makeup for psychoanalysis has waned over the last two decades. To be sure, one looks for honesty, perseverance, psychological-mindedness, and ego resilience in a potential candidate for psychoanalysis, but attention has now shifted to other, perhaps more important, questions in this realm. The following statement captures the essence of these questions: who is analyzable vis-à-vis what conflicts, during what era of their lives, by what sort of analyst, and under what circumstance?

3. Bion's choice of the letter "O" for this idea remains mysterious. At least three explanations have been offered: (1) Lopez-Corvo (2003) thinks that the letter "O" is taken from the word "origin" and is "related to the same term used to designate the center of the Cartesian coordinates that correspond to the point where the X and Y axes intercept; however it could have also been taken from the concept of "origin" in Zen Buddhism" (p. 197); (2) Symington (2008) believes that "O" stood for Ontos in Bion's mind, since he often used Greek letters to designate psychological realities and both "O" and Ontos denote ultimate reality and absolute truth; and (3) I, myself have proposed (2008) that Bion's "O" is a truncated form of Om, the Sanskrit word for the Omnipresent Creator; this is likely in light of the fact that Bion grew up till age eight in India, where he was taken care of by a Hindu maid who presumably took him to many Hindu temples and exposed him to the chants of the word Om.

4. When she persisted, I explained to her that by calling the spider a "poem," I was declining to discuss this matter along the reality-unreality dimension. To my mind, the issue was not whether the spider was or was not a reincarnation of the bird. The issue was her wishful imagination. My response also underscored the fact that the whole experience belonged to the "transitional area" (Winnicott, 1953) of the mind where imagination is born and paradox reigns

supreme. To be sure, my fondness for E. B. White's (1973) *Charlotte's Web* facilitated my attunement to the unfolding clinical material involving the spider.

REFERENCES

Abraham, K. (1911). On the determining power of names. In *Clinical Papers and Essays on Psychoanalysis,* pp. 31–32. New York, NY: Brunner/Mazel, 1955.

Akhtar, S. (1992). *Broken Structures: Severe Personality Disorders and Their Treatment.* Northvale, NJ: Jason Aronson.

———. (1996). "Someday . . ." and "if only . . ." fantasies: Pathological optimism and inordinate nostalgia as related forms of idealization. *Journal of American Psychoanalytic Association 44*: 723–753.

———. (2002) Forgiveness: Origins, dynamics, psychopathology, and technical relevance. *Psychoanalytic Quarterly 71*: 175–212

———. (2008). Introduction. In: *On Freud's "The Future of an Illusion,"* eds. M.K. O'Neil and S. Akhtar, pp. 1–8. London, UK: Karnac Books.

———.(2008). *The Crescent and the Couch: Crosscurrents between Islam and Psychoanalysis.* Lanham, MD: Jason Aronson.

Benedek, T. (1938). Adaptation to reality in early infancy. *Psychoanalysis Quarterly 7*: 200–214.

Bion, W. R. (1962). *Learning from Experience*. London: Karnac Books, 1984.

———. (1967). *Second Thoughts*. London, UK: Heinemann.

———. (1970). Lies and the thinker. In: *Attention and Interpretation*. London, UK: Tavistock.

Casement, P. (1991). *Learning from the Patient.* New York, NY: Guilford Press.

Coen, S. (2002) *Affect Intolerance in the Patient and the Analyst.* Northvale, NJ: Jason Aronson.

Cooper, A. (1988). Our changing views of the therapeutic action of psychoanalysis: comparing Strachey and Loewald. *Psychoanalytic Quarterly 57*: 15–27.

Eigen, M. (1981). The area of faith in Winnicott, Lacan, and Bion. *International Journal of Psychoanalysis 62*: 413–433.

Erikson, E. H. (1950). *Childhood and Society*. New York, NY: W.W. Norton.

———. (1959). *Identity and the Life Cycle*. New York, NY: International Universities Press.

Fonagy, P. and Target, M. (1997). Attachment and reflective function: Their role in self-organization. *Developmental Psychopathology 9*: 679–700.

Freud, S. (1914). Remembering, repeating, and working through. *Standard Edition* 12: 145–156.

———. (1927). The future of an illusion. *Standard Edition* 21: 3–56

Kernberg, O. (1976). Technical considerations in the treatment of borderline personality organization. *Journal of the American Psychoanalytic Association 30*: 795–829.

________ (1992). *Aggression in Personality Disorders and Perversions.* New Haven, CT: Yale University Press.

Levine, S. (2007). Nothing but the truth: Self-disclosure, and self-revelation, and the persona of the analyst. *Journal of the American Psychoanalytic Association 55*: 81–104.

Lewin, R. A. and Schulz, C. (1992). *Losing and Fusing: Borderline Transitional Object and Self Relations*. Northvale, NJ: Jason Aronson.

Lichtenstein, H. (1961). Identity and sexuality: A study of their interrelationship in man. *Journal of the American Psychoanalytic Association 9*: 179–260.

Loewald, H. W. (1960). On the therapeutic action of psychoanalysis. In: *Papers on Psychoanalysis,* pp. 221–256. New Haven, CT: Yale University Press, 1980.

Lopez-Corvo, R.E. (2003). *The Dictionary of the Work of W.R. Bion*. London: Karnac.

Modell, A. (1976). The holding environment and the therapeutic action of psychoanalysis. *Journal of the American Psychoanalytic Association 24*: 285–307.

Olinick, S., Poland, W., Grigg, K., and Granatir, W. (1973). The psychoanalytic work ego: Process and interpretation. *International Journal of Psychoanalysis 54*: 143–151.

Pine, F. (1997). *Diversity and Direction in Psychoanalytic Technique*. New Haven, CT: Yale University Press.

Pruett, K. D. (1988). *The Nurturing Father*. New York, NY: Warner Books.

———. (2000). *Fatherneed*. New York, NY: Basic Books.

Pulver, S. (1991). Termination and separation-individuation. In *Beyond the Symbiotic Orbit: Advances in Separation-Individuation Theory*, eds. S. Akhtar and H. Parens, pp. 389–404. Hillsdale, NJ: The Analytic Press.

Sandler, J. (1976). Countertransference and role- responsiveness. *International Review of Psychoanalysis 3*: 43–47.

Seelig, B., and Rosof, L. (2001). Normal and pathological altruism. *Journal of the American Psychoanalytic Association 41*: 179–190.

Symington, N. (2008). Generosity of heart: Source of sanity. *British Journal of Psychotherapy*, 24, 488-500.

Winnicott, D.W. (1953). Transitional objects and transitional phenomena: A study of the first not-me possession. *International Journal of Psychoanalysis 34*: 89–97.

________ (1960). The theory of parent-infant relationship. *International Journal of Psychoanalysis 41*: 585–595.

________ (1968). Use of an object and relating through identifications. In *Playing in Reality*, pp. 86–94. London: Tavistock.

Chapter Nine

Response to "Three Pillars of Therapeutic Attitude" by Salman Akhtar

Chris R. Schlauch

> "to recognize human limitation and variability is not to conclude that it is useless or foolish to attempt to set forth standards of excellence for analytic work. Nor is it to come to the conclusion that formulating the ideal analytic attitude is equivalent to idealizing, platitudinizing, or being oppressively perfectionistic. For it is on the individual analyst's efforts to approximate this ideal that the beneficial effects of analyzing largely depend ." —Schafer, 1983, p. 5

Researchers and practitioners of clinical care tend to advocate on behalf of one or another particular theoretical approach (orthodoxy) or technique (orthopraxy) as the only one among many that is valid. Endorsing their own perspective and dismissing alternatives, they typically focus on how properly to conceptualize diagnosis and treatment or, even more often, what replicable techniques properly should be carried out. Embedded in their diverse loyalties is an underlying assumption. Granting, following Kluckhohn and Murray (1948), that in some ways a person is like all people, in other ways like many other persons, and yet in other ways like no other person, these researchers and practitioners especially value the first premise and for the most part dismiss the other two. Having assumed that people are more alike than different, therapists can embrace a theory or technique—make it theirs—that they feel "mirrors nature" and is valid and reliable for everyone.

Teaching and practicing within a particular tradition, psychoanalytic, that is itself remarkably diverse, Dr. Salman Akhtar's reflections and his underlying assumptions depart from these norms. He focuses neither on theory nor practice alone but rather on a construct arising at their intersection: a clinical attitude.[1]

He is not invested in advancing, dogmatically, *the* right approach (to theory or practice) but more in imaginatively characterizing a viable one. Though he assumes, of course, that his particular ideas about clinical attitude will have merit for all interested readers, and toward that end he outlines "three pillars"—"survival, vision, and faith"—he is more intent, I believe, on exemplifying a project that each clinician must carry out in a *particular* way, finding and creating, as Winnicott might say, the pillars of her or his own viable clinical attitude.

My Response to Dr. Akhtar's chapter unfolds in five steps: *Explaining My Context, Key Concepts, "Opening Lines," The Three Pillars, and Observations and Questions.*

EXPLAINING MY CONTEXT

Research and scholarship—and thus an essay and a response—usually unfold within a particular field of study, for example, psychology. Those who participate in and extend a line of inquiry traditionally share common assumptions, concepts, and methods, in this instance, psychoanalytic. Readers of this response would thus naturally anticipate that Dr. Akhtar's paper on a psychoanalytic attitude would be discussed in terms of psychoanalytically oriented theory and practice. Though this response will fulfill that expectation, its focus is notably broader. For this reason I briefly explain my particular context and through that take steps to outline a rationale for this atypical way of proceeding.

My formal education and academic career as a professor in a research university have been expressly interdisciplinary, teaching and writing at the intersection of psychology, religion, and theology. Concurrently, my clinical training and my teaching and training of others have been similarly interdisciplinary and expressly psychoanalytically oriented, drawing especially on the work of Sigmund Freud, Heinz Kohut, and Donald Woods Winnicott. I thus engage Dr. Akhtar's essay as two different genres within two different sites: as a research document in the academy, it is a text to be read; as theory having to do with clinical case studies in the clinic, it is a report to be interpreted. Further, I read the text and interpret the report in conjunction with literature in three different fields: psychology, religion, and theology. In addition, I engage the work not only as a respondent to a presenter but as one clinician to another and one theorist of clinical attitude (Schlauch, 1993; 1995) to another.

This academic-clinical interdisciplinary response departs from intradisciplinary norms in the academy and the clinic, but its design actually expresses how human beings naturally function. Indeed, each person listens to or reads an essay, or a response to an essay, in a different way, registering more or less unique impressions, ideas, and conclusions that take into account a range of particular contexts, approaches, questions, needs, and intentions. A few brief comments on interpreting texts explain this more fully.

Some theorists assume that, "a text has only one true meaning, and that is the one that the author intended to communicate" (Brümmer, 1991, p. 451). Achieving this singular meaning requires that "the interpreter should systematically free himself from the conceptual assumptions and prejudices of his own historical and cultural situation, and should replace them with those of the author whose text he is interpreting" (Brümmer, pp. 451–2). I follow the lead of other theorists who "presume that no interpreter can, in fact, free herself from her assumptions and prejudices but can only become critically reflective about such influence in an engagement with a text." More specifically, ". . . it is part of the 'ontological possibility' of every text that it can always be understood in new ways. Every text has a surplus of meaning in the sense that it allows for a large number of *natural* (that is, non-contrived) interpretations. . ." (Brümmer, 1991, p. 453). As Paul Ricoeur (1970) elaborates, engagements with a text *naturally and inevitably* eventuate in multiple "readings." The meaning of a text for Reader A will differ from the meaning of that text for Reader B.[2] The (primary or central) meaning of a text for Reader A changes over time; Reader A will develop different readings of the same text.[3] Reader A carries out multiple (and notably different) readings, concurrently, of a text; she will find and create different meanings of the same text at the same time.

It is worth noting that Ricoeur's (1970) most extensive and complex analysis of multiple readings of texts emerged in his masterful study *Freud and Philosophy*, using psychoanalytic theories to interpret those ideas. As a result, the notion of multiple readings is thoroughly consonant with the theory and practice of psychoanalytically oriented clinical care: psychoanalytically oriented theorists and practitioners assume that a patient's report, a clinician's presentation to a case conference, a consultation with a colleague or supervisor, as well as a presentation at a professional conference carry a surplus of meaning that will be interpreted in numerous ways as others listen for "the music . . . behind the . . . words" (Kohut, 1957/1978, p. 243).

Though I have formally differentiated between genres (texts to be read, reports to be interpreted), sites (academy, clinic), and fields of study (psychology, religion, theology), the following comments express the interplay among them. After examining Dr. Akhtar's two central concepts, attitude and pillars, in conjunction with relevant literature, I turn to consider the title and rather suggestive "opening lines" of the presentation. I offer a way of rendering Dr. Akhtar's three pillars—survival, vision, and faith—and conclude with a series of observations and related questions.

KEY CONCEPTS

Attitude

The concept of "clinical attitude," though reasonably well known within psychoanalytic circles, has never been the subject of extensive research and is, for the most part, more or less neglected in other clinical approaches.[4]

The word "attitude" is common in everyday usage. We may have an attitude—a particular feeling or disposition, likely evoked, unfolding unreflectively—toward another person, idea, activity, or event. Each of us has many attitudes toward many things. The notion of "clinical attitude," by contrast, refers to a singular, intentionally developed form of engaging patients. It can be thought of as bearing a family resemblance to *a basic style, posture, stance, "cast of mind," mode of being-in-the-world,* or *"a way of seeing things"* (see, for example, Ajzen, 2005; Allphin, 2005; Aron, 2005; Berger & Kellner, 1981; Black, Fliegel, Silverman, Gill, Tolpin, 1987; Bloom, 1987; Cacioppo, Petty, & Green 1989; Fritsch, 2013; Hansell, 2008; Kaley, 1993; Lemma, 2012; Loewald, 1960; McClure & Hodge, 1987; Messick & Fritzky, 1963; Poland, 2002; Schafer, 1970/1976; 1983; Tuttman, 1987). This "characterological," more or less invariable, and enduring *attitude-in-general* is engaged and enacted flexibly. That is, one's attitude is a guide priming, loosely, but not determining, rigidly, how one experiences and relates to different patients in unfolding processes.

Several authors have acknowledged the pivotal role of the clinician's attitude. David Shapiro (1989) opens the "Preface" to his delightful and enlightening text *Psychotherapy of Neurotic Character* with these words:

> My teacher, Hellmuth Kaiser, once expressed a dilemma to me about the teaching of psychotherapy. He said it was no use teaching what to do or what to say because *the significance and effect of what the therapist did or said depended on the attitude with which it was expressed.* With the right attitude on the part of the therapist, he thought, all else would follow easily. (p. ix, emphasis added)

Hans Loewald (1960/1988), in an article entitled "On the Mode of Therapeutic Action of Psychoanalytic Psychotherapy" points, if only indirectly, to the influence of the clinician's attitude. In response to the question "How does treatment help?" he writes,

> Instead of addressing such [a] question head on, I shall try to give a general picture of various facets of the therapist's impact on the patient. Psychotherapists, if they are worth their salt, have certain characteristics in common with professions of a different cast, with priests, rabbis, ministers, the old-fashioned doctor, who at their best function also as *significant models of steady convictions, whatever their content, and of compassionate concern and dedication.*

> Therapists blend in with aspects of the conduct of the good parent, teacher, educator, or lover. (p. 55, emphasis added)[5]

Roy Schafer (1983) also concludes that the core of psychoanalytic practice is the attitude of the clinician. Writing in *The Analytic Attitude*, he observes that behind key concepts, metapsychology, and clinical technique lies the attitude of the practitioner. This attitude remains in the background, "behind the scenes," shaping all of what unfolds. Though typically outside of awareness and thus not a matter of discussion, the clinical attitude directly bears on all of the therapy relationship and process. Thus, for example, Schafer examines how the psychoanalytically oriented clinician attempts to be "neutral"; avoids either-or thinking; consistently analyzes; aims to be helpful; provides an atmosphere of safety; has an appreciation for the client; and seeks to be disciplined, empathic, and confident.

Attitude is deeply influential, also, in a more direct manner: the patient will be influenced not only by what is conveyed "through" the clinician's attitude but also by the conveying and learning "of" the attitude itself. Heinz Kohut (1987) writes, in a provocative article entitled "Extending Empathic Understanding, Sharing an Attitude":

> I teach the patient an attitude toward himself. I create an atmosphere—not artificially, however, because it truly is mine—in which a broadened understanding for oneself is encouraged. My own interest is in what is going on in the patient—not only in what he experiences, but also in how he experiences and relates to his difficulties. This is in essence an attitude of an expanded self-empathy—an expanded capacity to be empathic with one's own past, and with aspects of oneself that one really does not own, or does not own fully, including even aspects of oneself that have not yet expanded—in other words, one's future possibilities. (p. 188)

Approaching clinical attitude by way of two metaphors—as a hub of a wheel or a fulcrum—reveals some of its value as a heuristic. Attitude stands at the intersection, so to speak, of theory and practice. It cannot be reduced either to right theory or right technique but emerges from, informs, and is informed by both. Attitude moves within but also beyond psychological literature. As a term with colloquial origins and uses, its elaboration involves ideas emerging within many contexts and traditions. (For example, survival, vision, and faith have existential as well as religious overtones, and in that regard signal some connection to, if not needed elaboration through, ethical and religious sources.) Attitude, finally, expresses a tension between universal and particular (what is relevant to every patient and process, but different with each patient in each process) and between social and personal (what expresses a clinician's membership in a particular community and tradition, for example, psychoanalytic, but what is found and created in particular substance and form by each clinician).

Pillars

A search on Google Scholar reveals that "pillars" is not an uncommon concept. Consider these titles: *The Three Pillars of Zen* (1989); *The Seven Pillars of Partnering* (1990); "The Seven Pillars of Quality" (1990); *Six Pillars of Self-esteem* (1995); *Seven Pillars of Wisdom* (2000); *Pillars of Faith: American Congregations and their Partners* (2005); "Three Pillars of the Liberal Peace" (2005). Islam has traditionally been characterized in terms of five pillars, variously considered primary *beliefs*, or better, *obligations*: profession of faith, prayer, almsgiving, fasting during Ramadan, and the pilgrimage to Mecca.[6]

According to the *OED*, "pillars" has Anglo-Norman, Old French, and Middle French origins in the eleventh century and refers to "a tall vertical structure . . . used as a support," to "a person seen as a source of support or stability," as well as to "a fact or principle which is a main support or basis *of* something." It also referred, "In mythological contexts and *poet[ry]* [to] any of a number of props or supports upon which the earth, sky, heaven, etc. rests." Taking this together, one may wonder if pillars is intended to identify something that provides "structure," "support," "stability," "the basis" of things—*perhaps even all things in heaven and on earth*—and by its origin in something literally of stone, something substantial; something having a place; something there; something to lean on, and to build on.

"OPENING LINES"

Before formally discussing the subject matter Dr. Akhtar spells out in his title—"The Three Pillars of Therapeutic Attitude"—he quotes Winnicott: "If God is a projection, even so is there a God who created me in such a way that I have the material in me for such a projection? Aetiologically, if I may use a word here that usually refers to disease, the paradox must be accepted, not resolved—Donald Winnicott (1968, p. 205)". It seems to me that Dr. Akhtar intimates that discussing his pillars involves discussing "God." (I cannot know whether he means, descriptively, that "God" is a part of developing his own attitude or, more generally, that the task of developing an attitude inherently presupposes some consideration of "God," or, for readers who are not theists, taking into account what is "ultimate" or "sacred."[7]) By quoting Winnicott, Dr. Akhtar suggests that this kind of discussion—again, whether about his clinical attitude or about attitude more generally—is to be spoken in *the subjunctive*—or what we could call *the hypothetical*: "If God is a projection. . ." Again following Winnicott, Dr. Akhtar appears to encourage a kind of *humble agnosticism* that honors the inherent uncertainty of the space in which we move ("the paradox must be accepted, not resolved"). Our attitude is to be held lightly, not tightly, as a provisional map and not the territory (Smith, 1993), a guide, not a god (Kohut, 1977).[8]

THE THREE PILLARS

Dr. Akhtar's pillars themselves, individually and collectively, merit comment.

Survival

He provides a remarkable "visual icon" for purposes of characterizing the pillar of survival. "I suggest that a practicing psychotherapist (or psychoanalyst) is a human equivalent of the Weeble. He receives and absorbs 'shocks' from the patient's emotional outpouring, revelations, and attacks, but he steadfastly maintains his analytic posture" (p.106). In a clinical relationship and process, patients recreate a drama in which the clinician becomes a participant. As the target of multiple forms of transference or transference reactions, the clinician is by definition experienced only partially *as* her or himself but also in terms of the patient's "patterns of expectation" (Basch, 1980, p. 35): as an object, part object, transitional object, or selfobject (as contrasted with a subject) to be used by the patient. (She or he is, in this sense, not seen, partially rendered invisible, and so "destroyed.") The clinician may, in some instances, be the target of aggression, narcissistic rage, and destructiveness. In the midst of each and all of these processes, the clinician survives destruction and, in doing so, satisfies needs and wishes to be a target to be destroyed, but also competing needs and wishes—one might say hope—that she or he survives destruction. The clinician is stable, substantial: a pillar.

Vision

Dr. Akhtar lends his notion of the pillar of vision by way of the following visual icon: "Just the way the sculptor feels that all he has to do is to remove the unnecessary parts of the stone to let the statue emerge, the therapist can also envision, with more or less clarity, how the patient would be were their work to succeed in dissolving his neurotic structures" (p. 110). Patients enter a clinical relationship and process ambivalently, in conflict. On the one hand they seek help to resolve conflicts and/or resume development, while on the other hand they act to inhibit or restrict achievement of those goals as they express "resistance" or "self-protectiveness." The clinician enters the process mindful of this ambivalence, respecting activities to forestall change, yet aware of the shape next steps may take. By vision, Dr. Akhtar refers both to the particular contours of these next developmental steps and to the expectation (one might say promise or hope) that the patient will succeed in achieving those steps. (As if to say, "I have a vision of what you will look like and in doing so, I participate with you with the expectation that you can and will, in fact, achieve what we set out to accomplish together.")

Faith

Dr. Akhtar's description of his unusual and enormously evocative visual icon of the pillar of faith requires quoting at length. He writes:

> The best way I can conceptualize a visual metaphor for faith is to encourage the reader to undertake a thought experiment. Imagine yourself to be in a circus. Looking upward, near the top of the tent, you notice a man on a trapeze. He swings back and forth, building confidence or courage for a while. It is as if he is figuring something out, not on the level of overt cognition but somewhere deep in his muscles, in his spirit. And then, just as you are about to give up on his seemingly futile rumination, the magic happens. The man leaves the trapeze and, for a shining moment or two, is in mid-air, and then catches a second trapeze that was coming his way from the opposite end of the tent. It is all over in the blink of an eye. But let us suppose you had a high power camera and the necessary skill to use it and you shot a photograph of the man while he was mid-way between the two trapezes. Now print out a large size glossy copy and look at it. What you see there is a man of faith. Visibly captured. Pure and simple. (p. 113)

The process of change is, by definition, one of losing and finding, not having (grief and mourning) and having anew. Requisite to the project of changing is openness to leaving behind what is familiar (or familial) in reasonable expectation of receiving what may become familiar (or familial). We can think of this process on multiple levels, whether relinquishing a cherished object, a valued person, a prized community and tradition (and thus an identity as a member of that community and tradition), or a "stage" in development (as the metaphor suggests, a place or "foundation" on which one stands from which to view and on which to engage everything). Undergoing change (whether maturation, development, or "cure") thus involves a measure of hope (that what will emerge is good enough) and trust (trusting the process).

THE THREE PILLARS, COLLECTIVELY

The psychoanalytic literary critic Norman Holland (1985) suggests that when reading the corpus of an author one may detect recurrent images, motifs, plot lines, etc., and these resembling elements may be gathered and interpreted by way of the metaphor, variations on a theme.[9] With the help of Holland's metaphor, I would propose that Dr. Akhtar's pillars of survival, vision, and faith, to use Winnicottian language, collectively *address the fear of not going on being and affirm the prospect of going on being.*[10] With this in mind, we cannot but admit that patient and clinician naturally and inevitably engage in work having to do with being and non-being (Tillich, 1957), life and death.

In surviving[11], the clinician demonstrates that, despite her or his own fragility, vulnerability, finitude, and humanity, and despite being the target of human destructiveness (whether in being engaged, inevitably and ubiquitously, by way of transference, or in being the target of more explicit aggression and rage), the patient learns that her or his own needs and wishes are not lethal (and that she or he is not toxic), that intense and overwhelming conflict need not eventuate in the ending of a relationship (and the disconnection from the other).

In the clinician's ongoing envisioning, the patient registers, perhaps unconsciously, the clinician's hope and trust that change is possible. If surviving expresses an affirmation of the *clinician's* going on being, envisioning expresses an affirmation of the *patient's* going on being.

In faith, or one might say, following James Fowler, "faithing" (Fowler, 1981, p. 16), clinicians are practicing a habit, or enacting an elemental belief, that even as we let go we are holding on and being held. The capacity to let go (of one trapeze) and look for and catch something new (a second trapeze) presupposes the belief that there will be something there when one lets go. A belief is a habit of mind formed through experience. Letting go and looking for and expecting that there will be something there to catch presupposes holding on to the *memory* of having something there to catch after one has let go—holding on to the memory *by which one is held.* (It is worth noting that "holding" is the antidote to the "primitive agony" of "falling forever" (1963/1965, p. 58).) *We* (clinician and patient) will, in other words, go on being.

It is important to retrieve an idea introduced earlier, that in the relationship between patient and clinician the patient may "learn" or "internalize" features of the clinician's attitude. Or, to speak in more dyadic and relational terms, the patient, like the infant, child, adolescent, and adult, can only "learn" or "know" anything by *experiencing it with another.* Winnicott (1945/1975) puts it this way:

> . . . true relation to external reality is almost the whole thing.
> . . . In terms of baby and mother's breast . . ., the baby has instinctual urges and predatory ideas. The mother has a breast and the power to produce milk, and the idea that she would like to be attacked by a hungry baby. These two phenomena do not come into relation with each other till the mother and child *live an experience together*. (p. 152, italics in original)[12]

In living an experience together, the infant is going on being (and the infant and mother *as a unit* are going on being *together*). Similarly, in living an experience together, the patient is going on being (and the patient and clinician *as a unit* are going on being *together*).

OBSERVATIONS AND QUESTIONS

Specialized Fields of Inquiry and Practices of Care

The first observations and question in relation to this interdisciplinary conception of the clinical attitude have to do with what may be called *the myth and allure of the division of labor and specialization* as a context within which to consider how clinical theory and practice necessarily extend beyond the boundaries of what is psychological.

Stephen Toulmin (1982/1985) explains how researchers and scholars customarily restrict their attention to the problems and questions unique to their particular field. He observes how scientific inquiry evolved over centuries, increasingly carried out within independent "disciplines," each with its own kinds of questions and issues. The researcher's first step was to judge how the phenomena to be studied "presented themselves" as fitting in one discipline rather than any others. In doing so, the researcher was determining that the phenomena were now to be explained in terms specific only to that discipline (see Toulmin, 1982/1985, pp. 228–229).

Given this "division of knowledge" and corresponding "division of labor" (Toulmin, 2001), researchers and scholars may unwittingly commit what Anthony Flew called "the Specialist Fallacy": "a belief that the words 'I am only *paid* to know about these things' mean the same as 'I am paid to know *only* about these things'" (Toulmin, 2001, p. 41).

Researchers and scholars are socialized in the academy as specialists whose respective theories and practices ought to remain strictly within the boundaries of one's respective field or discipline. Similarly, clinicians and supervisors are socialized in the clinic to learn, teach, and practice care within the parameters of particular guilds and, more specifically, in the particular approaches unique and appropriate to one or another setting and/or population. It is intellectually suspect to theorize beyond the boundaries of one's field; it is ethically problematic to practice beyond one's areas of competence.

However, as Julie Thompson Klein remarks in one of her several texts on interdisciplinary research and scholarship, *"The real problems of society do not come in discipline-shaped blocks"* (Klein, 1990, p. 35, italics in original). Karl Popper observes, "We are not students of some subject matter, but students of problems. And problems may cut right across the borders of any subject matter or discipline" (Popper, 1963, p. 88, quoted in National Academy of Sciences, 2005, p. 16). More to the point, it is self-evident *that each person registers problems in mind of a wide range of contributions, personal as well as professional, and that the process of inquiry cannot but draw upon that wide range. Observation is,* to amend the well-known phrase, *theories-laden.*[13] Thus in the particular practice of clinical care, both clinician and patient *cannot* but observe and interpret everything in conjunction with a *range* of sources. If that is the case—*it is not truly possible for clinicians to practice and theorize about practice solely in psychological terms.*

Within this context, I would suggest that attitude, borrowing from Freud (1915/1957), is a "borderland concept"[14] —in three different but related senses. It lies on the border between the theoretical and the practical, as it points on the one hand to a construct through which we synthesize resources and orient attention and also on the other hand to what is embedded in every action, intrapsychic as well as interpersonal. It lies on the border, second, between the professional and the personal, as it bears the imprint not only of formal education and training but also of the lifelong history of learning in one's ever-widening circle of family and friends. Finally, it lies on the borders between psychological, moral, and religious, as it encompasses ideas that guide understanding and interpretation, judgments about good and bad, right and wrong, virtue and evil, and beliefs about who we are and whose we are, about what we hold dear.

A question that emerges from these observations is thus *if clinical theory and practice in general, and every clinical attitude in particular, involve moral action and ethical judgment as well as religious beliefs, should the teaching and training of clinicians involve studies in ethics, philosophy, religion, and theology as traditions of inquiry that illumine these complex topics?*[15]

Taking the Unconscious Seriously

A second observation and set of questions have to do with what it means to "take the unconscious seriously." We live on the boundary between being aware and not being aware. Some of what lies outside of awareness as nonconscious may at some point become conscious, while some of what lies outside of awareness as unconscious may inadvertently become conscious, however directly or indirectly, despite our efforts to keep it from consciousness. By definition, any and all theorizing we develop emerges on the boundary between, and reflects the given-ness of being, both unconscious and conscious.

Elaborating the implications of this fact, pastoral psychologist Merle Jordan (1988) differentiates between beliefs of which we are conscious and that we declare explicitly and elaborate thoughtfully, what he calls "professed theology," and nonconscious or unconscious beliefs that we enact or perform, what he calls "lived theology." This distinction illumines several important ideas: operative beliefs are not limited to what is consciously professed; some beliefs operate outside of awareness, and some may be kept from awareness; these tacit beliefs are performed, repeated rather than recollected (Freud, 1914/1958); and finally, others persons may, at times, be in a position to grasp a fuller notion of our beliefs than the believer herself.

Were we to extrapolate from these reflections, we are in a position to pose a series of important questions: *How does any clinician develop a clinical attitude given the fact that features of that attitude will be "professed" but others will be "lived"? To what degree is a clinician responsible for identifying and reflecting upon her or his "lived clinical attitude"?*

A second set of questions arises in response to the idea of taking the unconscious seriously. Consider a notion well known in the literature on metaphor: metaphors hide as well as show (see, for example, Lakoff & Johnson, 1980). Similarly, theorizing, or formulations of therapeutic attitude, hide as well as show. Julie Thompson Klein (1990) makes a similar point: all knowledge reflects reality, selects reality, but at the same time *deflects* reality (p. 56).

The myth and allure of the division of labor and specialization serve to hide from awareness that our theories and practices are not singularly psychological, and thus, more specifically, that our formulations of therapeutic attitude include psychological ideas, moral judgments, and religious beliefs. As such, is it incumbent on us to identify and not simply enact them, and further, to reconstruct them in conversation with relevant research and scholarship? With this in mind, *to what degree is a clinician responsible for problems and questions deflected by her or his clinical attitude?*

A great deal of recent research and scholarship in many fields of inquiry in the academy and in the clinic have exposed that and how theories and practices may be designed, wittingly or unwittingly, to benefit some communities but not others. With this in mind, *to what degree is a clinician responsible for ways in which care informed by her or his clinical attitude helps some people but not others, and may harm still others?*[16]

Taking into account that some of the features of our attitude remain unconscious to us but may be registered by others, we need to be mindful not only about what is taught but what is caught. *To what degree is a clinician responsible for working to identify, from their patients' experiences, what their patients may be taking to be their (the clinician's) clinical attitude? In what ways is it important not only to help a clinician identify and form a viable clinical attitude, but also to encourage her or him to attend to the attitude embedded in a* patient's *thoughts and actions? Related to that, in what ways ought we to pay more devoted attention to the congruence, competition, and conflict of attitudes between others and oneself—whether clinician and patient, supervisor and supervisee, teacher and student?*

Some researchers and scholars, like some patients as well as clinicians, find reward in achieving answers, resting places where what Charles Sanders

Peirce (1878) called "the irritation of doubt" has been "appeased." Others are at home in the project of inquiry, gathering tentative impressions and glimpses of ideas to be able to put into words, at last, questions worth addressing. My response to Dr. Akhtar's essay is, in the spirit of inquiry, less declaring beliefs or demonstrating theses than posing what I hope and intend are important questions meriting deliberate attention and reflection.

NOTES

1. Attitude is a conceptual synthesis of the "microtheories" (Holzman, 1969/1995) of which one's approach is constituted, yet it is embedded in and guides all mental and verbal actions. When thought of in terms of "action language" (Schafer, 1970/1976), neither as theory informing technique nor as technique expressing theory, attitude is "better conceptualized as actions and modes of action" (1983, p. 52).

2. In the Preface to his in-depth study of reading, *5 Readers Reading*, Norman Holland (1975) states the problem his study addresses, and the problem at the heart of any analysis of reading, quoting Blake.

> Both read the Bible day & night,
> But thou read'st black where I read white.

The question I would like to answer is: Why is this so? To be sure, Blake had in mind religious controversy as much as people's different readings of a text—

> The Vision of Christ that thou dost see
> Is my Vision's Greatest Enemy.
> Thine has a great hook nose like thine;
> Mine has a snub nose like to mine. (p. ix)

3. When someone reads a text, she or he makes guesses that express a temporary understanding of initial impressions. These serve not only as the basis for proceeding, as hypotheses that guide, but also are necessarily subject to testing and correction. Understanding is by definition evolving. The reader may at one moment treat a current understanding as more or less final, as if now understanding the text, or she or he may return, subsequently, to the text, read it again, move through another unfolding engagement, and along the way and at its conclusion arrive at another ostensibly final understanding. However, interpreting as a process can only eventuate in a reading that is—when compared to one's future reading—partial, provisional, and subject to revision.

4. Roy Schafer's (1983) collection of essays under the title *The Analytic Attitude* does cite a series of relevant contributors "from a very long list," including "Sandor Ferenczi, Karl Abraham, Anna Freud, Melanie Klein, Wilhelm Reich, Otto Fenichel, Edward Glover, John Strachey, Ella Freeman Sharpe, Theodor Reik, Ernst Kris, Rudolph Loewenstein, Anna Reich, Edith Jacobson, Kurt Eissler, Ralph Greenson, Leo Stone, Jacob Arlow, Charles Brenner, Merton Gill, and Heinz Kohut" (p. 3).

5. Loewald's wording, "steady convictions" as well as "compassionate concern and dedication," clearly suggests that an attitude is constituted not simply of claims made in one or another clinical theory but also more broadly of beliefs. His linking the clinician with "priests, rabbis, [and] ministers" further suggests that the beliefs embedded and expressed in a clinical attitude resemble those characteristic of religious traditions.

6. "Reading" the term "pillars" within a religious and theological context as a well-known way of speaking about Islam is not unrelated to "hearing" the term "pillars" with this religious

overtone, in conjunction with Dr. Akhtar's use of Winnicott's statement about "God" (see below).

7. Researchers and scholars in religious studies differentiate between regarding "God" as the name of a divine being (in certain religious traditions) and regarding "God" as a symbol of what may *function* as an ideal or ultimate in a person's world view.

8. Kohut's (1977) exact words are, "Ideals are guides, not gods" (p. 312).

9. Psychoanalytically oriented clinicians practice an analogous process when assuming that disparate elements in a patient's report are in fact related: the clinician sets about the task of synthesis in finding and creating a "red thread."

10. The phrase "going on being" (Winnicott, 1963/1965, p. 86) points to an abiding awareness of "a continuity of existence" (Winnicott, 1960/1965, p. 47) and "the continuity of being" (Winnicott, 1960/1965, p. 52). Winnicott (1987) writes, "The basis for all theories about human personality is continuity of the line of life . . . continuity which carries with it the idea that nothing that has been part of an individual's experience is or can ever be lost to that individual, even if in various complex ways it should and does become unavailable to consciousness" (p. 90).

11. Following Roy Schafer's (1976) idea of "action language," I am putting the pillars into verb form.

12. Thomas Ogden's (2001) discussion is illuminative. He writes,

> "*Live an experience together*"—what makes this phrase remarkable is the unexpected word *live*. The mother and child do not "take part in," "share," "participate in," or "enter into" an experience together; they *live* an experience together. In this single phrase, Winnicott is suggesting (though I think he was not fully aware of this as he wrote it) that he is in the process of transforming psychoanalysis, both as a theory and as a therapeutic relationship, in a way that involves altering the notion of what is most fundamental to human psychology. No longer will desiring and regulating desire (Freud), loving, hating, and making reparations (Klein), or object-seeking and object-relating (Fairbairn) constitute what is of greatest importance in the development of the psyche-soma from its beginnings and continuing throughout life. Instead, what Winnicott starts to lay out here for the first time is the idea that the central organizing thread of psychological development, from its inception, is the experience of being alive and the consequences of disruptions to that continuity of being. (pp. 314–315)

13. The well-known statement is, of course, "observation is theory laden." Explicitly changing *theory* to *theories* emphasizes the fact that *the theory with which all observation is laden, semantically as well as perceptually (see Schindler, 2013), is never and can never be "singular."* To make the point another way, everything we register in consciousness is "overdetermined."

14. Instinct is "a borderland concept" (1915/1957) between the mental and the physical (it transgresses artificial reified boundaries between mind and body).

15. Space does not admit elaboration, but the posing of this question indeed suggests this author's judgment that *one cannot achieve clinical competence (what is called "cultural competence") without more elaborate exposure to and reflection on contributions from these cognate fields of study.* Providing sound clinical care involves understanding patients, and understanding patients presupposes research and training in subject matter relevant to care. The division of labor among disciplines, fields, and guilds that has become normative eventuates in care that may be "efficient" but is not good enough, much less optimal.

16. Space permits only the most preliminary of observations in response to such a far ranging question. I am inspired to pose and begin to address it by a statement in the Talmud: "It is not upon you to finish the work; neither are you free to desist from it" (Aboth 2:21).

The pillars of any viable clinical attitude must, at some level, be meaningful and relevant to all persons, patients as well as clinicians. In my judgment, survival, vision, and faith, on their face, meet those criteria. At the same time, I am mindful that attitudes, like theories and practices of care more generally, too often neglect to identify and discuss, *explicitly*, a range of issues critical to culturally-sensitive clinical care, including race, ethnicity, gender, class, religion, age, sexual orientation, power, oppression, and violence. In this regard, Dr. Akhtar should be encouraged to elaborate his three pillars. More particularly, how would sound care require exploring *very different kinds of experiences* having to do with survival, vision, and faith among diverse patients? How would those experiences necessarily differ precisely because they bear the imprint of different social locations and embody *the impingement of different events* having to do with prejudice, ethnocentrism, xenophobia, racism, heterosexism, and classism, among other institutionalized expressions of violence?

REFERENCES

Ajzen, I. (2005). *Attitudes, personality and behavior.* Second edition. Berkshire, England: Open University Press.

Allphin, C. (2005). An ethical attitude in the analytic relationship. *Journal of Analytical Psychology, 50*: 451–468.

Aron, L. (2005). Acceptance, compassion, and an affirmative analytic attitude in both intersubjectivity and compromise formation theory. *Psychoanalytic Dialogues, 15* (3): 433–446.

Basch, M. F. (1980). *Doing psychotherapy.* New York, NY: Basic Books.

Berger, P., & Kellner, H. (1981). *Sociology reinterpreted: An essay on method and vocation.* Garden City, NY: Anchor Press/Doubleday.

Black, M. J., Fliegel, Z. O., Silverman, L., Gill, M. M., & M. Tolpin. (1987). The analyst's stance: Transferential implications of technical orientation. *The Annual of Psychoanalysis 15*: 127–172.

Bloom, A. (1987). *The closing of the American mind: How higher education has failed democracy and impoverished the soul's of today's students.* New York: Simon and Schuster.

Brümmer, V. (1991). Philosophy, theology, and the reading of texts. *Religious Studies, 27*(4) 451–462.

Cacioppo, J. T., Petty, R. R., & T. R. Green. (1989). Attitude, structure and function: From the tripartite to the homeostasis model of attitudes. In A. R. Pratkanis, S. J. Breckler, & A. G. Greenwald (Eds.), *Attitude, structure, and function* (pp.275–310). Hillsdale, NJ: Lawrence Erlbaum Associates, Publishers.

Fowler, J. W. (1981). *Stages of faith: The psychology of human development and the quest for meaning.* San Francisco, California: Harper & Row.

Freud, S. (1958). Remembering, repeating and working-through. In J. Strachey (Ed. and Trans.), *The standard edition of the complete psychological works of Sigmund Freud* (Vol. 12, pp. 145–157). London: Hogarth Press. (Original work published 1914)

Freud, S. (1957). Instincts and their vicissitudes. In J. Strachey (Ed. and Trans.), *The standard edition of the complete psychological works of Sigmund Freud* (Vol. 19, pp. 23–66). London: Hogarth Press. (Original work published 1915)

Freud, S. (1961). The ego and the id. In J. Strachey (Ed. and Trans.), *The standard edition of the complete psychological works of Sigmund Freud* (Vol. 19, pp. 23–66). London: Hogarth Press. (Original work published 1923)

Fritsch, R. C. (2013). Roy Schafer's contributions to psychological testing: From clinical sensibility to the analytic attitude. *The Psychoanalytic Quarterly, LXXXII* (1): 9–21.

Hansell, J. (2008). Psychoanalytic aims and attitudes. *The Psychoanalytic Quarterly, LXXVII* (4): 1179–1192.

Holland, N. (1975). *5 Readers reading.* New Haven, CT: Yale University Press.

Holland, N. (1985). *The I.* New Haven, CT: Yale University Press.

Holzman, P. (1995). *Psychoanalysis and psychopathology.* New York, NY: Jason Aronson. (Original work published 1969)

Jordan, Merle R. (1987). *Taking on the gods: The task of the pastoral counselor* Nashville, TN: Abingdon Press.

Kaley, H. (1993). Psychoanalysis in education: Attitude and process. *Psychoanalytic psychology, 10* (10: 93–103.

Klein, J. T. (1990). *Interdisciplinarity: History, theory, and practice*. Detroit, MI: Wayne State University Press.
Kluckhohn, C., & Murray, H. A. (Eds.). (1948). *Personality in nature, society, and culture*. New York, NY: Knopf.
Kohut, H. (1978). Observations on the psychological functions of music. In P. H. Ornstein (Ed.). *The search for the self: Selected writings of Heinz Kohut: 1950–1978* (pp. 233–253). New York: International Universities Press. (Original work published 1957)
Kohut, H. (1977). *The restoration of the self*. New York, NY: International Universities Press.
Kohut, H. (1987). Extending empathic understanding, sharing an attitude. In M. Elson (Ed.). *The Kohut seminars on self psychology and psychotherapy with adolescents and young adults* (pp. 188–202). New York, NY: W. W. Norton.
Lakoff, G., & M. Johnson (1980). *Metaphors we live by*. Chicago, IL: University of Chicago Press.
Lemma, A. (2012). Some reflections on the "teaching attitude" and its application to teaching about the use of the transference: A British view. *British Journal of Psychotherapy, 28* (4): 454–473.
Loewald, H. (1960). On the therapeutic action of psychoanalysis. *International Journal of Psychoanalysis, 41*: 16–33.
McClure, B. A., & R. W. Hodge. (1987). Measuring countertransference and attitude in therapeutic relationships. *Psychotherapy, 24* (3): 325–335.
Messick, S., & F. J. Fritzky, (1963). Dimensions of analytic attitude in cognition and personality. *Journal of Personality, 31* (3): 346–370.
National Academy of Sciences. (2005). *Facilitating interdisciplinary research*. Washington, D.C.: National Academies Press.
Ogden, T. H. (2001). Reading Winnicott. *Psychoanalytic Quarterly, LXX*, 299–323.
Peirce, C. S. (1878). How to make our ideas clear. *Popular Science Monthly, 12*, 286–302.
Poland, W. (2002). The interpretive attitude. *Journal of the American Psychoanalytic Association, 50* (3): 807–826.
Ricoeur, P. (1970). *Freud and philosophy*. (D. Savage, Trans.). New Haven, CT: Yale University Press.
Schafer, R. (1976). The psychoanalytic vision of reality. In *A new language for psychoanalysis*. New Haven, CT: Yale University Press. (original work published 1970).
Schafer, R. (1976). *A new language for psychoanalysis*. New Haven, CT: Yale University Press
Schafer, R. (1983). *The analytic attitude*. New York: Basic Books, 1983.
Schindler, S. (2013). Observation and theory-ladenness. In B. Kaldis (Ed.), *Encyclopedia of philosophy and the social sciences*, 15, 695–698.
Schlauch, C. R. (1993). Re-visioning pastoral diagnosis. In R. J. Wicks & R. D. Parsons (Eds.), *The clinical handbook of pastoral counseling, volume II* (pp. 51-101). New York, NY: Paulist Press.
Schlauch, C. R. (1995). *Faithful companioning: How pastoral counseling heals*. Minneapolis, MN: Fortress Press.
Shapiro, D. (1989). *Psychotherapy of neurotic character*. New York: Basic Books.
Smith, J. Z. (1993). *Map is not territory*. Chicago, IL: University of Chicago Press.
Tillich, P. (1957). *Systematic theology, Volume II. Existence and the Christ*. Chicago, IL: University of Chicago Press.
Toulmin, S. (1985). *The Return to Cosmology: Postmodern Science and the Theology of Nature*. Berkeley, CA: University of California Press. (Original work published 1982)
Toulmin, S. (2001). *Return to Reason. Cambridge, MA: Harvard University Press.*
Tuttman, S. (1987). Exploring the analyst's treatment stance in current psychoanalytic practice. *Journal of the American Academy of Psychoanalysis 15*: 29–37.
Winnicott, D. W. (1965). The theory of the parent-infant relationship. In *The maturational process and the facilitating environment: Studies in the theory of emotional development* (pp. 37–55). London: Hogarth Press. (Original work published 1960)
Winnicott, D. W. (1965). From dependence towards independence in the development of the individual. In *The maturational process and the facilitating environment: Studies in the*

theory of emotional development (pp. 83–92). London: Hogarth Press. (Original work published 1963)

Winnicott, D. W. (1975). Primitive emotional development. In *Through paediatrics to psychoanalysis* (pp. 145–156). New York: Basic Books, Inc. (Original work published 1945).

Winnicott, D. W. (1987). *Babies and their mothers*. Cambridge, MA: Perseus Publishing.

Winnicott, D. W. (1989). Playing and culture. In C. Winnicott, R. Shepherd, & M. Davis (Eds.). *Psychoanalytic explorations* (pp. 203–206). Cambridge, MA: Harvard University Press. (Original work published 1968).

Chapter Ten

Evocations

Thomas J. Cottle

"Words/Which speak of nothing more than what we are."
—William Wordsworth

The novelist V. S. Naipaul once remarked that the great novel both enlightens and evokes. The same, I suppose, may be said for a powerful paper delivered by one of the world's foremost psychoanalysts. In this essay, I respond less to the enlightening aspects of Salman Akhtar's paper, and more to what was evoked in me as I studied his writing, and then later, reflected on his words.

Well before encountering Dr. Akhtar's paper, I had come across some highly provocative and telling remarks from four cultural heroes. Their words seemed to touch directly on my work as a psychotherapist and researcher, and on looking back upon them I wondered how Dr. Akhtar might respond to these ideas. Do these four men speak to the notions of survival, vision, and faith that constitute a predicate of Dr. Akhtar's rich ideas? How, for example, would he react to T. S. Eliot's insistence that each of us requires a highly developed sense of fact? Do we even speak of facts in psychotherapy in the same way our colleagues in the sciences do? Surely, psychotherapy sits closer to the throne of fact than to the reality of a blog.

I wonder too, whether Dr. Akhtar would object to these words from the literary critic Lionel Trilling (McDonald, 2011)? "Literature takes the fullest and most precise account of variousness, possibility, complexity, and difficulty" (p. 23). In jotting down notes for my response I imagined him appreciating that term, "variousness," but I included a caution: namely, do those of us practicing psychotherapy get so caught up in the theories, procedures, or outright rituals of our work, that we fail to attend to our clients and hence fail to encounter the richness of their lives, the genuine possibilities they present to us, or what Trilling calls their "variousness"? Put differently, does an adherence to personal beliefs and theoretical predilections move us away from what might be considered an ethical imperative, captured in these words from the poet Mary Oliver: "To pay attention, this is our endless and proper work"?

On a similar note, and I leave this for the reader to consider, can the act of psychotherapy tolerate this admonition from Randall Jarrett (McDonald, 2011)? "The self is an instrument through which art is seen. So that the work will seem everything to him, and his own self nothing" (p.23). Do psychotherapists properly see themselves as nothing when they encounter their clients? Doubtful. But there is some delicate connection here for me. Or is this merely another evocation?

I leave the best for last. Herein words from the literary critic Alfred Kazin (McDonald, 2011). They perfectly capture, what does one even call it, my friendship with psychoanalysis: "…a profound inner struggle between what has been and what must be, the values he is used to and those which presently exist… This struggle with oneself as well as with the age…" (p. 23). It has been many years since my own analysis, and a host of other theoretical perspectives have entered all of our lives. Truthfully, when I read a paper like Dr. Akhtar's I find myself slipping back in time to a period when, quite frankly, I imagined psychoanalytic theory was all and all. Who in their right mind would doubt the power of the unconscious, and the self-evident truths contained in constructs like the Oedipus complex and defense mechanisms? Ingenious, isn't it, the idea of the ego, seemingly impotent in the face of a hard driving id, figuring out ways essentially to distort reality and thus trick it? Now really, who would dare question any of this?! But question we have, moved on we have, wondered (and wandered) more and more we have.

So there is that inevitable tug between the golden past and a present—I won't even mention the future—that makes me question whether I fit anywhere in this modern scheme. Do I have sufficient strength and courage to try on new theoretical coats, or has my past slipped away and taken a good measure of me with it? Have I been set adrift somehow? In this light, Kazin speaks to the struggle one experiences between what one has been and what one must be, and the consequent demand that we drop values which for decades we deeply cherished. I wonder whether Dr. Akhtar would consider placing this notion in any of his categories comprising attitude? It would seem to fit in all three: survival, vision, and faith. Part of one's faith, after all, necessarily involves a certain devotion to something, to someone, a transcendent figure perhaps, or some ideal conception or conceptualization. It involves, as well, a certain attitude of hopefulness, a theme I surely detect in Dr. Akhtar's words, and thus a new evocation, several in fact.

Arising in me first is the writing of Erik Erikson (1950), and more specifically that in each of eight stages of development, stages well known to most students of psychology, a unique dilemma is meant to be resolved. From this resolution, furthermore, will emerge either a mal-development, a pathological status, or what Erikson labels a strength or virtue. Does it seem strange to think of Erikson as advancing the development of the virtuous person? Might we agree that taken together his eight virtues, hope, will, purpose, competence, fidelity, love, care, and wisdom constitute a rather virtuous soul? Is this the soul that William James would recognize as virtuous? Was it not James (1907), after all, who claimed that the prime result of a good education was the ability to recognize a virtuous person? More to the point, in reflecting on Dr. Akhtar's attitudes, one wonders how often those of us practicing psychotherapy ever conceive of our clients in terms of their virtuousness.

Another piece evoked by Dr. Akhtar's paper arrives in one word: This is a kind man, a kindly man, I find myself thinking, benevolent as well. Excusing the pun, there is a patient curiosity about him. I am convinced he has come across Mary Oliver's words, which like his own, never drown in a sea of sentimentality, a theme to which I shall return in a moment. I suspect he is able to see the personality and soul of a patient emerging from the yet to be fully carved rock to which he refers. Or is it more precise to aver that he aids in the sculpting and hence deliverance of that personality and soul? He must, I conclude, or he would not be considering the particular issues he raises and with which he is fascinated in the first place. If he speaks about the mother's gaze, then we are bound to imagine the power of his own gaze, which makes one wonder whether in the somewhat irreal context of the therapeutic encounter, anyone gazes upon us as assiduously as the psychotherapist? Gaze, after all means little more than looking steadily, intently, and with fixed attention. It is what Mary Oliver alerted us to, is it not? Parents may well look ahead of their children, keep them from falling, prepare them for some imagined version of the future, imagine their potential, or perhaps even perceive it, which is yet another piece of the survival attitude. But their supreme gift is an ability to gaze upon their children with a power to render a certain strength to their children that later on will make it possible for the children not only to survive, but also to make friends with their own potential, capacities, and possibilities, what Trilling called their variousness. The notion brings to mind Donald Winnicott's (1987) concern that one feel real to oneself, not merely a phantom. I suspect that a healthy gaze provides a way of diminishing the danger of an impending sense that mine is a phantom self. Do not worry, Dr. Akhtar assures us, there will always be people to help us. I pray this is so.

There was a point I reached in perusing Dr. Akhtar's paper when I felt as though I was encountering a tone poem. Surely when he points out to his patient that her story of the spider is perhaps a poem, one can well imagine the entire piece being one grand poem. "Poetry is not a turning loose of emotion," T.S. Eliot (1921) wrote, "but an escape from emotion; it is not the expression of personality, but an escape from personality. But, of course, only those who have personality and emotions know what it means to want to escape from these things" (p.33). It is strange to think of the therapeutic intervention as one part escape, one part poetry. Still, if this seems far-fetched, consider, alongside Dr. Akhtar's biographical and hence more personal sections of the paper, these words from the critic Steve Wasserman (2007): "It is through the work of novelists and poets that we understand how we imagine ourselves and contend with the often elusive forces—of which language itself is a foremost factor—that shape us as individuals and families, citizens and communities..." (p. 53). Would the reader agree that a willingness, albeit reluctant in the beginning, to undertake this escape is in fact a testament to the power of the *survival* notion Dr. Akhtar advances, and furthermore, that the willingness to shape one's own personality, compose one's poem, we might say, is made possible through first a particular *vision* of the therapeutic process, and second, a *faith* in the person bearing witness to this emerging poem, this emerging form born from the rock? Again from Mary Oliver (1994): "Poetry is a life-cherishing force. And it requires a vision, a faith, to use an old fashioned term. Yes, indeed. For poems are not words, after all, but fires for the cold, ropes let down to the lost, something as necessary as bread in the pockets of the hungry" (p. 122).

Dr. Akhtar speaks directly to these themes when he alludes to the unconventionality of therapeutic interventions. Who, after all, sits beside us as we launch an escape into a mythical or mythopoeic examination of ourselves? Talk about a trapeze act requiring a net of faith, and someone to catch us, not to mention an exquisite code of ethics! From one perspective, the therapeutic intervention looms as utterly unconventional. From another perspective, it appears utterly human. Then again, does a poem ever seem genuinely unconventional?

There is another layer here to which the author remains sensitive. Freud viewed psychoanalysis as both a learning and research enterprise. Dr. Akhtar clearly does as well. And why not? Most significantly, as Jung taught, there is a pedagogy occurring in our offices; all parties must be learning. Jung (2001) himself employed the word "education" in his third stage of therapy, in which he spoke of "the ill tree growing straight." He spoke too of confession (the first stage of therapy), a phenomenon resting, surely, on faith. "How can I be substantial if I fail to cast a shadow?" (p. 35) Jung challenges us.

Granted, there must be a willingness to engage in the process, both parties rising above, or perhaps momentarily pushing aside their resistance to the enterprise, and the poetry, even to commence. Jung (2001) wrote: "At first we cannot see beyond the path that leads downward to dark and hateful things—but no light or beauty will ever come from the man who cannot bear this sight. Light is always born of darkness, and the sun never stood still in heaven to satisfy man's longing or to still his fears" (p. 35). But once underway, Jung counseled, once the light begins to appear, once both parties reveal to one another the degrees of capability and responsibility this sacred trust demands, once the vision is safely internalized, both are altered. "If there is any reaction," Jung intoned, "both are transformed" (p. 49).

What then is the actual curriculum of the therapeutic process? More precisely, in Akhtar's terms, how is this *vision* of an examination of a self, this birth of a poem enacted? One answer may be found in the writings of Robert Kegan (1982) who reminds us that the fundamental act of being human is making meaning. Notice carefully his language: "There is thus no feeling, no experience, no thought, no perception, independent of a meaning-making context in which it becomes a feeling, an experience, a thought, a perception, because we are the meaning-making context" (p. 11). Which further suggests that it is essential we remain vulnerable to the world, interior and exterior alike, all the while remaining aware that this vulnerability in no way detracts from our evaluative and critical stance toward the world, and ourselves.

So we are poets as well as meaning makers, both activities requiring vision, faith, and belief in survival. But we still are uncertain of the actual curriculum. What is it that emerges as the product of our meaning making? For this the philosopher Michael Oakeshott (1989) may have the final word, arguing as he does that essentially what makes us human is the ability to articulate for ourselves what it means to be human. But notice here that to reach this point we must have learned some things, a host of things, and hence we cannot disentangle being human from learning. In a word, we are what we have learned. Which in turn means that, in some manner, a vision, a faith, and a sense of survival have been passed over to us by teachers, and if Jung is to be believed, by fellow transformers. But how is this accomplished in psychotherapy, in families, in classrooms?

I return to that passing reference to a doctor's kindness and willingness to subscribe to the almost medical edicts put forth by Mary Oliver. Inherent in this mysterious curriculum is the capacity found in the ideal of Caritas, namely, to will the good of the other. Requiring that we remain careful to think realistically, Caritas shows itself as mercy to sinners. With its authentic conception of human nature, a civilization of Caritas is necessarily a civilization acutely aware of human sinfulness. Caritas is love aimed at the real, not the apparent, good of the other. It is built upon realistic judgments, not mere illusions or appearances. That sea of sentimentality about which we spoke earlier has no place here. Caritas liberates as it nourishes, and always it demands that we respect the human person as the originating source of human action, the "imago Dei." Like psychotherapy itself, Caritas inspires a form of work meant to assist others in forming relationships predicated on dignity, solidarity, trustworthiness, courtesy, reliability, creative imagination, and, most significantly, justice.

One more note will serve to close this section. If the notion of Caritas is to be accepted, I am not certain that the concept of human development, as Dr. Akhtar appears to suggest, ought properly to be envisioned as mere peripheral matter. We may wish to agree that the psychotherapeutic intervention is irreal, but not unreal. Put it this way: Human development represents an equation, the left-hand side of which reflects Trilling's human variousness, possibility, complexity, and difficulty, and the right-hand side economic, political and social opportunities, all of which form the bedrock out of which variousness arises. Can we not legitimately speak of something called a sociopolitical stress? John Steinbeck, as cited in Mallon (2012) alluded to this equation thusly: "… no single organism could be understood without observing and comprehending the entire colony." And now Thomas Mallon (2012) commenting on Steinbeck: "This is not a hymn to collectivism; it's simply a realization that humans become themselves only when twitched into life by other humans."

Much of this, of course, is the common plea for an ecological perspective, what Caritas delineates as the cardinal virtues of human ecology necessary for human flourishing and a sentiment, finally, captured by David Brooks (2012):

> When you look over the domestic policy landscape, you see all these different people in different policy silos with different budgets: in health care, education, crime, poverty, social mobility and labor force issues. But, in their disjointed ways, they are all dealing with the same problem—that across vast stretches of America, economic, social and family breakdowns are producing enormous amounts of stress and unregulated behavior, which dulls motivation, undermines self-control and distorts lives (p. A31).

There it is, near the end of an eloquent book review of what appears to be an extraordinary volume, *When I Was a Child I Read Books* by Marilynne Robinson (2012), the phrase that unknowingly I have been hunting for: "It's hard to deliberate when you're certain," Michael Washburn (2012) writes. He is referring to Professor Robinson's (2012) observation that "certainty is a relic… a husk we ought to have outgrown" (p. 197). Granted, knowing generates all varieties of precarious postures and predilections; stolid assurance sits alongside unalloyed dogmatism. What is required in psychotherapy, and in writing the tone poem in which that variousness theme is delicately dissected, is perhaps the purest form of deliberation, itself the child of contemplative knowing wherein we remain attentive, open, and willing to embrace, for one extended moment even, the obverse and contradictions that buzz in our heads.

Examination of Dr. Akhtar's three attitudes, and more importantly the manner in which he approaches ideas and persons, yields an insight into what has come to be called contemplative knowing, defined here as attentiveness, openness, and an ability to embrace the obverse and contradictory (Zajonc, 2008). The appreciation of the other in concert with the capacity to look into the soul of another (or at least imagine that one is doing this) emerge in the forms of *Eros* and insight. Reminding us of the quality of attention inherent in the spirit of Caritas, philosophers tell us that contemplative knowing becomes an act of reimagined love. Neither sentimental nor purely self-satisfying, contemplative knowing provides the foundation for the forms of education and self-transformation we continually observe in psychotherapy.

Does it sound outrageous in this context to suggest that the psychotherapeutic intervention is a form of Eros and insight, and hence an act of true love? Does it sound outrageous to allege that the psychotherapeutic intervention may be viewed as an invitation to both parties to engage in acts of healing, blur distinctions between practice and theory, sensation and rationality, and uphold separation and longing as the fundaments of conscious being? Art and science, after all, may be considered distinct but superficially different ways of knowing, and the psychotherapeutic enterprise reveals ways of knowing transcended by a commonality of human longing for wholeness, a longing arising from an acknowledged condition of consciousness and utterly human fragmentation. Rightly then, we acknowledge Dr. Akhtar's inherent challenge to the conventional separation of art and science, as when he seats $E=mc^2$ alongside the Oedipal Complex.

Contemplative knowing, enduring surely in each of us, brings our attention to ideas like the search for meaning, the need to know what it means to be human, or how to mold the self in such manner that, in the words of Rilke (2004), we begin to recognize that knowing is a form of "wandering mourning" (p.81). If we can arrive, as Dr. Akhtar suggests in the section of his paper devoted to survival, at the sort of awareness required to overcome the murderous rage we all possess, even in its most benign forms, and if, moreover, we arrive at a point where we are able to conceive of the spiritual somehow ranking higher in our consciousness than the physical, then we may discover the sort of unfolding consciousness present in the therapeutic process. We may begin to feel, furthermore, what it is to heal and to learn, as Eliot (1971) writes in *Little Gidding*, that all true love, especially the sort found in therapy through Eros and insight, is always a beginning. "Quick, now, here, now, always" (p.49).

Would it be appropriate to suggest, therefore, that survival, vision, and faith provide groundwork for the posture taken by Dr. Akhtar? Similarly, might one allege that the psychotherapeutic process as described by this gifted psychoanalyst in fact represents the summit of ethical transactions? If this were the case, then Dr. Akhtar would have to appreciate the writings of the philosopher Emmanuel Levinas (1969) who insisted that in all human engagements the ethical must always be present. Preceding reason, the ethical presents itself only upon our recognition that we *are* the relationships we safeguard, exactly as Heidegger had proposed, and discover, further, that we have taken responsibility for the other. Notice here that we do not choose the other; it is almost as though the other has chosen *us*. . . . As Derrida (1990) notes: "We did not choose this responsibility, it imposes itself upon us" (p. 92). Adding to the gravity of this position, Levinas insists that the debt of human responsibility for the other is never fulfilled; it extends to eternity (Steiner, 2001).

Levinas (1969) speaks of being held hostage by the gaze of the other. Surely provocative words, "held hostage" means nothing more than a pledge for lodging. The gaze constitutes the domain of concrete existence. Paraphrasing Levinas (1985), the other person is felt as a weight that I encounter pushing against me. . . a weight existing on my behalf, constantly refusing my atavistic desire to become one with it, or devour it, a notion akin to Dr. Akhtar's notion of survival, as is this proposition: "In his face the Other appears to me not as an obstacle, nor as a menace I evaluate, but as what measures me" (p. 116). In this same manner, the act of affirmation, inherent one must assume in the psychotherapeutic enterprise, is intended for both of us; I affirm myself as I affirm yourself. It is the act of affirmation that forever assures you that I shall not destroy you (Cottle, 2003). Levinas reminds us, if we welcome only those we know, we have not welcomed strangers; we have affirmed no one. If we first know the other then respond to his or her summons, we have not acted ethically. We affirm before knowing, before reasoning, even. Levinas, E. and Kearney, R. (1986) himself cited the words of Alyosha in *The Brothers Karamazov*: "We are all responsible for everyone else, but I am more responsible than all the others" (p. 31). Without this life force there cannot be a genuine knowledge and sense of self. Nor can there be anything in the society resembling genuine justice. From Nel Noddings (1984): "We love not because we are required to love but because our natural relatedness gives birth to love. It is this love, this natural caring *that makes the ethical possible*" (p. 43, emphasis added).

Now, for those wondering about the relevance of faith, consider these words on Levinas from Denis Donoghue (2001): "It follows that Levinas's aim is to displace the priority of knowledge by the priority of faith: not faith in God but in the sublime existence of other people than oneself. Not faith in their mere bodily proximity on the street, but in their mode of existence as persons for whom I hold myself responsible" (p. 56). This rudimentary concept of responsibility, moreover, is predicated neither on reason nor duty. Again from Donoghue: "The primary act is the spontaneous one by which I address another person as 'you.' I ground my own mode of existence solely upon that act" (p. 53). I cannot, therefore, become me, much less develop my own concept of self without acknowledging you, and taking responsibility for you.

When Levinas speaks of having taken responsibility for another and genuinely ethical behavior, one again is put in mind of the ideals of psychotherapy. Ethical behavior for this one philosopher does not derive from logical reasoning. Nor does it sit somewhere in space, ready, somehow, to be activated. Rather, it appears to be born in the encounter with the patient, the stranger. In symbolically moving toward the patient as we do in the act of empathy (Kohut, 1978), we have roused in ourselves a call, as it were, to our humanness. The noblest of empathic experiences, by hearing the stranger's words, we feel her as a stirring (being) inside us. This of course assumes that we practice in a manner that allows our self to be open, vulnerable, not just to the patient, but also to the reverberations in ourselves that we experience as a function of encountering the patient. In genuine affirmation, in what Levinas called "sensibility," we find ourselves not only summoned by the other, but also roused by the other without ever having previously known anything about her. Aware of it or not, we have created a just relationship.

To say the least, this notion of discovering that one has taken responsibility for another is a profoundly complex matter. Granted, we all experience in our lives some form of precariousness requiring, we imagine, someone to assume responsibility for us. Granted too, precariousness is a general condition of human life, but some people, patients in therapy perhaps, are more precarious than others. And while I prefer not to consider the ways in which I discriminate people and hence fail to assume responsibility for them, I am in the same moment confronted with the Levinasian problem of how do I include the face of the other who cannot be known? Can I truly see the oppressed other? Can I recognize, as Mari Ruti (2013) suggests, that the other is as woundable as I am? Will I, moreover, suspend responsibility in the name of self-defense? Equally relevant is what I will do with the face of the other who wishes to diminish or even destroy another? How possibly can anyone require me to act responsibly before the faceless face of the monster? Less severely, can I respect differences, and the different ones, or do I only respect those whom I like? How possibly am I meant to humanize the face of the other? Is the other even knowable to begin with? I ask myself. How do we relate to a face to which we feel we can't relate? We are responsible, says Levinas, even if the other is evil, like the face of a terrorist.

It is Judith Butler's (2005) claim that we condemn subjectivity when we cannot find a way to be compassionate, but subjectivity is inherently part of ethics. Justice only commences, she instructs, when I deal with those I do not know; in Levinasian terms, this single, or is it singular, act transcends the fetish of the face. Indeed, it might be suggested, and here students of Dr. Akhtar will do more than raise an eyebrow, that justice may require a certain coldness. How else could we take responsibility for a new patient, a new friend, someone who moments ago was but a stranger, or perhaps someone who will forever remain to us as stranger? Perhaps genuine ethics must be possible without the face of the other. Ethics, Ruti notes, are founded on the studied indifference of the other. While we initiate the process of the ethical by dealing with categories of sameness, we must hold in mind that this is only a starting point. Eventually we are compelled to deal with the inevitable distinctions between and among people, and furthermore, respect these distinctions. Is it possible, therefore, that the face of the other is merely a decoy for exploring justice?

Therapy is hardly the only realm obliging us to find commonality as well as similarity with others. We need not maintain identical experiences, but we must locate the parallels in our lives. And while some people, as therapists know all too well, have trouble being seen as people, we, the so-called responsibility takers, tend to trap some people in narrow and self-serving categories, like nationalism, or race, or gender, or ethnicity. And thus the philosopher inquires, can one be human without being black, or white, or Jewish, or male? Egotism without recognizing the other is a black hole, Levinas claims. From grasping the other, he teaches, one finds oneself grasped.

Survival, vision, and faith, Akhtar instructs, are rooted in the landscape of the psychotherapeutic experience. They creep into our conceptions of time and space, just as they appear to us in their utterly practical and still mystical forms. They remind us, perhaps, of the existentialists' notion of *Existenz* which speaks to the primordial, spontaneous depth of each self, a portion of the self meant to be actualized. When the shallow life doesn't work, Abraham Maslow (1954) wrote, there occurs a call to fundamentals, a call that symbolizes fundamentals of being. We would add that these fundamentals reside in the realm of *Existenz*, a realm requiring us to break out of patterns, build new knowledge, and examine new ideas regarding the spirit, art, morals, and religion (Rogers-McMillan, 2008). And isn't this what occurs in psychotherapy? Isn't this what psychotherapy encompasses, a word favored by Karl Jaspers (1971)?

But psychotherapy, and especially the forms delineated by Dr. Akhtar, demands at least one thing more: transcendence, the being beyond all objectivity. Borrowing from the writing of Thomas Dukes (2009), we might allege that it is the so-called boundary situation that describes the circumstance from which we suffer and with which we struggle. In the main, the boundary situation cannot be transformed; we cannot modify it; we may only make it lucid by entering it with eyes wide open, or working with someone who intends to make certain that indeed our eyes remain wide open. Like psychotherapy itself, the boundary situation, demanding as it does fundamental notions of survival, vision, and faith, makes us aware of our very being, and thus represents an essential ingredient of our capacity to construct meaning. Yet the meanings I derive are something other than myself, more than mere expressions or projections of myself; they push me toward meanings both within and outside of myself. If, as Robert Nozick (1989) alleged, the self dwells in its own capacity to change, a capacity in which those of us practicing psychotherapy rather strongly believe, then our aim must be to help those wishing to seek the deepest parts of themselves, and even more, by embracing the notion of faith, and the spiritual, connect or at least resonate to what we imagine to be the highest things there are.

In the end, psychotherapy, as the concept of *Existenz* portends, causes us to do something, or *will* something in order to become ourselves. If we are to give life meaning, we must transcend these so-called boundary experiences and hence the limits of our own physical life. Without the capacity for transcendence we lose more than a bit of the impact of Dr. Akhtar's ideas surrounding survival, vision, and faith. More significantly, transcendence of the self is the core of resilience. Perhaps only through this aspect of psychotherapy do we encounter our authentic selves and hold these selves fast in our minds. Even bolstered by ideas of survival, vision, and faith, psychotherapy requires what William James (1890) called "mental effort" (p.301), and all of it is undertaken, as we have noted, with eyes wide open. The patient consents to the process, consents to examine the yet still unforeseeable. She consents to stretching beyond her present visions of her own potentials, her own variousness. She consents to the covenant of reaching outward, and inward, to the so-called good and virtuous life, and hence she emerges as hero. This reach for the deepest parts and simultaneously the highest spheres, if not the divine, captures the essence of performing at the highest level, not to mention the concept of resiliency. And might these experiences, inherent in psychotherapy, experiences drenched by ideas of survival, vision, and faith, reflect those times when we feel most human!

It is intriguing, surely, to witness fads and behaviors come and go, and various folks emerge as charismatic and iconic, that overworked term. Equally intriguing is to recognize how one's identity probably is formed by one, but rarely more than two, eras. Now for me those eras are gone. I have written elsewhere, I don't struggle with my age; I struggle with my age. Still, a single pilot light refuses to fade, and so I live with a fading glow of fear. Should something happen, will there be a sufficient number of people to keep me safe? Will enough people eschew certitude in favor of insight (and Eros), and perceive us all as equals, thereby making it possible for them to embrace Paul Ricoeur's (2000) lovely prescription for justice, namely that we ought to treat equals equally? Will enough people recognize that homeland security comes in various forms, each with the power to extinguish someday and for good a pilot light flickering in more citizens than some would ever imagine, or even dare to discern? And might these notions too, be part of the concepts of vision, faith, and most especially survival that limn the world of psychotherapy?

REFERENCES

Brooks, D. (2012, September 27). The Psych Approach. *New York Times.* page A31.
Butler, J. (2005). *Giving an Account of Oneself.* New York: Fordham University Press.
Changeux, J., & Ricoeor, P. (2000). *What Makes Us Think.* Princeton, NJ: Princeton University Press.
Cottle, T. (2003). *A Sense of Self: The Work of Affirmation.* Amherst, MA: University of Massachusetts Press.
Derrida, J. (1990). The Other Heading. *PMLA, 108* (92).
Donoghue, D. (2001). *Adam's Curse: Reflections on Religion and Literature.* Notre Dame, IN: University of Notre Dame Press.
Dukes, T. (2009). Self-understanding as a protective factor: Adolescent identity consolidation and the nurturing of resilience. Unpublished doctoral dissertation. Boston University School of Education. Boston, MA.
Eliot, T. S. (1921). *The Sacred Wood: Essays on Poetry and Criticism. New* York: Knopf.
Eliot, T. S. (1971). *Four Quartets.* Orlando: Harcourt.
Erikson, E. *Childhood and Society.* New York: Norton, 1950.
James, W. (1890). *Principles of Psychology, Volume 1.* New York: Henry Holt.
James, W. (1907). *The Social Value of the College-Bred.* Address Delivered at a Meeting of the Association of American Alumnae at Radcliff College.
Jaspers, K. (1971). *The Philosophy of Existence*, translated by Richard F. Grabau. Philadelphia: University of Pennsylvania Press.
Jung, C. (2001) *Modern Man in Search of a Soul.* New York: Routledge.
Kegan, R. *The Evolving Self.* Cambridge, MA: Harvard University Press.
Kohut, H. (1978). *Search for the Self, Volume 2*, Paul Ornstein (Editor). New York: International Universities Press.
Levinas, E. (1957). Philosophy and the idea of the infinite. *Revue Philosophique de la France et de l'Etranger.* Paris: Presses universitaires de France.
Levinas, E. (1969). *Totality and Infinity: An Essay on Exteriority.* translated by Alphonso Lingis. Pittsburgh: Duquesne University Press.
Levinas, E. (1985). *Ethics and Infinity.* Pittsburgh: Duquesne University Press.
Levinas, E., & Kearney, R. (1986). Dialogue with Emmanuel Levinas. In *Face to Face with Levinas: Neighborhood Reinvestment and Displacement.* Richard Cohen (ed). Albany: SUNY Press.
Mallon, T. (2012, October 28). Review of Tom Wolf's *Back to Blood. New York Times Book Review.*
Maslow, A. (1954). *Motivation and Personality.* New York: Harper and Row.
McDonald, J. (2011, January 2). Masters of the Form. *The New York Times Book Review.* p. 23.
Noddings, N. (1984). *A Feminine Approach to Ethics and Mortality.* Berkeley: University of California Press.
Nozick, R. (1989). *The Examined Life: Philosophical Meditations.* New York: Simon and Schuster.
Oakeshott, M. (1989). *The Voice of Liberal Learning.* New Haven: Yale University Press.
Oliver, M. (1994). *A Poetry Handbook: A Prose Guide to Writing and Understanding Poetry.* Boston: Houghton Mifflin.
Oliver, Mary (2003). *Owls and Other Fantasies.* Boston: Beacon Press.
Ricoeur, P. (2000). *The Just.* Translated by David Pellauer. Chicago: University of Chicago Press.
Rilke, R. M. (2004). *Sonnets to Orpheus.* New York: Northpoint Press.
Robinson, M. (2012). *When I Was a Child I Read Books.* New York: Macmillan.
Rogers-McMillan, S. (2008). Diminishing Egocentricity: A Secondary Analysis of Longitudinal Data. Dissertation Proposal, Boston University School of Education. Boston, MA.
Ruti, M. (2013). The Other as Face in Post-Levinasian and post-Lacanian Ethics. Paper presented at Psychology and the Other Conference, Cambridge, MA.
Sarker, S. (2008). *T. S. Eliot: Poetry, Plays, and Prose.* New Delhi: Atlantic Publishing.
Steiner, D. (2001). Levinas' Ethical Interruption of Reciprocity. *Salmagundi*, Spring/Summer.

Washburn, M. (2012, March 25). Review of "When I Was a Child I Read Books: Essays" by Marilynne Robinson. A cautionary defense of patriotism, in the voice of faith. *The Boston Globe.*

Wasserman (2007, September 18). The State of Criticism. *Columbia Journalism Review.*

Winnicott, D.W. (1987). *The Child, The Family, And the Outside World.* New York: Perseus Publishing.

Zajonc, A. (2008). *Meditation as Contemplative Inquiry: When Knowing Becomes Love.* Great Barrington, MA: Lindisfarne Books.

Conclusion

Merle Jordan

I would like to add my own perspective on the conference topic, because I have a unique perspective on the integration of psychology and spirituality, and I realize that there aren't many people in the field who might agree with me, except for some of my former students. My fundamental thesis is this: All psychotherapy is really clinical theology. One's understanding of the depths and facets of another's life is best held in the context of the person's story and struggle being seen as implicit, internal drama. This idea began with the work of the Austrian analyst Wilfried Daim who, out of his studies, came to the belief that all people (though he was focusing mainly on neurotics) come to their struggles by making an ultimate power out of some experience they've had in human relationships. Certainly the authors collected here, Dr. Wallin in particular, have really highlighted how true that was in their own life experience.

The other dimension of this that is very significant for me is a kind of double idolatry. An illustration of double idolatry would be the person who has critical, perfectionistic parents who dominate the individual's emotional life. In order to cope with these parental authorities, who function as ultimate authority, a person develops a strategy of survival, such as being acquiescent and passive in regard to these authorities. The image of the dominant parents and the process of surviving them both function as ultimate processes. The second idolatry is thus how you become your own savior, living with harsh and cruel or perhaps distant and passive authorities. And so we all learn ways of survival. When I was six years old, I stood in the kitchen of my family home in South Portland, Maine, and my mother said to me with tears coming down her face and with great emotional struggle, "I need you to know that when you were just a baby, your birth mother died. I think I am your mother, but I'm afraid that your knowing about your other mother will mean that you won't want me as your mother." My world was turned upside down just like that. But I was also so sensitive to the fact that she was very upset and anxious about my taking care of her and continuing to love her that I immediately moved to reassure her: "of course I love you, and you are my mother." Never again in my childhood, with either my stepmother or my father, did I ask a single question—it didn't feel safe. I had one person, a cousin of mine, who would tell me stories, like her memory of my birth mother and my father having the radio on in the kitchen, and they were dancing. And my cousin would tell me about how she would go with my mother to the theater in Portland, Maine, and enjoy stage shows. So in a few weeks I am flying out to San Diego, where this cousin now lives, because she is celebrating her 95th birthday, but also because she is special to me as the one link to my mother. And would you believe that with all of the therapy that I've had and all the kinds of supervision I've participated in, I am finally learning that I don't have to give up being who I really am in order to survive in this world. It has been difficult for me to perceive that this world is a place in which I am safe to really be me and to go on in a constructive way.

Some of you know that my favorite way of teaching is to tell a story, so I'm going to make my final comments a story that comes from Henry Nouwen and has been adapted by Wayne Dyer. It goes like this:

> Imagine the following scene if you will: two babies are in utero, confined by the walls of their mother's womb, and they are having a conversation. For the sake of clarity, we'll call one Ego and one Spirit.
>
> Spirit says to Ego, "I know you're going to find this difficult to accept, but I truly believe there is a life hereafter."
>
> Ego responds, "Don't be ridiculous! Look around you—this is all there is. Why must you always be thinking about something beyond reality? Accept your lot in life, make yourself comfortable, and forget about all this 'life after birth' nonsense."
>
> So Spirit quiets down for a while, until her inner voice won't allow her to stay silent any longer. "Ego," she says, "now don't get mad, but I have something else to say. I also believe there is *a mother*."
>
> "A mother?" Ego guffaws. "How can you be so absurd? You've never seen a mother! Why can't you accept that this is all there is? The idea of a mother is crazy! All you have is being here alone with me. This is your reality. Now grab hold of that cord, go into your corner, and stop being so silly. Trust me, there is no mother."
>
> So Spirit reluctantly stops the conversation with Ego, but soon her restlessness gets the better of her. "Ego," she implores, "please just listen to me without rejecting my ideas. Somehow I think that these constant pressures we both feel—these movements that make us so uncomfortable sometimes, that continual repositioning and all of that closing in that seems to be taking place as we are growing—are getting us ready for a place of glowing light, and we will experience it very soon."

> "Now I know you are absolutely insane," says Ego to Spirit. "All you've ever known is darkness. You've never seen light. How can you even contemplate such an idea? Those movements and pressures that you feel are your reality. You are a distinct, separate being. This is your journey, darkness and pressures and a closed-in feeling are what life is all about. You'll have to fight it as long as you live. Now grab your cord and please stay still."
>
> So Spirit relaxes, just for a while. But finally she can contain herself, again, no longer. "Ego, I have only one more thing to say and then I will never bother you again."
>
> "Go ahead," Ego says impatiently.
>
> "I believe all of these pressures and all of this discomfort are not only going to bring us to a new celestial light, but when we experience it, we are going to meet mother face-to-face, and it will be an ecstasy we have never experienced up until now."
>
> "You are really crazy, Spirit. Now I'm truly convinced of it."

And this story simply encourages all of us to keep that faith in the unseen, that we will yet experience the reality of a love that stands at the heart of the meaning of the universe and of human life. That that love which is healing can sustain us and also is there before us after we move through death to the life beyond. May you know that love and that light and may it fill your life with its overwhelming joy. Amen.

Index of Names

Index of Subjects

About the Contributors

Salman Akhtar, MD is Professor of Psychiatry at Jefferson Medical College and Training and Supervising Analyst at the Psychoanalytic Center of Philadelphia. He is the Book Review Editor of the *International Journal of Applied Psychoanalytic Studies*, Film Review Editor of the *International Journal of Psychoanalysis*, and has served on the Editorial Board of the *Journal of the American Psychoanalytic Association*. He is the author of a number of books, including *Broken Structures, Inner Torment, Objects of Our Desire*, and *Turning Points in Dynamic Psychotherapy*. He has also contributed to many edited books. Dr. Akhtar is the recipient of several awards including the Best Paper of the Year Award and Edith Sabshin Award from the American Psychoanalytic Association and the Sigmund Freud Award for Distinguished Contribution to Psychoanalysis from the American Society of Psychoanalytic Physicians.

Celia Brickman, Ph.D., LCPC is the Director of Education at the Center for Religion and Pyschotherapy of Chicago, where she is also a member of the faculty and clinical staff. She received her doctorate at the University of Chicago's Divinity School in Religion and the Human Sciences. She is the author of *Aboriginal Populations in the Mind*: *Race and Primitivity in Psychoanalysis*, which was nominated for a Gradiva award by the National Association for the Advancement of Psychoanalysis, in addition to several book chapters, reviews, and articles.

Thomas J. Cottle, Ph.D. is Professor of Education at Boston University. He is the author of numerous articles and more than thirty books, including almost six hundred articles, essays, and reviews. His books include, *Hardest Times: The Trauma of Long Term Unemployment; Mind Fields: Adolescent*

Consciousness in a Culture of Distraction; A Sense of Self: The Work of Affirmation; At Peril: Stories of Injustice; When the Music Stopped: Discovering My Mother; and *Drawing Life: Narratives and A Sense of Self.*

Marie T. Hoffman, Ph.D. is Assistant Clinical Professor of Psychology (Adjunct) at NYU Postdoctoral Program in Psychotherapy and Psychoanalysis. She is Co-Director of Society for Exploration of Psychoanalytic Therapies and Theology, Director of Brookhaven Institute for Psychoanalysis and Christian Theology, and Co-Director/ practicing psychoanalyst and clinical psychologist at Brookhaven Center in Allentown, PA. In addition to journal articles and book chapters, she is author of *Toward Mutual Recognition: Relational Psychoanalysis and the Christian Narrative.* Dr. Hoffman lectures and consults on the interdisciplinary integration of psychoanalysis and Christian theology.

Merle Jordan, Th.D., is Emeritus Professor of Pastoral Psychology at Boston University, where he taught, supervised, advised, and mentored students from around the world in the integration of spirituality and psychotherapy from 1969 to his retirement from Boston University in 1996. He served as Executive Director of the Danielsen Institute from 1972–1981, guiding the Institute to the forefront of pastoral counseling and pastoral psychology training and education. Dr. Jordan is a pioneer and leader in the field of the integration of spirituality and psychotherapy and has published widely on this topic. His books include *Taking on the Gods: The Task of the Pastoral Counselor, Reclaiming Your Story: Family History and Spiritual Growth,* and *Addiction and Spirituality: A Multidisciplinary Approach* (co-edited with Oliver Morgan).

Nancy McWilliams, Ph.D. teaches at Rutgers University's Graduate School of Applied & Professional Psychology and practices in Flemington, New Jersey. Author of *Psychoanalytic Diagnosis* (1994, rev. ed. 2011), *Psychoanalytic Case Formulation* (1999), and *Psychoanalytic Psychotherapy* (2004), and associate editor of the *Psychodynamic Diagnostic Manual* (2006), she is a former president of Division 39 (Psychoanalysis) of the American Psychological Association. She is one of three psychotherapists chosen by APA Press (2011) to be videotaped for purposes of training in a comparison and contrast of major psychotherapeutic approaches.

Steven J. Sandage, Ph.D. is the Albert and Jessie Danielsen Professor of Pastoral Psychology and Theology at Boston University and Director of the Center for Research in Religion and Psychology at the Danielsen Institute. He is co-author of three books, *To Forgive is Human, The Faces of Forgiveness: Searching for Wholeness and Salvation*, and *Transforming Spirituality*:

Integrating Theology and Psychology and has a forthcoming book with American Psychological Association Books on *Forgiveness and Relational Spirituality*. He and theologian LeRon Shults received the Narramore Award for the Integration of Psychology and Theology from the Christian Association of Psychological Studies. He has also authored articles and chapters in areas such as forgiveness and related virtues (e.g., hope, humility, gratitude, and justice), spiritual development, marriage and family therapy, relational development (e.g., attachment, differentiation of self), narcissism, intercultural competence, and suicidology.

Chris Schlauch, Ph.D. has been at Boston University since 1985, initially as Assistant Director for Professional Services at the Danielsen Institute and Adjunct Assistant Professor; in 1988 he became a full-time faculty member. Since 1997, he has served as Chair of Area C—Religion, Culture, and Personality—in the School of Theology, and as Coordinator of two Ph.D. programs in the Graduate School: Counseling Psychology and Religion, and Psychology of Religion.

Daniel Shaw, LCSW is a psychoanalyst in private practice in New York City and in Nyack, NY. His book, *Traumatic Narcissism: Relational Systems of Subjugation*, was recently published by Routledge for the Relational Perspectives Series.

Phillis Isabella Sheppard, Ph.D. is a womanist practical theologian, psychoanalyst and sometime poet. She completed her Ph.D. at Chicago Theological Seminary in Theology, Ethics, and the Human Sciences combined with certification in Pastoral Psychotherapy (Center for Religion and Psychotherapy, Chicago) and has earned certification in Adult Psychoanalysis (Chicago Institute for Psychoanalysis). Dr. Sheppard's research engages the intersection where the social and the intrapsychic meet. Her recently published *Self, Culture and Others in Womanist Practical Theology* addresses serious lacunae in pastoral theology, psychology of religion, and psychoanalytic theory.

George Stavros, M.Div., Ph.D. is the Executive Director of the Danielsen Institute at Boston University. His teaching and research interests are in psychotherapy, psychotherapy training, Religion. He is currently working on a manuscript on the writings of Donald Woods Winnicott and religion and spirituality in clinical practice. He is a licensed psychologist and holds a Master of Divinity from Holy Cross Greek Orthodox School of Theology. He and his wife Despina are parents to four daughters.

David Wallin, Ph.D. is a clinical psychologist in private practice in Albany and Mill Valley, CA. A *magna cum laude* graduate of Harvard College who received his doctorate from the Wright Institute in Berkeley, he has been practicing, teaching, and writing about psychotherapy for nearly three decades. His most recent book, *Attachment in Psychotherapy* (Guilford, 2007), is presently being translated into nine languages. He is also co-author (with Stephen Goldbart) of *Mapping the Terrain of the Heart: Passion, Tenderness, and the Capacity to Love* (Jason Aronson, 1996). He has lectured on attachment and psychotherapy in Australia, Europe, Canada, and throughout the United States.

CPSIA information can be obtained at www.ICGtesting.com
Printed in the USA
BVOW01*1547140914

366588BV00002B/3/P

9 781442 234482